GW00691933

BREAKING FEMINIST WAVES

Series Editors:

LINDA MARTÍN ALCOFF, Hunter College and CUNY Graduate Center
GILLIAN HOWIE†, University of Liverpool

For the last 20 years, feminist theory has been presented as a series of ascending waves. This picture has had the effect of de-emphasizing the diversity of past scholarship as well as constraining the way we understand and frame new work. The aim of this series is to attract original scholars who will offer unique interpretations of past scholarship and unearth neglected contributions to feminist theory. By breaking free from the constraints of the image of waves, this series will be able to provide a wider forum for dialogue and engage historical and interdisciplinary work to open up feminist theory to new audiences and markets.

LINDA MARTÍN ALCOFF is professor of Philosophy at Hunter College and the City University of New York Graduate Center. Her books include *Visible Identities: Race, Gender and the Self*; *The Blackwell Guide to Feminist Philosophy* (coedited with Eva Kittay); *Identity Politics Reconsidered* (coedited with Moya, Mohanty, and Hames-Garcia); and *Singing in the Fire: Tales of Women in Philosophy*.

GILLIAN HOWIE was professor in the Department of Philosophy at the University of Liverpool. Her work includes *Deleuze and Spinoza: Aura of Expressionism*; *Touching Transcendence: Women and the Divine* (coedited with Jan Jobling); *Third Wave Feminism: A Critical Exploration* (coedited with Stacy Gillis and Rebecca Munford); *Menstruation* (coedited with Andrew Shail); and *Gender, Teaching and Research in Higher Education* (coedited with Ashley Tauchert).

Titles to date:

Unassimilable Feminisms: Reappraising Feminist, Womanist, and Mestiza *Identity Politics*
    by Laura Gillman

Further Adventures of The Dialectic of Sex: *Critical Essays on Shulamith Firestone*
    edited by Mandy Merck and Stella Sandford

Hegel's Philosophy and Feminist Thought: Beyond Antigone?
    edited by Kimberly Hutchings and Tuija Pulkkinen

Femme*nism and the Mexican Woman Intellectual from Sor Juana to Poniatowska: Boob Lit*
    by Emily Hind

Between Feminism and Materialism: A Question of Method
    by Gillian Howie

Resonances of Slavery in Race/Gender Relations: Shadow at the Heart of American Politics
    by Jane Flax

The Many Dimensions of Chinese Feminism
by Ya-chen Chen

Rousseau in Drag: Deconstructing Gender
by Rosanne Terese Kennedy

Undutiful Daughters: New Directions in Feminist Thought and Practice
edited by Henriette Gunkel, Chrysanthi Nigianni, and Fanny Söderbäck

A Theory of Freedom: Feminism and the Social Contract
by Shay Welch

Theory on the Edge: Irish Studies and the Politics of Sexual Difference
edited by Noreen Giffney and Margrit Shildrick

THEORY ON THE EDGE

Irish Studies and the Politics of Sexual Difference

Edited by

Noreen Giffney
and
Margrit Shildrick

THEORY ON THE EDGE
Copyright © Noreen Giffney and Margrit Shildrick, 2013.

All rights reserved.

First published in 2013 by
PALGRAVE MACMILLAN®
in the United States—a division of St. Martin's Press LLC,
175 Fifth Avenue, New York, NY 10010.

Where this book is distributed in the UK, Europe and the rest of the world,
this is by Palgrave Macmillan, a division of Macmillan Publishers Limited,
registered in England, company number 785998, of Houndmills,
Basingstoke, Hampshire RG21 6XS.

Palgrave Macmillan is the global academic imprint of the above companies
and has companies and representatives throughout the world.

Palgrave® and Macmillan® are registered trademarks in the United States,
the United Kingdom, Europe and other countries.

ISBN: 978–1–137–30697–5

Library of Congress Cataloging-in-Publication Data

Theory on the edge : Irish studies and the politics of sexual difference /
edited by Noreen Giffney and Margrit Shildrick.
    pages cm.—(Breaking feminist waves)
    Includes bibliographical references.
    ISBN 978–1–137–30697–5 (alk. paper)
    1. Feminism—Ireland. 2. Sex—Ireland. 3. Ireland—Social policy.
4. Ireland—Civilization. 5. Ireland—Social life and customs. I. Giffney,
Noreen. II. Shildrick, Margrit.

HQ1600.3.T54 2013
305.4209417—dc23   2012048225

A catalogue record of the book is available from the British Library.

Design by Newgen Imaging Systems (P) Ltd., Chennai, India.

First edition: June 2013

Theory on the Edge *is inspired by, and dedicated to, Ailbhe Smyth, whose energy, persistence, activism, and scholarship have been central to extending the legacy of Irish women's political and social struggles into academia*

Contents

Part II   Culture

SERIES FOREWORD

Breaking Feminist Waves is a series designed to rethink the conventional models of what feminism is today, its past and future trajectories. For more than a quarter of a century, feminist theory has been presented as a series of ascending waves, and this has come to represent generational divides and differences of political orientation as well as different formulations of goals. The imagery of waves, while connoting continuous movement, implies a singular trajectory with an inevitably progressive teleology. As such, it constrains the way we understand what feminism has been and where feminist thought has appeared, while simplifying the rich and nuanced political and philosophical diversity that has been characteristic of feminism throughout. Most disturbingly, it restricts the way we understand and frame new work.

This series provides a forum to reassess established constructions of feminism and of feminist theory. It provides a starting point to redefine feminism as a configuration of intersecting movements and concerns, with political commitment but, perhaps, without a singular center or primary track. The generational divisions among women do not actually correlate with common interpretive frameworks shaped by shared historical circumstances, but rather with a diverse set of arguments, problems, and interests affected by differing historical contexts and locations. Often excluded from cultural access to dominant modes of communication and dissemination, feminisms have never been uniform nor yet in a comprehensive conversation. The generational division, then, cannot represent the dominant divide within feminism, nor a division between essentially coherent moments; there are always multiple conflicts and contradictions, as well as differences about the goals, strategies, founding concepts, and starting premises.Nonetheless, the problems facing women, feminists, and feminisms are as acute and pressing today as ever. Featuring a variety of disciplinary and theoretical perspectives, *Breaking Feminist Waves* provides a forum for comparative, historical, and interdisciplinary work, with special attention to the problems of cultural differences, language and representation, embodiment, rights, violence, sexual economies, and political action. By rethinking feminisms' history as well as their present, and by unearthing neglected contributions to feminist theory, this series intends to unlock conversations between feminists and feminisms and to open up feminist theory and practice to new audiences.

LINDA MARTÍN ALCOFF AND GILLIAN HOWIE

Acknowledgments

Our thanks are extended to all those who have contributed to *Theory on the Edge* either by offering written pieces or by supporting us in other ways. The initial idea came from Noreen and once we had formed an editorial team and started seeking out ideas for the collection, we were delighted with the alacrity and enthusiasm with which everyone accepted our invitations. Following the withdrawal of our first contract due to unforeseen circumstances on the publisher's side, Gill Howie, of University of Liverpool, suggested that we resubmit to the Palgrave *Breaking Feminist Waves* series which she coedited with Linda Alcoff and that has proved an excellent match. The final contributors have been extremely patient and we would like to acknowledge their continuing goodwill during the delay.

Following Gill's untimely death during the late stages of the production process, Margrit, in particular, wishes to acknowledge her longterm personal friendship with Gill and the many impassioned and productive intellectual exchanges that we both so enjoyed.

We gratefully acknowledge permissions granted by *Women's Studies International Forum* to reproduce the opening piece—"Women's Studies and the Disciplines"—by Ailbhe Smyth. Gerardine Meaney's chapter contains previously published material from her book *Gender, Ireland and Cultural Change: Race, Sex and Nation* (Routledge). Meaney's chapter originally appeared in *The Irish Review.* An earlier and shorter version of Noreen Giffney's chapter appears in *Irish Postmodernisms and Popular Culture*, ed. Wanda Balzano, Anne Mulhall, and Moynagh Sullivan (Basingstoke and New York: Palgrave Macmillan, 2007).

Note on Cover Image: Lisa Fingleton

The image of Ailbhe Smyth on the cover of the book is from a conference where she is saying "Let me speak." She passionately argues that she wants to be allowed to speak rather than being invited to "chair" meetings. The image is set against the backdrop of the Irish Sea. Ailbhe has always been an advocate for the thousands of women who have been forced to cross the Irish waters seeking abortions.

Introduction: Emergent Strands or Theory on Edge?

Margrit Shildrick

The manifestation of feminism in Ireland, north and south, has followed some very specific pathways that reflect a history that is quite unlike that of its nearest neighbor, the United Kingdom; and even though the north is politically aligned with Britain, and is in some ways socioculturally distinct from the republic, there is still an overall sense of otherness. Ireland as a whole has been disregarded and romanticized in turn, a place of abjection and dreams according to the context. For feminists, there has always been the example of some very strong women to look back on, but also a sense in which the repressions that have assailed Ireland over many centuries have taken their toll on the social and political promotion of women in particular. That is not to say that women have been silenced—and the myth of Irish "backwardness" that outsiders have used as a lazy explanatory model has been comprehensively critiqued, not least by Linda Connelly (2002) in her exposition of the Irish Women's Movement—but that, as elsewhere, women's specific concerns have been deemed less important than other more "gender-neutral" matters. The priorities of the state in Ireland, whether represented by Dublin or London, are rarely directed toward women in any liberatory sense, while the enduring strength of the Church, both Roman Catholic and Protestant, throughout the twentieth century, has actively blocked the development of a social agenda that would redress historical inequities. Nonetheless, feminist voices have been persistently raised—even if not always self-identified as such—and no-one in the early twenty-first century would doubt that Ireland has a rich history of gender politics. In bringing together this collection of essays from both north and south of the border, we have wanted to demonstrate the depth and variety of Irish feminism as it has developed both in response to, and despite, both local and universal conditions.

The emergence in recent years of a strong theoretical underpinning to Irish feminist thinking, then, both mirrors wider Eurocentric and Anglo-American trajectories and gestures toward, or explicitly references, the specificity of its own location. The politics of conflict between states, religions, genders, sexualities, class, and differential rights are inextricably linked and mark feminist theory as always intersectional and dynamic, never finished nor intending to offer definitive answers. Rather than making Women's and Gender Studies themselves the closed referents of the collection, the aim, then, is to highlight the points of intersection and divergence of a number of theoretical perspectives and research areas that run through Irish Studies more generally, and in which sexual difference—even when unacknowledged—is a common thread. Feminist theory is in that sense always on the edge, and on edge, responsive to new developments and powerfully enabling, both unwilling and unable to settle. It is theory that is rooted in material issues, but always asks "why" rather than just "how." As I write, for example, the Irish republic—the Celtic Tiger state of the 1990s and early part of this century that belied the knowingly dismissive image of Ireland as a poor cousin of its western European neighbors—is under enormous economic, political, and social pressure. However one views its base reality, the financial crisis is already cited as the justification for substantive retrenchment in many spheres, not as a gender-neutral matter, but as one that impacts disproportionately on women. But rather than expecting feminism to pull back from theory to refocus on material changes, perhaps we should hope also for a further development of feminist economic theory to shake up the tired old conventions that seem to provide only ineffective tinkering around the edges. For most feminists now, it would be a truism to assert that theory is inseparable from practice, and it is clear that many essays in this collection—though none yet that addresses the economic situation—take off from specific "events" in the Irish context to formulate theory that influences what is yet to come. In that context, it is no surprise that Ailbhe Smyth, one of the most influential scholars of contemporary Irish feminism, who has been the inspiration for this collection, should so clearly exemplify in her own work the symbiotic relation that is evident throughout.

For just that reason, we have chosen to open the text with an early piece by Smyth that appeared in 1992, shortly after she had founded the Women's Education, Research and Resource Centre (WERRC) at a none-too-enthusiastic University College Dublin. Although her major theme is the tension in academia between the development of a newly buoyant and autonomous Women's Studies and a more integrationist, discipline-based approach that built on existing models, her paper speaks too to the related tension—or supposed tension—between theory and practice. When Smyth declares her preference for a permanently "undisciplined" Women's Studies, she does so in part precisely because she does not want to lose sight "of the material and political realities in which women's lives are embedded" (17).

In the event, WERRC maintained its independence for almost two decades, nurturing self-named activists and theorists alike, bringing perspectives and voices together to great effect. Not only did the scholarship emerging from the Centre help propel academic Irish feminism to its present prominence—and it is notable that the majority of the pieces included in this collection directly cite Smyth herself—but it established outreach programs that brought a different flavor of feminism to women who would have had no expectations of a university-based approach. The contribution here of Aideen Quilty, who held a long-term post at WERRC, traces some of that remarkable development, while Smyth's own trajectory through academia and activism is laid out more clearly in the closing piece of the collection, where she talks openly in a recent interview with Medb Ruane.

The book is divided into two sections—politics and culture—both preeminent concerns for Smyth, which are not to be taken as distinct. Although some pieces clearly gravitate more toward one term than the other, it would in effect be an impossibility to separate the two elements as having any independent meaning, and to speak of one necessarily entails unpacking its intersection with the other. Indeed, as Debbie Ging notes, it is precisely the conflation of the cultural with the political that "makes the contemporary genderscape so nebulous" (281). In her trenchant piece on postfeminism in the contemporary Irish context, Ging deftly analyzes both the myths and the challenges of understanding feminism as a set of discursive responses rather than as either a traditional form of political activism or as a coherently developed ideology, and she offers a strong insight into why theory should be always on the edge. That is not to say that in some other contributions there is not—on a descriptive level—often a bias toward a less complex focus, but once meaning is invoked and analysis begins, then the political, the social and cultural, and the historical, not to mention the psychic underpinnings of all of those, cannot be kept apart. To take one example from the text, although the intermezzo piece by Paula Burns on the Armagh Women's dirty protest is positioned in the politics section, and Olga Cox-Cameron's literature-heavy chapter, "Enjoying Substance," is in the culture section, both rely on an understanding of the psychic imaginary to tease out the significances. And whether the substantive concerns are material or abstract—itself a somewhat unsustainable division—what matters is how the analysis throws light on the situated nature of the theory produced. Even though the contributors employ a range of perspectives, there is little doubt that postmodernism has greatly impacted the apparent certainties and singularities of second-wave feminism to push theory into a postconventional mode better suited to the changing "realities" of cultural and sociopolitics.

For readers unfamiliar with the specificities of recent Irish politics and religion as they impact on women, Ivana Bacik's comprehensive survey on sexual difference puts in place a highly grounded sense of what has been at stake in Irish feminism. The situation in the North is inevitably somewhat different, but it should not be forgotten that although the relationship between the state and the Church works within different parameters, the dominant religion of the North is no less conservative and pervasive than it has been in the republic. The widespread segregation of primary and secondary education on religious grounds, and the inevitable perpetuation of community tensions, comes as something of a shock to outsiders. Despite my own several years' experience at WERRC, I was certainly taken aback when I took up a lecturing post at Queen's University, Belfast, to realize that first-year undergraduates might be encountering others from across the religious divide for almost the first time, at least in any extensive way, and equally I had failed to anticipate the influence of the organized Church in the North. In both geographical locations, then, material specificities are powerful drivers of how the theoretical field is shaped; yet those substantive issues cannot be read apart from the domain of sexual, familial, and religious beliefs and values. As Gerardine Meaney picks up the thread in "Race, Sex and Nation," the question of national identities is deeply tied up with the persistent trope of Mother Ireland, the appeal to an abstracted embodiment that bears little resemblance to the systematic inequities endured by individual women. Turning to postcolonial theory, Meaney deftly unpacks notions not simply of Ireland as an historically colonized nation, but the racialized and gendered discourse in which Irish identity itself figures a certain appeal to purity actively promulgated by both Church and state. Where Meaney's observations are addressed to the Republic, it would be instructive to reflect on the question of such purity in relation to cross-border mobilizations in which many historically shared attitudes and values are challenged by very different political and economic developments.

While the historic roots of Irish feminism's recent concerns are fully evident in issues such as abortion—which, as Sandra McAvoy outlines, remains an unresolved point of discord in Irish politics—or in the male-dominated postconflict reconstruction in the North that Margaret Ward writes of, the problematic of sexual difference and agency is always there to be excavated. Too often the official record makes scant reference to the part played by women at the political level, even less to the effects on the lived experiences of women. When Ward refers to "male begrudgery," we might consider her somewhat generous, but what she and others offer is not the option of head-on confrontation but a persistent and informed critique that indicates why sexual difference might indeed make a difference. In contrast, in Burns's account of the Armagh Women's dirty protest, which in many ways paralleled the men's hunger strike led by Bobby Sands, the imprisoned women—who did not directly identify with feminism— did confront male power, but nonetheless in a manner that could only be inherently female. Their innovative challenge to the prison authorities and to wider state policy, using their own menstrual blood as a form of protest, was, nonetheless, widely ignored not only in the mainstream, but in the Republican press. The sexual difference of substantive fluid bodies was—and still is, if the paucity of archival material is to be conceded—simply beyond acknowledgment. In such a light, it is fascinating to make the link across to the wealth of Irish literature—not least to James Joyce who remains a dominant marker within the humanities—to see how clearly politics has suppressed a keen appreciation of differential embodiment.

In any case, it would be entirely misleading to suggest that Irish Studies devolves only on questions of nation, religion, and state. As Breda Gray makes clear in her chapter "Affecting Trans-feminist Solidarity," the contemporary feminist agenda is firmly transnational and intersectional in its concerns and implications. In addressing the vexed issue of solidarity across putative boundaries, Gray turns to the politics of emotion to rethink the old divides of geopolitical and sexual difference among other forms and to suggest that empathy has a part to play in an ethically reconfigured global politics. That Irish Studies has never been a mere regional concern recalls too a longstanding history of emigration and the force of the Irish diaspora worldwide. Although the majority of contributions in *Theory on the Edge* are written by those living now in Ireland, the question of crossing geographic borders is a powerful element of reflection that engages with both the empirical reality and the wider significance of displacement and belonging. While not ignoring the historic motivators in play, Eithne Luibhéid's short piece on queer migration studies, for example, decisively deconstructs the conventional approach to Irish emigration to open up the task of "rethinking migration and sexuality regimes in relation to logics other than that of the neo-liberal and neo-colonial" (p. 91). What is sometimes missing from the empirical picture, however, is that Ireland, like most other western European countries, is the destination of many new immigrants, precisely those with whom Luibhéid, and Gray, would wish to make common cause. Where many of the incomers are accounted for within the legal system, with asylum seekers occupying a painfully unresolved area of uncertainty, the darker underside concerns those who are trafficked, often from the Far East. Edith Shillue, whose work in the North brings her into direct contact with women who have recently arrived, often illegally via the routes operated by snake-head gangs, reflects on a different type of diaspora that calls into question what constitutes belonging. As a Mandarin speaker, Shillue is well placed to hear the language of personal stories that she deftly relates to the dispersal of a unique Irish national identity.

In framing of the "real" stories of immigration, Shillue's piece, like so many others, turns to the wealth of Irish literature that pervades popular culture as much as academic study. For her, Joyce is a powerful presence, as it is for Olga Cox Cameron who sets out to engage with the "the lure, the pleasure, the disabling 'hit' of great literature" (256) from the very different perspective of her own discipline of Lacanian psychoanalysis. In a demanding but invigorating chapter, it is the notion of jouissance—precisely the excessive "feminine" principle celebrated by Joyce to the discomfort of the Irish establishment—that prevails. Turning to more recent literature, Moynagh Sullivan takes up the work of feminist poet Rita Ann Higgins, which like that of Joyce has a certain uncontainable exuberance. And as Sullivan points out, the intertwining of the politics, aesthetics, and culture of contemporary Ireland is characteristic not only of Higgins, but of Ailbhe Smyth herself. The short opening piece to the collection does not reveal it—although it emerges more clearly in the concluding interview with Medb Ruane—that Smyth is as well known for her often deeply touching, creative writing as for her straight sociopolitical commentaries. Indeed, it would be misplaced to try to draw a line between them, and it is significant that many of the contributors, whatever their own approach, go to Smyth's more overtly "poetic" output when they reference her work. As editors, we wondered about including just such a piece in its entirety, but have felt that there are so many quotations embedded in the existing chapters that it was perhaps superfluous. The facility with which Smyth makes powerful political points about sexual difference through her "poetic" voice pervades not only her written scholarship, but her many public and academic presentations. It is a great shame that there is no adequate way of representing that here.

The question of sexual difference is the thread that links together this collection and it is one that greatly exceeds any simplistic appeal to gender. As with most progressive feminist theory, the very concept of sexual difference figures a wide array of ideas and issues that encompass identity, race, nationalism, religion, sexuality, embodiment, and, in recent years, the queering of all those elements. Fintan Walsh turns his attention to the relation between politics and queer performance, taking as his text the Dublin Pride parade of 2009, until then a long-established and vibrant event in the capital that was not seen as especially controversial. Walsh's account tracks the particular tensions emerging in 2009 when acceptance of the colorful visibility of the queer community was destabilized by an emergent reality—a proposed Civil Partnership Bill—that reinvigorated political performativity. In contrast, Anne Mulhall focuses on the playing out and deconstruction of queer identity within a recent Irish novel, *Breakfast on Pluto* (McCabe 1998), which was subsequently made into a Neil Jordan film. Working through all the tropes of Irish nationalism, sexuality, and identity, Mulhall takes apart the narrative's oedipal structure to show how the unresolved and edgy queerness of the novel is subtly subverted in the "new queer multicultural national family" (300) that marks the film's conclusion. Clearly, the term "queer"—particularly as it is increasingly heard in Irish feminist discourse—comes with an extensive range of possible meanings and deployments, which Noreen Giffney subjects to a rigorous exploration in her piece "Quare Theory." For Giffney, *quare* theory has a specifically Irish context in the intersections of queer theory, feminism and lesbian studies, and she insists that the term should be understood as pertaining to methodological issues rather than to identity. It is, as she says, not another category to "come out" into, but a highly useful tool for exploring the insights and limitations of existing terms (340). As the co-convenor of several queer/quare studies groups in Dublin, Giffney has been highly instrumental in creating theory on the edge.

I would like to end this Introduction on a more personal note. When Noreen Giffney first asked if I should like to join her in coediting this book, my response was emphatically positive, not least because

I had experienced first hand the generosity with which Ailbhe Smyth has promoted the careers and interest of other feminists while dealing with a stream of obstacles to her own progression as a feminist academic. At a point where, having reached the end of a research contract, I was finding it difficult to find a new full-time post in the United Kingdom that spoke to my experience and expertise, I was welcomed by Ailbhe to WERRC at University College Dublin with the remit to conduct a series of higher-level seminars on feminist theory and its application to some very specific issues such as disability, identity politics, and sexuality. There are undoubtedly many points of feminist concern on which we do not see eye to eye, but she was invariably part of the discussion, raising a range of acute questions and comments, which greatly facilitated the whole learning experience for all of us in the group. It was at that time that I first met Noreen—then a PhD student in another department of University College Dublin—whose own work was exemplary of the innovative directions in which feminist-inspired output could go, given the kind of support that WERRC so effectively provided. For everyone involved, whether from Dublin universities, the local community, or further afield, the sessions hosted by WERRC spoke to a shared excitement about the multiple possibilities of feminist theory and to a commitment to openly explore the uncertainties of postconventional thinking. The same delight in working through a range of problematics was evident in WERRC's Masters program, and although I was not directly involved with the outreach initiatives, their very endurance and popularity spoke to a real sensitivity to the differential concerns of all those involved. As the director of the Centre, Ailbhe Smyth showed herself not only as a first-rate scholar of Women's Studies, and more generally Irish Studies, but as an inspired motivator for an array of women who might have thought themselves to have nothing in common. And whatever it is called, and whatever its alignments and guises, Irish feminism continues to thrive. For all of us involved in the development of a politics of sexual difference in Ireland, there is much to thank her for.

REFERENCES

Connelly, Linda (2002) *The Irish Women's Movement: From Revolution to Devolution*. Basingstoke: Palgrave Macmillan.

McCabe, Patrick (1998) *Breakfast on Pluto*. New York: Harper Perennial.

Women's Studies and the Disciplines

Ailbhe Smyth

In Women's Studies, "I" am both speakable and speaking, not decontextualized, disembodied, neutralized, and neutered. I take great pleasure in that "I," mine and yours, particular and plural, whatever that "I" may be, however questioned.[1]

The autobiographical statement is now, I suppose, *de rigueur* in feminist writing/teaching/speaking, almost a commonplace, although not common in that, very precisely, it speaks from and to the differences among us, of place, and many other things. And while it doesn't matter much to you (although it does to me), whether I have three cats or five children or seven lovers (or all of these), it does matter (I think), if we are to speak to one another, that we be precise about how we place ourselves, and how we are placed, in and in relation to Women's Studies and "the disciplines."

In her wonderfully clear background paper to today's discussion, Dearbhal Ni Charthaigh reminds us of the continuing tension between the two major "models" for the development of Women's Studies within the academy: an integrationist, discipline-directed strategy and the establishment of autonomous Women's Studies. Many of us, of course, find ourselves doing "both/and": working simultaneously to develop Women's Studies as an independent area *and* trying to change "our" disciplines from within. Often, and pragmatically, there is no choice and we do what we have to do. But the question is, do we *want* to be doing both, should we be trying to do "both/and"?

Let me say straight away that I now consider myself, after years of mind, soul, and job searching (in a manner of speaking), to be (quite) undisciplined. It has taken literally years to extract myself from "my discipline of origin," as the phrase goes (although who wants to originate in a discipline, I wonder?) and I most certainly do not intend to return there (who wants to die in a discipline?).

Of course, long years of (any) discipline leave their mark and I am constantly irritated and dismayed to discover my narrow habits of thought, my one-track perspective, the gross limitations of my understanding of what we need and might want to know and how we can come to know it. But the point is that I actively and positively do not want to be locked into disciplinary/disciplined narrowness.

Doing "both/and"—simultaneously integrating and separating—seems to me to be an impossible contradiction. Trying to integrate—or rather more radically to transform—a discipline (or even "the disciplines") must involve an acceptance, at some level, of both the idea of disciplinarity and the reality of "the disciplines." Trying to develop Women's Studies separately, independently, autonomously, or whatever necessarily involves a questioning, at the very least, of the validity and value of disciplinarity and a rejection, at some level, of the capacity of "the disciplines" to generate the kinds of knowledge that (all kinds of) women do or might need and want.

I do not want to do both at once: (a) because I think it is impossible anyway, and (b) most important for me, because I believe that Women's Studies is, must be, about moving outside and beyond academic disciplines with their narrow habits and rigid boundaries. "Moving beyond" is actually not a very satisfactory phrase because it constitutes Women's Studies as deriving from, marked by, and therefore still existing in relation to "the disciplines" (like myself).

It is impossibly Utopian to desire a Women's Studies that is not connected to historically disciplined knowledge, and impossibly contradictory to then believe it (Women's Studies) can be "placed" within the academy at all. However, given a choice between the impossibilities and contradictions of Utopia and those of Women's Studies "in" the disciplines, I will choose Utopia any day.

The problem is, we do not usually have much of a choice, so I will try to address the questions raised for today's discussion more directly.

Has Women's Studies Had an Impact on Academic Institutions?

Yes and no.

The very existence of Women's Studies programs, centers, and (more rarely) departments means that, of course, Women's Studies has had some impact on academic institutions and structures. The introduction of a new element must always displace existing elements in some way or another. But I am not sure how much this forces the existing elements into a significantly new configuration (of power). True, there is now space for (some) students and (some) teachers/researchers to do feminist work at least some of the time, but I do not see that the *balance of power* has shifted much, if at all.

In my own university and at this very moment, the main opposition (a quite virulent strain) to the expansion of Women's Studies stems from a fear that more Women's Studies will mean fewer students and therefore fewer resources for some disciplines within the Humanities. I take this both as a sign of the "success" of Women's Studies (i.e., its impact on the distribution of students within the university has been noted) and as a warning signal. What I think the institution is saying to us in Women's Studies is: If you stay quiet, and small, in your allotted corner we will let you be—leave our system undisturbed and we will not disturb you; we will even pay you (a little) to stay small and quiet.

And there, surely, is the crux of this particular question. If Women's Studies minds its manners and stays quiet, we cannot make any significant impact on the system. On the other hand, if we decide to be obstreperous, can we survive more than two minutes? Staying quiet is to accept recuperation while shouting looks like hara-kiri. Either way, it can feel like a no-win situation for Women's Studies and the survival, intact, of a remarkably powerful and powerfully resistant institution. (Actually, shouting is more Utopian; so we are shouting, and when you think about it, there is not so very much to lose.)

Has Women's Studies Had an Impact on the Curriculum?

Yes and no.

The curriculum appears to be remarkably *unmarked* by Women's Studies, almost totally impermeable to its advances in the Sciences, Medicine, Engineering, Architecture, and not much less so in the Social and Human Sciences. The malestream flows on, as oblivious to our developmental phases as to our reconceptualizations. A course added here and a text tacked on there do not constitute an impact. You would retire in deepest depression if that was all there was to it.

But it is not. Where I think Women's Studies has had an enormous impact is on *Women's Studies*. That is not, really, such a tautology. Women's Studies itself has been changing, becoming both broader and deeper over the past two decades. When you consider the huge number of books, articles, journals, research projects, programs, and courses on all manner of topics and issues, it is clear that Women's Studies is becoming stronger and more confident and vibrantly energetic all the time.

Which is why the interrogation and expansion of knowledge taking place *within* Women's Studies in myriad ways is not crossing the Great (Disciplinary) Divide. That vital and dynamic process is, I think, what most threatens our institutions. It is that which leads them to seek to confine and contain Women's Studies and to intimidate us (not always explicitly) with threats of (an impossible?) extinction.

I think, to disagree with Dearbhal Ni Charthaigh, that Women's Studies is indeed developing a "robust alternative feminist theory capable of presenting a clear challenge to the dominant paradigms." I also think that the dominant paradigms are perfectly resistant to recognizing the challenge for what it is. Ignoring change is precisely what enables them to survive powerfully and overpoweringly intact.

When did we (seriously) think it would or could be otherwise? Do we (i.e., in Women's Studies) either need or want to cross the Divide right now? I think we should be focusing on what *Women's Studies* needs, not dissipating ever-vulnerable energies in a multiplicity of different "models," strategies, and directions. Whatever the difficulty of moving "beyond," moving "into" the disciplines does not feel like a survival strategy to me. I have no desire to drown.

So it may be (at least for some of us) that we shall never make the crossing because to row back toward the disciplines would be to undo the undisciplining that has taken so long to achieve. I think we need to explore even more fully, vigorously—and subtly—what a truly *undisciplined* Women's Studies could achieve.

What Has Been the Impact of Women's Studies on Students' Expectations?

I do not think this is quite the question I want to be answering.

Women's Studies has certainly given (some) students the opportunity to explore issues and topics that I did not expect when I was a student—did not even know they existed or could be "spoken" in the academy. Those students come to Women's Studies with complex expectations (intellectual, political, emotional, and social). Sometimes, those expectations are met, sometimes our students make quite other, unexpected, discoveries. But there are, relatively, so few students in Women's Studies and so very very many women not in the academy at all.

What, I ask myself, is Women's Studies doing *for women*? What is its impact on the lives, life-chances, expectations, whatever, of all kinds of women? If it is too soon to expect us (in Women's Studies) to have the answer, it is most certainly too soon for us to forget the question. I emphatically do not want a Women's Studies, which, its cap set firmly on "integrating the disciplines," loses sight of the material and political realities in which women's lives are embedded. And those realities, shifting though they be, are the origin of Women's Studies. Not "my discipline."

I happen to think that looking outward is, will be, both more *disruptive* of academic knowledge and more *constructive* of the many kinds of knowledge(s) women variously need to discover ourselves and expand our freedoms.[2] So I would like to finish with Adrienne Rich's question, to which I want Women's Studies to be a constantly developing answer:

What does a woman need to know to become a self-conscious, self-defining human being?

NOTES

1. An earlier version of this short essay was presented at a GRACE (Commission of the European Communities Women's Studies Project 1990–1992) seminar in Brussels on the theme "The Impact of Women's Studies on the Curriculum." A background paper was prepared for the seminar by Dearbhal Ni Charthaigh to which speakers were asked to respond. The issues raised included a reflection on the history and future direction(s) of Women's Studies in the academy, specifically in the context of developing EC (European Community) policy in the area. This chapter is reprinted from *Women's Studies International Forum*, Vol. 15, Nos. 5/6, pp. 615–617, 1992.

2. Almost 20 years later, I am not at all inclined to change my mind. In my own case, the academy proved to be a far more dangerous place than any Utopia I might have imagined. And I still prefer shouting.

PART I

Politics

The Politics of Sexual Difference: The Enduring Influence of the Catholic Church

Ivana Bacik

In order to understand anything about Irish society and the politics of sexual difference in Ireland today, it is necessary to understand the enduring influence of the Roman Catholic Church. "The Church," as it is usually called, has wielded considerable power for centuries in this country. In the late eighteenth century and early nineteenth century, the drastic restrictions imposed upon the rights of Catholics by the British government through the Catholic Relief Acts merely served to strengthen the Church's position in society, and the will of the people to practice their chosen faith. Catholicism thus became the religion of social and political defiance, of nationhood and patriotic identity—inevitably, this makes for a potent cocktail.

Catholic emancipation was formally secured in 1829. Since then, the Church has amassed significant power in Irish society. Although this was especially notable after independence in 1922, the Church was placed in a powerful position much earlier, with the passing of the Charitable Bequests Act, 1844, for example, which recognized it alongside the established Church (the Church of Ireland). The Catholic Church gained the power to have ownership and control of many schools, hospitals, and social services across Ireland, confirming its role as a social-services provider in the absence of a national government, and even prior to independence.

In the twentieth century, the fight for independence was finally won, and the Church moved into alignment with those in power in the new Free State, and with successive governments, making its influence felt in every sphere of public life. As academic Maura Adshead has written, "The Irish State, from the beginning, was ostentatiously Catholic" (2003: 172). The power of the Church reached its peak during Eamon de Valera's first terms of office as head of the Irish government (1932–1948), with the infamous influence of Catholic Archbishop John Charles McQuaid on the drafting of the 1937 Constitution, Bunreacht na hEireann. The influence of Catholic doctrine upon the wording of the fundamental rights Articles is especially notable. Although the reference in the Constitution to the "special position" of the Catholic Church as "the guardian of the Faith professed by the great majority of the citizens," originally contained in Article 44, was removed in 1972 by a referendum, the strong influence of Catholic doctrine and religious belief is still clearly evident in the text of the Constitution, the Preamble of which begins

> "In the Name of the Most Holy Trinity, from Whom is all authority and to Whom, as our final end, all actions both of men and States must be referred" and which goes on to "humbly" acknowledge "all our obligations to our Divine Lord, Jesus Christ."

Ever since independence, the Catholic Church has thus had enduring power in Ireland—it is no coincidence, in the land where the president, every member of the Council of State, and all judges are required to take an oath beginning "In the presence of Almighty God" and where the national broadcaster still carries a denominational religious message (the "Angelus") at 6 p.m. every evening, that when we speak of "Church and State," Church always comes first.

In part, this is through sheer force of numbers, as it has always been the Church of the vast majority of the population. Even now, most recent census figures indicate that the vast majority of the population is still identified as Roman Catholic (84 percent in the 2011 census, representing however a significant drop from almost 92 percent in 1991). However, a total of 269,800 people declared themselves as having no religion in the 2011 census—a 45 percent increase in this category from 2006, making those of no religion the next biggest belief group after Roman Catholics. By contrast, a total of 129,000 people identified themselves as belonging to the Church of Ireland, the next largest religious grouping after Catholics.

Apart from its numerical strength, the Catholic Church has also maintained significant power in Ireland through its substitution for the state in the provision of social services, particularly in education, health, and welfare. The importance in Ireland of the "third sector," or community and voluntary sector, in delivering social services usually provided by the state in other systems is well known. The Community and Voluntary Pillar was even regarded as one of the social partners during national pay and partnership negotiations in the 1990s. Long before then, the Catholic Church had taken on a key role in lieu of state responsibility:

> Voluntary activity, especially by religious orders and their concern with charity and the poor, played a major role in providing supplementary welfare provision. The church-based education system—at primary and secondary level—and voluntary hospitals, predate the foundation of the State. The primary role of church-based voluntary organisations and services provided by religious orders in meeting education and social welfare needs continued after the foundation of the State. (Government of Ireland White Paper, 2000: 48)

Indeed, as the White Paper points out, the roots of the voluntary sector in Ireland today can be traced back to the Church-based philanthropic organizations of the eighteenth century. Although the state gradually after the 1950s began to take on a wider role in funding voluntary activity, notably with the enactment of the Health Act 1953, religious groups continue to play a strong role in service provision through the voluntary sector. The state and laypersons are increasingly filling the gaps that have appeared in voluntary service provision due to the decline in religious vocations—but many of the services remain under the effective control of the Church and Church-run institutions.

The powerful influence of Catholicism thus continues to this day. The *nature* of the Church's role may be changing, and even reducing, but the Church continues to exert a strong influence on the everyday lives of all Irish citizens—and on the sexual politics of Irish society.

In the areas of education and health, in particular, the institutional Church continues to have great power, with both control by the Church and indirect subsidy of the Church by the state built into the structures of our education and health systems. In education, over 90 percent of the 3,200 state-funded primary schools ("national schools") are owned and controlled by the Catholic Church, with religious instruction in the Catholic doctrine provided throughout the entire school day by means of an "integrated curriculum." The state may pay the teachers, but the Church calls the tune. Less than 70 schools nationally are run on a multidenominational basis by the "Educate Together" organization—yet parents are increasingly demanding this model of education for their children. There are at last welcome signs of change with the establishment by the Minister for Education in 2011 of a National Forum on Patronage and Pluralism in the primary sector, and a commitment given by the Minister in 2012 to ensure that some Catholic schools are to be transformed into multidenominational schools; but this will be a slow process, and there are already clear signs of resistance from within the Church.

In welfare provision, too, through its lay organization the St Vincent de Paul Society, the Catholic Church continues to act as a sort of "shadow welfare state." Catholic bishops continue to wield huge power within Irish society, through their role in education and welfare in particular, despite scandals over extensive sexual abuse of children in their care and the care of Catholic religious orders until recent times, and despite grave public concern over the way in which the Church attempted to deal with that abuse and to protect those alleged abusers within its ranks.

Of course, religious practice is a comfort and a necessity to a huge number of people, regardless of their chosen belief system, and they should all have the right to practice their chosen religion. The nub of the problem with the role of religion in Ireland is however that the Catholic Church as an institution still retains disproportionate influence in civil society. In today's pluralist Ireland, a multicultural society with an increasingly secular population that is growing ever more disillusioned with revelations about abuses of power perpetrated by those in the institutional Catholic Church over the years, especially following publication of the Ryan Report (2009) and the Murphy Report (2010), this is quite simply an antiquated and unsustainable state of affairs.

In his comprehensive work on sexual policy and Irish society, *Occasions of Sin*, Diarmaid Ferriter (2009) suggests that our sexual history is as complex as in many other countries. What emerges from his work however is the sense that while there may have been little uniqueness about Irish sexuality, the Irish state responded with laws that were uniquely submissive to the doctrines of the dominant Church. From independence in 1922 onward, he writes that the Catholic Church wielded a pervasive influence. Its leading ideologue, Archbishop McQuaid, appeared to find sex itself intrinsically sinful, apparently finding any public airing of issues to do with the female body or reproduction distasteful. Despite McQuaid's influence, Ferriter argues that Ireland was not unusually sexually repressive in some ways, compared to, for example, Italy or Spain at comparable periods in each country's history. However, those countries moved to legalize contraception and divorce long before Ireland, and the state appeared less submissive to the doctrines of any one church.

Truly unique to Ireland was the extent of the state's reliance on religious orders to provide institutional care to children. Indeed, as the Ryan and Murphy Reports on child abuse in religious-run institutions have so graphically illustrated, thousands of children in Ireland suffered years of systematic abuse, physical and sexual, in those institutions for many decades between the 1930s and the 1970s. A climate of fear was pervasive in those institutions, as documented by the Reports and by personal accounts of the survivors of abuse.

Readers of Ferriter's book, of the Ryan and Murphy Reports, and of other accounts of child abuse over this period, will become increasingly angry about the failures of policy makers over many decades to confront Catholic Church doctrine on sexuality. Undoubtedly, the Church's view of sex as sinful was a causal factor in the infliction of enormous unnecessary human suffering. Women who became pregnant outside marriage, and their children, were treated particularly harshly both by the Church and by society. Perhaps, the harshest punishment was reserved for those unfortunate women who entered the "Magdalen laundries," institutions run by orders of nuns like the Good Shepherd Sisters. These women and girls were abandoned by an uncaring state, made to give up their babies for illicit adoption, and forced to work in conditions of slavery. In this context, the introduction of a state allowance for unmarried mothers in 1973 was hugely significant, and followed by the almost equally important right to paid maternity leave. Despite these important advances, however, it would be 1987 before the status of illegitimacy was finally abolished.

By then, the influence of the Church was greatly diminished, although the "sexual revolution" usually defined as occurring during the 1960s did not really begin in Ireland until the 1970s. Indeed, the battle over the legalization of contraception dominated the debates on sexuality in Ireland throughout the 1970s and 1980s. The campaign to legalize contraception, led by brave individuals like Dr Michael Solomons (a key founder of the Irish Family Planning Association) and Mary Robinson, whose contraception bills in the Seanad helped to force change, was of course finally successful in 1992.

Another lengthy campaign, which was instituted to reform the law on homosexuality, finally succeeded in the passing of decriminalizing legislation in 1993. In the decade preceding that development, courageous activists like David Norris led the way in securing progressive legal change. Since then, civil partnership for gay couples has been legalized through legislation in 2010, but the campaign for marriage equality continues.

In the development of the Irish education and welfare systems, just as in the development of social policy, it is clear that the Catholic Church has had a strong influence. This influence is also clear in the development of the Irish health-care system. As a result, there have been serious implications for the way in which sexual and reproductive health matters are treated. Like education, health care in Ireland has traditionally been controlled and run by the Catholic Church. This has had a huge impact both on the way the health service is structured and on the way individual hospitals are run. That some sort of national direction has been lacking from our health system until now may well be a legacy of the handing over of control of hospitals and nursing homes to a myriad of religious orders, each of which brought different management structures to bear. What each had in common was the Catholic ethical code, and this in turn influenced, and limited, the types of services made available to patients.

This has been true for a very long time. The most famous, or notorious, example is of course the Church's vicious role in cutting down Minister for Health Noel Browne's proposed health-care scheme, the "Mother and Child Scheme," in 1949. The success of the Church in forcing the government to abandon a health program that would have vastly improved the health of mothers and children caused Browne to write bitterly in his autobiography, *Against the Tide*, that in his view, the hierarchy had become the factual instrument of government on all important social and economic policies in Ireland. As early as the 1940s, senior political figures were deeply concerned about the impact of the Catholic Church on the health system. In truth, an organization primarily concerned with the health of the soul could not have been able to prescribe accurately and objectively for the health of the physical body, nor, for that matter, for the body politic.

One of the biggest problems arising from Church influence in medical matters was, as with the Mother and Child Scheme, the curtailing of medical procedures made available to patients. In particular, the Church's influence on dictating the kinds of reproductive health services available persists to this day, although happily not to the same extent as in the past—but this limiting of the Church's role has been very hard won, and there have been many casualties in the process.

The barbaric practice of symphysiotomy, for example, was apparently routinely carried out in some Irish maternity hospitals right into the 1980s for so-called ethical reasons. This procedure, performed during childbirth, involved sawing through the pelvis so it opened like a hinge. Many of the women upon whom it was performed have suffered lifelong incontinence, difficulties in walking, and other physical and psychological effects as a result. Almost none of the women was consulted before the performance of the symphysiotomy and none was asked for her consent.

The procedure, allegedly carried out for Catholic doctrinal reasons, was performed on a woman where otherwise her child could only have been delivered by way of caesarean section. The symphysiotomy procedure facilitated future vaginal births, avoiding repeat caesareans, an unwelcome prospect that, it was feared, might induce women to resort to contraception or sterilization. Because women can deliver only a small number of children by way of caesarean section, the support group "Survivors of Symphysiotomy" say that the procedure was seen by some Catholic doctors as preferable because it enabled a woman to give birth an unlimited number of times. The attendant pain, discomfort, and damage to the health of the women upon whom the operation was performed were apparently all overlooked by those ruling over the hospitals' all-powerful ethics committees.

How this barbaric and usually unnecessary practice could have persisted in Ireland until the 1980s, when caesarean section offered an infinitely better alternative for women's health, is a question that remains unanswered, despite ongoing lobbying by support groups representing over 200 women affected by the procedure.

Other examples of Church influence in reproductive health services have been more persistent. Well into the 1990s, for example, male vasectomy operations were performed at only one hospital in Ireland—a hospital known for its Protestant ethos. Female sterilization remains difficult to obtain, and abortion unavailable. Contraceptives have only been fully legally available in the last decade. Until May 2002, a new morning-after pill, Levonelle, was unavailable in Ireland because the Irish Medicines Board took the view that it could be classified as an "abortifacient."

Although Levonelle has now been licensed and is available on prescription, the morning-after pill generally continues to be administered on prescription only, by doctors acting in a legal vacuum. Prenatal screening to detect fetal abnormalities is not available in Irish hospitals to the same extent as elsewhere in Europe, apparently in case detection of an abnormality might cause some women to consider termination of their pregnancy. Abortion of course remains a criminal offence under 1861 legislation. In addition, a constitutional amendment inserted in 1983 equates the rights to life of the "mother" and the "unborn." This amendment was interpreted by the Supreme Court in the 1992 X case as permitting abortion where necessary to save a woman's life. However, very few life-saving terminations are performed in Irish hospitals, and instead thousands of women travel annually to England for abortion.

In 2002, during the course of the government's ill-conceived referendum aimed at rolling back the Supreme Court judgment in the 1992 X case to rule out suicide risk as a ground for termination, it was revealed that women were being forced to carry dead fetuses to term because doctors were refusing to terminate pregnancies even where they knew that there existed a fetal abnormality inconsistent with live birth. The 2002 referendum was defeated, and the restrictive nature and lack of clarity in Irish abortion law was found to have breached the rights of women in a landmark 2010 European Court of Human Rights judgment (the ABC case). However, legislation both to clarify when life-saving abortion may be carried out and to deal with the cases of fatal fetal abnormality is still awaited.

Ethics committees still operate in many hospitals, and to this day, many of them specifically refer to an underlying Catholic doctrine. In addition to the insidious and often overt religious influence on the structures of and service delivery within the health system, religious influence is also highly visible in practical terms. Most hospitals, like most Irish schools, continue to use religious iconography throughout their premises: pictures, crucifixes, and statues. Most of them also employ religious nomenclature, with wards named in honor of individual saints.

Extensive reform of the health-care system in Ireland is promised; but whatever structural changes are carried out, the ongoing influence of the Catholic Church on the provision of health services should be reviewed at the same time. The malign impact of religious teaching and ethics codes upon the health of women should not be allowed to endure any further. Clearly, as vocations fall away, the influence of the Church over health is diminishing over time—but it has not gone away.

Apart from the ongoing issue of religious influence within hospitals, much attention has focused of late on one very specific area of religious welfare provision: the homes and institutions run on behalf of the state by religious orders for the care of children. Just as the Catholic Church had assumed a dominant role in the provision of health and education services in the nineteenth century, so too at that time did it effectively take over control of juvenile justice institutions. Irish Catholic MPs at Westminster defeated a Bill for the Better

Care and Reformation of Juvenile Offenders in 1856, on the purported basis that it might expose juvenile offenders to the activities of Protestant proselytizing societies (O'Sullivan, 1998). This group of MPs demanded that any reform schools for juvenile offenders should be managed by people from the same religion as that of offenders. As a result, in 1858, a new Reform Schools Bill was passed for Ireland, permitting religious control. From that date on, separate reformatory and industrial schools were opened and operated by the Catholic and Protestant churches. By 1898, there were 71 such schools in Ireland: 17 for Roman Catholic boys (3,975 children); 44 for Roman Catholic girls (3,975); 4 for Protestant boys (586); and 5 for Protestant girls (409). There was one other, mixed industrial school—but that was mixed gender, not mixed religion!

The large numbers of children incarcerated in these institutions—more than in England, Wales, Scotland, or Northern Ireland—continued well into the twentieth century. This anomaly was due to the use of Irish industrial schools primarily to house destitute children, or children whose parents could not adequately care for them for whatever reason; children who had committed criminal offence made up just one-tenth of those incarcerated. The corrupting effect of poverty was recognized, as was the need to "save the souls" of these children, particularly the girls. This was another unique feature of the Irish juvenile detention system: that right up until 1969, there were always more girls detained in industrial schools than boys. O'Sullivan writes, indeed, that the production of docile young women was integral to the mission of the Catholic nuns who ran most of the institutions.

Many of these girls were also incarcerated in the Magdalen institutions referred to earlier. These institutions were originally established in Ireland in the eighteenth century as homes for women engaged in prostitution, but gradually they became used for the incarceration of girls and women who had had children while unmarried (or "fallen women," as they were charmingly known), or who were regarded as "wild" or uncontrollable, or who had intellectual or learning disabilities. Inmates of the institutions effectively became enslaved, often unable to leave, forced to work without pay in the laundries, and subjected to brutal treatment and abuse from the nuns in charge. Many died in the institutions, and not all of those who died were properly accounted for.

An interdepartmental enquiry into the Magdalen institutions was finally instituted by the government in 2011. Chaired by Senator Martin McAleese, its remit was to examine the extent to which the state was involved in the confinement of so many women and girls within the laundries. The report of this enquiry, published in February 2013, established conclusively the extensive level of state involvement. Later the same month, on February 19, the Taoiseach gave a formal apology on behalf of the state to all those women and girls who had been incarcerated in the Magdalen laundries over the 76 years in which they remained in existence, from 1922 to 1996. Redress will also be provided by the state for the survivors of the institutions.

In recent years, public attention has focused on the unfortunate children who were incarcerated in this way, in industrial schools, Magdalen laundries, and other institutions, as more and more revelations emerge about the extent to which they were abused, physically, emotionally, and sexually, while in the care of the religious orders. Perhaps, the most appalling aspect of the child-abuse scandal is the negligence of the state in this area—having handed over responsibility for control of the institutions to religious orders, it failed to provide any sort of monitoring of the conditions in which the children were kept.

However, as the full extent of abuse upon children resident in such institutions has come to light, there have been attempts by the state to make amends, through the establishment of commissions of inquiry, which led to the publication of reports like the Ryan and Murphy Reports referred to earlier. In addition, the Residential Institutions Redress Board was established by the state in 2002 with the role of making "fair and reasonable" awards of money to those who were abused as children while resident in industrial schools, reformatories, or other institutions subject to state regulation or inspection. However, the "indemnity deal" concluded between the state and the Catholic Church as to who will end up paying for the redress has been subject to extensive criticism. It now appears that the state will end up footing the vast bulk of the bill, while the Church has got off exceedingly lightly

This indemnity agreement was made between former minister for education, Dr Michael Woods, and the relevant religious orders, in the dying days of the outgoing Fianna Fáil/Progressive Democrat coalition government in 2002. It limits the religious orders' contribution to the costs of redress, leaving the state (i.e., the taxpayer) to meet the rest of the costs. It now seems that the orders' contribution will be substantially less than half of the total amount that may be paid out to survivors of abuse, even though it was the members of the orders, rather than anyone in the employment of the state, who actually inflicted the abuse upon the complainants. This could amount ultimately to a staggering bill for the state and for taxpayers.

In 2003, due to growing public concern, the Oireachtas Public Accounts Committee carried out an examination of the Church–state deal. It emerged that the first time the details of the indemnity were discussed by officials, including officials from the Attorney General's Office, was on April 19, 2002, just five days before the dissolution of the Dáil prior to the May 2002 election. Furthermore, it became clear that the attorney general had not been represented at two key meetings between government representatives and the religious orders in November 2001 and January 2002.

Finally, there is ongoing controversy about how the orders' contribution will be paid: They have pledged to contribute some cash, while the rest is to be paid in kind through the transfer of land and property to the state; the terms of ownership of at least some of the lands are disputed. This whole affair, borne of a previous government's willingness to negotiate with the Church in a uniquely partisan manner, is likely to continue rumbling on for some time.

This brief review demonstrates the negative and often malign influence that the Catholic Church has had over the development of our health and institutional welfare systems, and thus over the evolution of politics around sexuality and sexual difference. It also demonstrates how for so many years the state effectively abandoned its responsibility to citizens and handed over control of the most vulnerable members of our community to the churches, and to one church in particular. Even in less important areas—control over rituals like wedding ceremonies and funerals—the churches, and particularly the Catholic Church, clearly until now have retained significant power.

Despite welcome changes toward a more secular society, the persistent nature of Church power represents a continued challenge for those who wish to see a more secular social system develop in Ireland, and a more tolerant and respectful official approach to matters of sexuality and sexual difference. Although much progress has been made in recent years toward greater equality for all, irrespective of sexuality, there is still undoubtedly much more to be done. The campaigns continue.

References

Adshead, Maura (2003) *The Encyclopaedia of Ireland*. Dublin: Gill & Macmillan.

Browne, Noel (1986) *Against the Tide*. Dublin: Gill & Macmillan.

Bunreacht na hEireann/Constitution of Ireland (1937). Dublin: Government Publications.

Ferriter, Diarmuid (2009) *Occasions of Sin: Sex and Society in Modern Ireland.* London: Profile Books.

Government of Ireland White Paper (2000) *A Framework for Supporting Voluntary Activity.* Dublin: Government Publications.

McAleese Report (2013) *Report of the Inter-Departmental Committee to Establish the Facts of State Involvement with the Magdalen Laundries.* Dublin: Government Publications.

Murphy Report (2010) *Report of the Commission of Investigation into the Dublin Archdiocese Chaired by Judge Yvonne Murphy.* Dublin: Government Publications.

O'Sullivan, Eoin (1998) "Juvenile Justice and the Regulation of the Poor," in Bacik and O'Connell (eds), *Crime and Poverty in Ireland.* Dublin: Round Hall.

Ryan Report (2009) *Report of the Commission to Inquire into Child Abuse Chaired by Judge Sean Ryan.* Dublin: Government Publications.

CHAPTER 2

Rethinking the Armagh Women's Dirty Protest

Paula Burns

On February 7, 1980, in Northern Ireland (NI), 32 female republican inmates, held in Armagh Women's Prison, joined their 400 male comrades in Long Kesh men's prison in what is known as the "dirty protest." Unlike the hunger strike that would commence in 1981, the dirty protest represented a new form of challenge to authority that had no pattern in existing political culture, but was one that entailed the use of bodily waste as a political weapon. For the same reasons as their male comrades, the 32 women were protesting against British colonialism. However, the similarity between the protests was negated by the presence of menstrual blood that tapped an experience of the feminine excluded from NI's conservative public discourse. This meant that in order to deploy their own protest of utilizing dirt, the Armagh women needed to fight essentialist ideals present in the dominant establishments of the time. These included the male-dominant republican movement, the unitary feminist movement, and the patriarchal Catholic Church. On reflection, it became apparent that the women required a female voice; one that rejects sameness, equality, and a shared identity; one that acknowledges difference and destabilizes phallic language to question cultural hegemonic images of femininity. Drawing on a variety of theoretical resources, this essay rethinks the Armagh women's dirty protest in order to underline its feminist significance.

Most people have heard a sentence that begins: "As feminist I think..." It is a sentence that speaks of a wish that an agreed way of being a feminist should exist; and from the 1960s and 1970s, this is how feminists angled their appeal—at a very high level of generality. The unity of the movement was assumed to derive from a potential shared identity between women (Delmar, 1994: 7). However, despite the comparative success of the modern women's liberation movement, in recent years, this identity-based unity has turned out to be a very fragile matter, particularly in NI where coming to terms with difference has never been an easy task. This difficulty was reflected in a published report by Margaret Ward of a feminist conference held in Belfast in 1983, called *A Difficult, Dangerous Honesty: Ten Years of Feminism in Northern Ireland*. The feminist movement in NI had initially hoped to foster a unitary women's identity that would rise above the polarized ethnic divide between nationalist and loyalist women. Ward's report, as well as other Irish feminist writings, provided an important window into the difficulties and ambiguities that infused the political identity of feminist women and caused fragmentation throughout feminist discourse. Women were identified as Marxist, radical feminist, or black, to name but a few, operating in isolation and ignoring others except to criticize them. What then can the specifically republican action of Armagh bring to feminist understanding?

From the 1990s, many feminist theorists have joined sympathies with the postmodern and post-structuralist critical project in a process aimed at destabilizing modernist feminist theory. In short, they reject the claim that there is a single theory that can explain the oppressed position of women in society, or that there is any unitary essence to the concept "woman" and suggest instead ways in which the diverse interests of women can be pursued. And despite much criticism from conventional feminists like Stevi Jackson (1992: 4), postmodern feminists have used for their point of reference male theorists such as Lacan, Derrida, and Foucault, who, one the one hand, have been accused of being andocentric and unsympathetic toward feminism (Jackson, 1992: 4), yet on the other, provide an analysis and critique which can make the project of "knowing women" a challenging and exciting one. In this chapter, I rethink the Armagh dirty protest by using a number of contemporary feminist interpretations of some of these ideas. The underlying irony, however, is that at the beginning of the protest in 1980, the significance of the event was firmly rejected by mainstream feminists such as the Northern Ireland Women's Rights Movement (NIWRM)—a feminist organization founded in 1975—which was largely hostile to nationalism in general and republicanism in particular. They regarded the protest as not being a feminist issue at all, a view justified on the grounds that the Armagh women were mimicking their male comrades (Aretxaga, 1997: 143). In contrast, Women Against Imperialism (WAI)—a small group of republican and anti-imperialist left-wing women based in Belfast and Derry—fought to get the Armagh protest recognized, but by and large, they believed that women's liberation was only possible after British withdrawal from the north of Ireland (Loughran, 1986: 63). Finally and most importantly, the majority of women involved in the dirty protest did not consider themselves feminist and they viewed the feminist movement in NI as pro-British. In other words, the fact of being either nationalist or loyalist in NI was not an element that could be encompassed within the image of an essential woman. From a contemporary standpoint, all these unsettled aspects highlight two things: first that feminism can never be a transparent system in that it is always engendered by particular positions in a social universe; and second that the concept of feminism in NI at that time was almost impossible to pin down. I shall argue, therefore, that newer concerns with the fluidity of identity, language, power, and feminist agency are called for when analyzing the Armagh women's dirty protest, rather than earlier concepts such as equality and sisterhood. As Audre Lorde points out: "It is not our differences which separate women, but our reluctance to recognize those differences" (1992: 50).

By applying a contemporary feminist analysis to the dirty protest, and making the voices of the Armagh women heard, it becomes possible to escape from the confinements of masculinist thought and language that echoed throughout the protest. Many ideas regarding language and differences have their origins in the work of Lacan and Derrida, and in addition, Foucault's work plays a significant role in a number of different discourses relating to the dirty protest, not least in his view of surveillance as it might operate here both within Armagh prison and on the bodies of the Armagh women.

After the withdrawal of political status from prisoners, the republican women in Armagh went on a work strike refusing to do compulsory jobs for regular inmates. This protest carried with it loss of human rights such as visits, parcels, and education. As opposed to their male comrades, the women in Armagh were not required to wear prison uniforms, as was true for all women prisoners in Britain. However, the Armagh women used their own garments, berets, and black skirts to improvise Irish Republican Army (IRA) uniforms that would symbolize and reassert their denied political identity. It was in search of those small pieces of apparel that kicking and punching, military men in full riot gear entered the cells of the women prisoners. For the women, the events of February 7, 1980, triggered their "protest of dirt." For more than one year, 32 women, the majority of whom were under 24 years of age, lived in cells without washing, amid their own menstrual blood and bodily waste, to protest against British colonialism. Despite similarities with the ongoing male protest, there is no doubt that the dirty protest was different for the men and the women. The fact that there was "blood on the walls of Armagh prison" gave rise to deep concern among one section of the community and to expressions of disgust at such unwomanly behavior on others (Hill, 2003: 231).

Journalist, Tim Coogan, visited the jail at the time and wrote:

> I was taken into inspect "A" wing where the dirty protest was in full swing. This was sickening and appalling. Tissues, slops consisting of tea and urine, some faeces, and clots of blood obviously the detritus of menstruation lay in the corridors...I found the smell in the girls' cells far worse than at Long Kesh and several times found myself having to control feelings of nausea. (1980: 215–216)

What Coogan expresses with his body—it literally makes him sick—is the horror and repulsion triggered by the sight of what constitutes a specular and linguistic taboo; a horror that he cannot fully articulate (Aretxaga, 1997: 137). Lacan's psychoanalytic ideas on the symbolic order of language, what he calls the second stage of a child's development, are helpful here. In brief, Lacan sees language as essentially a masculinist phenomenon and he suggests this is why boys and girls view the world differently, insofar as girls have to use a language through which they cannot fully express themselves. Influenced in different ways by Lacan's theories, post-structuralist feminists, like Moira Gatens, have argued that language is phallocentric and that male-dominated language is incapable of expressing both feminine sexual pleasures and, in this case, feminine taboos (1999: 231).

The failure of language was starkly evident too after the dirty protest ended. The Armagh women recognized that they were more reluctant to talk about the dirty protest than the men. An example of this was expressed by a female observer at a rally in which a young woman released from Armagh spoke about what it was like for the prisoners during their periods. The observer explained that it was very hard for the ex-prisoner to talk about menstruation, to say that even during that time, they could not get a change of clothes, could not get washed. And some people at the rally including republican men were saying, how can she talk about that? (cited by Aretxaga, 1997: 141). Another former prisoner, Brenda, said that talking about the protest produced strong feeling of vulnerability and embarrassment (Aretxaga,

1997: 128). The difficulty of the women to speak in detail about their protest was not one that their male comrades shared; yet many of the women found themselves at a loss as to why this was so. I would suggest that the answer is evident within both Coogan's reaction and the Irish Catholic culture itself: Menstruation is an unmentionable subject. Any traces of, or reference to, menstruation are hidden away especially in households with men. There is a feeling of psychological dirtiness, shame, and susceptibility at the exposure of menstrual blood and the inability to wash it away. Such a taboo excludes women's experience from language because it is lost within the phallic language of the father. Drucilla Cornell, however, suggests ways in which a transformation of masculine language can occur in that meaning, inasmuch as it is established in a chain of signifiers, can always slide, thereby producing new meaning in the process (1993: 184). At the same time, a second form of transformation can be triggered by the transgression of a taboo and the eruption of a feminine experience that is suppressed in normative language. This is what Julia Kristeva has called the "abject of sexual difference" (1982: 5). Hence, for the Armagh women, the menstrual blood acted as a transgressive symbol of femininity that was normally excluded from existing fields of discourse. Unintentionally, the female protesters brought to the fore a feminine language, one that was systematically obscured in Catholic and nationalist culture.

The crucial difference between the men's and women's dirty protest, nonetheless, has not always been acknowledged, partly to show that gender was irrelevant in a male organization like the IRA, where there has been a consistent downplaying of women's difference and an interiorization of male standards. An example of this again concerns the power of language. Consider a statement in the Andersonstown News on May 10, 1980, that the parents of the prisoners claimed that "(t)he dignity, spiritual rights, and self-respect of the girls had been violated to a serious degree in Armagh prison." The key word here is "girls"; female prisoners were constantly thought of as girls. If girl is the signifier, one will visualize a female child not an adult woman as the signified. This relates to Aretxaga's view that the Armagh women's cultural space was in this sense liminal; neither men, nor completely women, they were perceived at a social level as gender neutral (1997: 138). It is notable that the Catholic Church also repeatedly referred to the Armagh prisoners as girls in an attempt to desexualize women whose image threatened to disrupt Catholic moral discourse regarding the female ideal. In contrast, the feminist groups that were trying to break the silence on the women's suffering referred to the prisoners as women to highlight the fact that they needed a voice.

Post-structuralist feminists, such as Cixous, take the whole concept of deconstruction one step further. Cixous and Clément (1987)
argue that phallocentic language is based around binary opposition,
which—in the context of the gender binaries dominant throughout
the dirty protest—includes head/heart, Jesus/Virgin Mary, IRA/
Cumman na mban, and republican martyr/wife. As she makes clear,
such oppositions are always hierarchical, with the masculine term
ranking higher that the feminine. Yet, Derrida's notion of undecid-
ability can undermine the claims of masculinity, radically disrupt-
ing masculinist certainties, and effecting a rethinking of difference.
When the Armagh women joined the IRA, then, and went on to par-
take in the dirty protest, initially, they negated gender differences and
stated that their struggle was the same as that of the men. Yet, this
attempt to be recognized as "equal" to their male comrades meant
they had to reject the feminine. Moreover, the claim to equality failed
with the appearance of menstrual blood, which materialized their
sexual difference. Two things are highlighted here: The dirty protest
entailed a refiguration of the feminine insofar as it was not the shared
identity celebrated by mainstream feminism; and it illustrates that it
is no good simply claiming equality. Rather, as Cixous suggests, the
struggle of the women was to develop ways of expressing their femininity and difference and be able to articulate what Spivak has called
"the space of what can only happen to a woman" (1997: 142).

Moving on from linguistic concerns, consider too the concept of
Foucauldian power that encompasses both material and discursive
effects. Foucault has extensively elaborated the importance of disciplinary techniques over the body in the production and deployment
of power, particularly as it is visible in total institutions like prisons.
And rather than trying to punish through physical pain, control is
far more effective if it is productive of "docile bodies." Even though
Foucault himself is ambivalent about the relevance of gender to the
disciplinary dimensions of power, it was undoubtedly central in relation to the Armagh women's protest. As he argues, power works by
creating normativities, especially about the body and sexuality, and
the male officers' assault on the women—which triggered their dirty
protest—can be interpreted as both an institutionalized attempt to
discipline through punishment and an assertion of male dominance
over the bodies of women. The challenge of the dirty protest, then, is
not only that the idea of any unwashed female body is repugnant and
brings to the fore psychological disgust, but that an unwashed, undisciplined, female body is almost incomprehensible in Irish society. Like
all others, the Armagh women had been socialized and normalized

to the everyday habits of femininity—including "hygienic" practices, especially during menstruation—that once internalized train the body in docility and obedience. Yet, they steeled themselves to live without washing and surrounded by their own excreta, urine, and menstrual blood in bare tiny prison cells. On the one hand, it is the threat to the normativities of a woman's body that provoked both the horrified reaction of the screws and the silence of the women themselves. But on the other hand, it was precisely the appearance of menstrual blood that so radically challenged the power of normalization. What Foucault has not fully addressed are the points at which the tools of normalization break down, the moment in which rational disciplines of the body fail to produce docile subjects, because the subjects, in this case the women prisoners, refused to be normalized, even at the cost of intense suffering and pain, as well as constant humiliation. For the Armagh women, it was worth subjugating their conventional feminine identities in order to assert their political identities.

As Foucault understands it, power always provokes resistance, and the appearance of menstrual blood on the walls of Armagh prison not only contests the power of surveillance to ensure self-normalization, but has a double dimension. The first is the psychological and physical dirtiness the women willingly endured; the second is the paradoxical empowerment this dirtiness gave the women. Moreover, in a phenomenological sense, the dirty protest is a paradigm of the break from conventional body expressions and habits to the use of the body for political purposes. In other words, the women became embodied, active subjects by crossing the normative boundaries of femininity; each decided, in Iris Marion Young's words, to stop "throwing like a girl." The Armagh women's bodily waste was their anchorage in the world, and the escalation of their tactics, such as rubbing their menstrual blood on their cell walls, illustrates how the embodied subject can seize and transform a given situation even during imprisonment.

More particularly, as Kristeva recognizes, "(t)he transgressive power of menstrual blood comes from an excess of signification that threatens the boundaries that constitute the social order" (1982: 65). She divides polluting objects into two types, excremental and menstrual.

> Excrement...stands from the dangers to identity that comes from without: the ego threatened by the non-ego...Menstrual blood on the contrary stands for the danger issuing from within identity (social or sexual); it threatens the relationship between the sexes within a social aggregate and through internalization, the identity of each sex in the face of sexual difference. (1982: 71)

In other words, for the Armagh women to display the marks of sexual difference is to question the construction of gender identity. It was this symbolic dimension to their material action that triggered the reaction of horror in the outside world, while coincidentally, it was precisely the transgressive power of menstrual blood that empowered the women themselves. Yet, living surrounded by menstrual blood and excrement was extremely difficult to endure, as one of the released protesters, Maureen Gibson, makes clear: "They [the nationalist community] don't understand what the women are going through both physically and psychologically. You go through a lot with your menstrual cycle" (Republican News, September 27, 1980). However, at the same time, the supposedly polluting bodily substances were a weapon deployed against the screws. The dirtiness of the women became a dreaded source of contamination, at least in imagination, and the screws wore masks, insulating suits and rubber boots to shield themselves against the threat of the prisoners. Screws did not like coming into contact with anything belonging to the women, and most of all they did not like touching the polluted bodies of the women themselves. In effect, the women's menstrual blood became embodied as a personal weapon, which protected them from beatings; it became their shield, their bodyguard, but most importantly, it became their focus of resistance, and their rejection of docility.

In conclusion, I have aimed to show how the Armagh women's dirty protest, which took place amid the rise of conservative second-wave feminism in NI, could greatly benefit from a postconventional feminist analysis. And unlike those who view many postmodern theories as interesting but dangerous for feminism as a whole, I would suggest that, in relation to the dirty protest, such approaches are central. At the very least, they problematize some of feminist doxa of the time, such as equality, a shared unity, and an agreed definition of feminism, all of which have proved to be elusive concepts. For me, the analysis of the Armagh dirty protest exemplifies the advantages of exploring the multiple meanings that can be read through contemporary feminist theory. By highlighting that language—including notions of gender—does not simply transmit thought or meaning, but that thought and meaning are constructed through language, it is possible to rethink the dirty protest. Nothing has a stable unambiguous meaning, and as the unpacking of power/knowledge reveals all discourses are constructed from specific positions. Finally, I would suggest that the dirty protest is an example of how we can look beyond Merleau-Ponty's "narrow gaze" and focus on the agency of women's bodies as central to the expression of political dissent. The Armagh women were left with no other means of fighting for their political identity other than through their bodies. By deploying the bodily performance of the dirty protest, it became possible for them to act meaningfully in the world and to contest dominant political "realities." What this brief analysis of their protest exemplifies is that the exploration of the postconventional dimensions of difference and of the feminine enables a productive new understanding of the material conditions of our recent history.

REFERENCES

Aretxaga, B. (1997) *Shattering Silence: Women, Nationalism, and Political Subjectivity in Northern Ireland*. Princeton, NJ: Princeton University Press.

Cixous, H. and Clément, C. (1987) *The Newly Born Woman*, trans. B. Wing. Manchester: Manchester University Press.

Cornell, D. (1993) *Transformations: Recollective Imagination and Sexual Difference*. New York: Routledge.

Coogan, T. P. (1980) *On the Blanket: The H-Block Story*. Dublin: Ward River.

Delmar, R. (1994) "What is Feminism?" in A. Herrmann and A. Stewart, (eds), *Theorizing Feminism*. Boulder, CO: Westview Press.

Foucault, M. (1991) *Discipline and Punish: The Birth of Prisons*. London: Penguin.

Gatens, M. (1999) "Power, Bodies and Difference," in J. Price and M. Shildrick. *Feminism Theory and the Body*. Edinburgh: Edinburgh University Press.

Hill, M. (2003) *Women in Ireland: A Century of Change*. Belfast: Blackstaff Press.

Jackson, S. (1992) "The Amazing Deconstructing Woman." *Trouble & Strife*, 25: 25–28.

Kristeva, J. (1982) Power of Horror: An Essay on Abjection, trans. Leon S. Roudiez. New York: New York University Press.

Loughran, C. (1986) "Armagh and Feminist Strategy." *Feminist Review*, 23: 59–80.

Spivak, G. in Aretxaga, B. (1997) *Shattering Silence: Women, Nationalism, and Political Subjectivity in Northern Ireland*. Princeton, NJ: Princeton University Press.

Ward, M. (1986) *A Difficult, Dangerous Honesty: 10 Years of Feminism in Northern Ireland*. Belfast: Women's News.

CHAPTER 3

Vindicating Women's Rights in a Fetocentric State: The Longest Irish Journey

Sandra McAvoy

But while the farce-makers act out their sadistic joke on the public stage, women in Ireland considering or seeking abortions abroad continue to do so in private anguish, uncertain about the legal status of their actions and without the information and practical support which would help to make their journey less traumatic.

—Smyth, 1992: 10

Ailbhe Smyth's statement above captured the anger and frustration felt by many in 1992, the year in which the Attorney General (AG) of Ireland, Harry Whelehan, obtained an injunction barring a 14-year-old girl, who had been raped by a family friend, from having an abortion in England. Her case, known as the X case, brought home how savagely Ireland's ban on abortion could impact on a young girl and her family. This anger, particularly of women, also threatened ratification of the Maastricht Treaty when it emerged that, in 1991, the government had negotiated a secret protocol to the Treaty ensuring that European Community law could not override Article 40:3.3 of the Irish Constitution, the prohibition on abortion (Smyth, 1992: 17–21). In effect, it denied Irish women future rights under European law enjoyed by women in other states. Thousands demonstrated in the streets to support the girl and her family and protest against a regime in which those seeking abortions, and anyone helping them, were criminalized (Bacik, 2004: 117). Smyth accurately summed up events in 1992 as a "tragic farce" played out in a male-controlled society, where the "foetocentric rhetoric and ethics" of the dominant Catholic Church dictated policy on reproduction (Smyth, 1992: 22). An appeal to the Supreme Court, however, resulted in the landmark decision that Ireland's constitutional ban on abortion did not apply if "it is established as a matter of probability that there is a real and sub-stantial risk to the life, as distinct from the health" of a woman includ-ing (as the girl was by then suicidal) the risk of suicide. The Court also indicated that a woman's right to travel might be restricted when there was no risk to her life (Supreme Court A.G.v X [1992] IESC 1; [1992] 1 IR [March 5, 1992]). Freedom to travel was established in one of the 1992 abortion referenda that followed from the X case. In the 20 years thereafter, no guidelines were issued and no legislation enacted to lay down the circumstances under which a termination of pregnancy might be legal in Ireland. How that "real and substantial risk" was to be assessed and how, or by whom, the risk of suicide might be judged was not established, nor were reproductive health facilities provided to deal with cases that met the X case criteria. Instead, the courts have been required to determine the entitlement of a number of young girls, in the care of the state, to travel outside it for terminations (Schweppe, 2008: 349–369). Abortion on health grounds, in cases of rape, incest, and fetal non-viability, has remained criminalized. Nevertheless, even at the time of the X case, 12 women a day—those who could afford to—traveled to British clinics (Irish Family Planning Association [IFPAa]).

The question of legislation came to the fore again following a December 2010 European Court of Human Rights (ECHR) deci-sion in cases against Ireland. These cases brought by three courageous women, known only as A, B, and C to protect their identities, captured a sense of the indignity, stigmatization, and exposure to health risks experienced by those forced to travel outside the jurisdiction to termi-nate their pregnancies. The third case, involving a Lithuanian woman resident in Ireland and suffering from cancer, appeared to meet the X case test in that there was a threat to her life. The ECHR accepted that the 1992 Supreme Court judgment had established that abortion is legally permissible in Ireland when there is a substantial risk to the life, though not the health, of a woman. Its judgment was critical of both Ireland's use of the courts as means of deciding abortion cases (ECHR Judgement: para. 258) and government inaction in the face of recommendations from members of the judiciary and three state committees (All Party Oireachtas Committee: Constitutional Review

Group Report, 1996; Green Paper, 1999; All Party Oireachtas Committee, 2000) that legal clarity was required (paras. 258–259. It found that failure to legislate or provide guidelines following the X case meant there were no "effective and accessible procedures" by which a woman in C's position might "establish her right to a lawful abortion in Ireland" (para. 263), and that this dereliction of duty violated C's right, under Article 8 of the European Convention on Human Rights and Fundamental Freedoms (ECHRFF), to "effective respect for her private life" (paras. 267–268).

Might this ruling mean that Ireland is on the cusp of change in its abortion policy or will the pretence continue that the state is abortion free while thousands of Irish women travel for terminations? In June 2011, the government submitted a brief "action plan" to the European Council of Ministers (representing the 47 signatory countries of the Convention). It made clear that the Fine Gael–Labour coalition government's response would be the commissioning of a further report on the issue, this time involving an "expert group, drawing on appropriate medical and legal expertise" (Action Plan Press Release). Its terms of reference confined it to clarifying the implications of the ECHR Judgement for health-care provision for pregnant women and advising on "constitutional, legal, medical, and ethical" aspects of policy implementation. They also suggested that a speedy response was required (Action Report: 1–2). The group was expected to submit its report in July 2012, but at the time of writing, that deadline has been pushed back to autumn. Its "expert" members include obstetricians, a psychiatrist, general practitioners, lawyers, and policy makers. Its composition is a reminder of how abortion policy is determined by political and professional elites, while women seeking abortions have been criminalized and silenced and those arguing for abortion rights sidelined and defined as a polarizing minority. Such stigmatization may have contributed to successive governments' apparent distrust of women and indifference to their exclusion from discussion on the issue. It may also be among the reasons why a majority of Irish politicians turn their faces against the idea that access to abortion might be a human rights matter.

This chapter looks, from a pro-choice, feminist, social historian's perspective, at some of the consequences of criminalization for those in crisis pregnancies and at recent developments in Ireland where the A, B, and C cases have been important in opening up a space in the media for discussion of abortion as a complex issue. This has given some women, and their partners, courage to speak publicly about why they decided to terminate pregnancies and the ordeal involved in traveling abroad. Among other sources, the chapter draws on selected comments on abortion in the Irish press, and on aspects of women's published personal stories, to highlight the apparent disconnect that exists between understandings of abortion expressed by those with practical experience of crisis pregnancy and by representatives of the Irish state who present opposition to abortion as a matter of nationally agreed principle. It also raises questions about the assertion—made by the AG during the A, B, and C cases—and crucial to the decisions of all but six of the seventeen ECHR judges—that addressing such issues runs counter to the cultural values and moral position of the Irish as a nation, as expressed in referenda in 1983, 1992, and 2002. It concludes by looking briefly at recent political developments, including the introduction, in April 2012, of a private members' bill on abortion provision to suggest that women voicing their stories have made some impact.

"Psychologically and Physically Arduous"

The ECHR did not rule in favor of A or B. The first had accessed abortion outside the jurisdiction for social and personal reasons and the second, who did not wish to be a lone parent, had used emergency contraception and was fearful of an ectopic pregnancy when it failed (ABC Case: Statement of Facts). Its judgment did, however, accept that being forced to travel abroad for an abortion was "psychologically and physically arduous" for both women and that it was "additionally so for the first applicant given her impoverished circumstances" (para. 239). It is not difficult to imagine the stress suffered by those stretched to the limit to find the €500 to close to €2,000 needed to pay for an abortion abroad, or unable to pull together the additional sums required for accommodation and travel in time to comply with the 24-week time limit on terminations in Britain. (In 2012, prices in Marie Stopes clinics ranged from £450 for a medical abortion, up to nine weeks, to £1,846 for a termination at more than 19 weeks.) Clearly, Ireland has a two-tiered system in which those with access to funds exercise their right to end their pregnancies outside the state and those in poverty cannot. For some, it takes time to raise money and Irish medical organization *Doctors for Choice in Ireland* (*DFC*) has expressed concern that, for such women, this may mean later abortions with "invasive procedures, under general rather than local anaesthetic" and risks to health that would be avoided if abortion services were available in Ireland (*DFC* leaflet: undated).

A doctor who performs an "unlawful" abortion or a woman who has a backstreet abortion in Ireland, or attempts self-abortion, faces up to life imprisonment under the British 1861 Offences Against the Person Act, inherited at independence in 1922. This archaic Irish law is out of step with that of our European neighbors. The ECHR Judgement recognized that A and B could have obtained abortions on request in 30 of the contracting states of the Council of Europe, that 40 provided for abortion for reasons of health and well being, and 35 on the ground of well-being (para. 235). Although it is perfectly legal to access such services abroad, within Ireland, criminalization and strident anti-abortion discourse have had their effect. A few lines from the statement of facts in one of the ECHR cases provide a snapshot of what a woman may go through, including how, even when worrying symptoms and infection occur, she may hesitate to seek post-abortion medical assistance:

> She had to travel to England alone, in secrecy and with no money to spare, without alerting the social workers and without missing a contact visit with her children. On her return to Ireland she experienced pain, nausea and bleeding for eight to nine weeks, but was afraid to seek medical advice because of the prohibition on abortion. (ABC Case: Statement of Facts)

More than 150,000 women resident in Ireland have had abortions abroad since the 1970s. The state's own 1999 *Green Paper on Abortion* (166) noted that at that time, the ratio of abortions to live births in the state was 1 to 10. Numbers of Irish residents seeking abortions in Britain have fallen in recent years, from 6,673 in 2001 to 4,422 in 2009, to 4,149 in 2011 (*Statistical Bulletin*, table 12a, and IFPA Abortion Statistics). This drop may be the result of greater openness about contraception, including the "morning-after-pill," only approved for use in Ireland in 2001, though clandestine imports of medical abortifacients like RU486, ordered online may be a further factor. Statistics gathered in the Netherlands indicate that 451 Irish women had abortions there in 2007, 351 in 2008, and 134 in 2009, but that by 2010, the figure had fallen to 31 (*Health Service Executive* [*HSE*] Press Release, May 25, 2010, and IFPA Abortion Statistics). It has been no secret in Ireland that banning abortion does not prevent it and inflicts oppressive journeys on vulnerable women. Few of those who traveled over the years revealed their identities when they spoke publicly about their experiences. None gave evidence to the All Party Oireachtas Committee on the Constitution that reported on abortion in 2000. Their stories have, however, been increasingly told in publications like the *IFPA*'s 2002 compilation *The Irish Journey*,

Rossiter's (*2009*) *Ireland's Hidden Diaspora*, and the 2010 Human Rights Watch (HRW) Report, *A State of Isolation*.

During the 2002 abortion referendum campaign, considerable impact was made by a radio interview with one woman, Deirdre de Barra, and by her letter to the editor of the *The Irish Times* (February 25, 2002), which spoke of the "inhumane treatment of women in this State" and her shocking discovery of how the state could "violate my rights and dignity." She described being forced to travel after learning that her baby was suffering from a chromosomal abnormality and would not survive after birth. Pressed on such cases by journalist Nell McCafferty, at a press conference, the Masters of the Irish maternity hospitals expressed sympathy and agreed that traveling for abortions created problems, such as the absence of postmortem information, and affected doctors' ability to counsel on future pregnancies (Coulter, 2002). In 2007, there was much publicity around a court case in which a 17-year-old girl in the care of the state, whose unborn baby was diagnosed with anencephaly, sought permission to travel (Schweppe, 2008). In the period 2002–2012, however, no attempt has been made by the state to face up even to this question of fatal fetal abnormalities although, as pointed out by *DFC*, Ireland has the second highest rate of neural-tube defects in the world (*DFC* Press Release, 2007).

During the years 2009–2012, more women have spoken publicly about both the stresses traveling imposed on them and their reasons for ending their pregnancies. For example, one 2009 newspaper report talked of a woman "fainting in the airport as she waited five hours for her return flight to Ireland, and the guilt, shame, and above all secrecy, which added their weight to this daunting experience" (Devlin, 2009). A 2010 Irish Examiner article reported the views of two women, one named and one anonymous. The first spoke of choosing abortion because her pregnancy occurred at the wrong time "emotionally, psychologically or financially. I was in a rebound relationship and I couldn't go ahead with the pregnancy." Both made clear their view that decisions on terminations were matters solely for the woman involved (Barry, 2010). A December 2010 *Irish Times* report, published days after the delivery of the ECHR Judgement, brought home both the implications of the failure to define the words "real and significant risk," after the 1992 ruling, and how disempowered a pregnant woman is in the process of deciding the level of threat cancer poses to her life. The woman involved had been told her cancer treatment would be delayed because she was pregnant. Balancing the risks, she discussed a termination with her doctors in Cork University Hospital.

The question was passed to the hospital's ethics committee, described as a group with "medical and non-medical" members. The report quoted a Health Service Executive statement suggesting that the committee's role was to deliberate on "any case brought before it in the light of the Irish Constitution" (O'Brien, 2010). Another item in the same paper noted that such committees had no statutory basis and that there was "little clarity or consistency about their role" (Coulter, 2010). Yet, such a committee was empowered by a hospital to make potentially life and death decisions while the applicant was excluded from its deliberations. It reportedly rejected the request, a decision that forced a sick woman to travel. She and her partner described how they borrowed money from family members, for a journey to England on which she was "stressed out," "weak," "nauseous and vomiting" and on which they could not afford the taxi fare to the London hospital. They also confided that, after her return, a scan indicated that the cancer had spread to her brain (O'Brien, 2010).

In spring 2012, with the introduction of a private members' bill, the Medical Treatment (Termination of Pregnancy in Case of Risk to Life of Pregnant Woman) Bill (discussed later), a number of women and some of their partners were interviewed by *Irish Times* journalist Kathy Sheridan. One couple had learned, at 21 weeks, that their baby might die in the womb and had little chance of surviving after birth. They described the world of evasion that arises in part from legal uncertainties in Ireland, including, perhaps, lack of clarity about the implications of the restrictive Regulation of Information (Services outside the State for Terminations of Pregnancies) Act 1995, interpreted as making it illegal for a doctor to refer a patient to abortion services abroad or make an appointment with a clinic on her behalf. They noticed that medical professionals avoided the word "abortion" and that an Irish hospital would not forward records directly to an English one. It faxed them to the IFPA as an intermediary. They described the physical and psychological stress involved in travel but also how meaningful had been the reassurance by an English midwife that they "were doing the right thing for their baby" when "no other medic" had offered such solace (Sheridan, 2012a). Another story highlighted an insidious result of forcing women to travel. It hugely reduces their opportunity to change their minds or postpone the procedure at the last minute, particularly if they are close to the 24-week deadline; have organized child care; taken leave from work; made a difficult journey; and invested large sums in travel, accommodation, and clinic fees (Sheridan, 2012a).

IMMUTABLE VALUES?

The *Irish Times* stories also contained a call from a man who spoke of his feelings on finding that his girlfriend had terminated her pregnancy. Explaining that he was "not an advocate for or against abortion," he asked for an end to the pretence that abortion did not exist in Ireland and for a new "collective understanding as a society" of the issues involved (Sheridan, 2012b). As long ago as 1999, the *Green Paper on Abortion* acknowledged that in Ireland "there is much private sympathy and concern for the personal, social and moral anxieties of those facing crisis pregnancies, particularly where rape, incest, or other grave circumstances are involved" (16). Politicians have, however, stood firm against the idea that such women should be permitted access to reproductive choices within Ireland. In external arenas, the position taken by the state is that the Irish, as a nation, oppose legalized abortion. For example, at a Council of Europe meeting, in 2008, this was at the heart of Ireland's opposition to the decriminalization of abortion in member states (O'Brien, 2008), although a Council report demonstrated that criminalization had public health impacts, created "abortion tourism," and exposed women to late, unsafe, or illegal terminations (Council of Europe Doc. 11576). Before Ireland's second vote on the Lisbon Treaty, the government sought guarantees from its European Union partners that nothing in it "affects in any way the scope and applicability of the protection of the right to life" under the Irish Constitution (European Council Conclusions, June 2009), much as, in 1991, Ireland had arranged the insertion of the secret protocol to the Maastricht Treaty.

That the Irish people stand firm against abortion was asserted in the pleading of the Irish AG, Paul Gallagher, during the December 2009 hearing of the A, B, and C cases when he argued that: Ireland's constitutional protection of the "unborn" reflected "profound moral values, deeply imbedded in the fabric of Irish society, and arrived at through a wholly democratic process involving, in all, three referenda" (ECHR podcast). The influence of the state's argument on the deliberations of the ECHR judges was clear. Accepting that national "authorities" are more capable than judges of international courts of understanding the moral values of their citizens (ECHR, para. 223) was central to the court's according Ireland a "margin of appreciation." That is, the extent to which a majority of judges accepted that the cultural and moral values of Ireland had to be taken into account when determining whether it met its obligations under the ECHRFF. For example, the majority judgment noted that A and B were unable to terminate their pregnancies in Ireland on grounds of health and well-being, although they could have done so in most European states. Because it took account of the "profound moral views of the Irish people," as suggested by the AG, it found that "Ireland had struck a fair balance" between the right of women to "respect for their private lives" and the rights of the fetus (para. 241).

Questions must arise for Irish women about the universality of human rights when permitting such a margin endorses the practice of weighing up the rights of a woman and a fetus and judging the woman's subordinate. Given the consensus on women's rights in other countries, the effect of this practice is to delineate Irish women as lesser citizens than most of their sisters in Europe. There is an issue too about the gendered nature of the values, Ireland's adherence to which impacts so severely on women's lives, health, and well-being. This is particularly so when they were inculcated by a male Catholic hierarchy, immutable in its opposition to women's reproductive rights (including use of contraceptives), and when they have been defended, over decades, by an overwhelmingly male political elite, most of whom were educated by that church. (Women won only 25 of the 166 seats in the 2011 election.) Nor are Irish public representatives or public servants compelled to divulge membership of church societies such as Opus Dei or the Knights of Columbanus that might have an interest in ensuring that public discourse and legislation reflect Catholic values.

The dissenting opinion of six ECHR judges did question the basis of the majority verdict. It foregrounded the "strong" consensus on abortion, among the majority of contracting states of the Council of Europe, that not just a woman's life, but also her "well-being and health, are considered more valuable than the right to life of the foetus" (ECHR Dissenting Opinion, para. 2), and that, in matters of human rights, such consensus "decisively narrows the margin of appreciation" (paras. 4–5). These six judges indicated that they would have found in favor of A and B, as well as C, in relation to Article 8 of the Convention, on the ground that permitting a woman to travel abroad, with the costs and other problems involved, did not meet the Convention's requirements regarding respect for her private life. Additionally, they expressed concern that their co-judges had "disregarded" the existence of a European consensus on the basis of "profound moral views," particularly as there was uncertainty about whether these views were still shared by the majority in Ireland. They posited that doing so marked "a real and dangerous new departure" for the court (paras. 8–9).

Referenda as Measures of Profound
Moral Values Held by a Majority

How can something as abstract as national values be measured? With regard to referendum results, is there a basis for the state's assertion that its abortion policy reflects a consensus arrived at democratically? Abortion is a matter of constitutional as well as criminal law in Ireland and constitutional amendments on the issue were put to voters in 1983, 1992, and 2002. Can the results of these referenda be taken as measures of a nationally agreed position on abortion, as implied by the AG? It is important to note two points. First, that no amendment intended to liberalize abortion law has been put to or rejected by the people. Second, for reasons of political stability, the outcome of a constitutional referendum must be understood as an expression of the democratic will of the people. In Ireland, however, no minimum turnout is required and decisions are made by a simple majority of those who vote, even if as few as 43 percent of those registered go to the polls, as in the 2002 referendum (*Elections Ireland* website). Clearly, an amendment may be accepted without the vote reflecting the views of the majority of citizens.

With a largely Catholic population, and with that church opposed to abortion, over decades, there has been little questioning of the state's apparently majoritarian, and Catholic, position. Do referendum results vindicate it? An examination of voting statistics suggests that only in 1992 can the outcome be read as a clear representation of the will of a majority of those registered to vote. In that year, three proposals on matters that arose from the X case were put to the people on a general election day. This factor contributed to a high turnout. Far from expressing a deeply held opposition to abortion, voters rejected government attempts to tighten the constitutional ban by ensuring that risk of suicide was removed as a ground for abortion and that the courts could not in future interpret a woman's right to life as implying a right to health. The proposed amendment read:

> It shall be unlawful to terminate the life of an unborn unless such termination is necessary to save the life, as distinct from the health, of the mother where there is an illness or disorder of the mother giving rise to a real and substantial risk to her life, not being the risk of self-destruction. (Referendum (Amendment) (No 2) Act 1992)

Around 68 percent of the electorate cast their votes on this "substantive issue," as it was euphemistically known, in 1992. Of these, only

34.65 percent (less than a quarter of the total number of registered voters) voted in favor of inserting the proposed restrictions in the constitution. 65.35 percent (almost 45 percent of those registered) voted against (*Elections Ireland* website). If such figures were an expression of national moral solidarity on the question of abortion, they imply sympathy with the girl in the X Case and distaste for further constitutional restrictions. Mahon (2001: 170) notes that, as anti-abortion groups were split on whether the proposal would limit or increase access to abortion, some anti-abortion voters contributed to the defeat of the referendum. As discussed below, confusion amongst the electorate and conflicting interpretations of the implications of the proposed wording have been features of each referendum campaign. Mahon (169–170) does, however, point to a finding in the 1990 European values study (Hornsby-Smith and Whelan, 1994: 36) that 65 percent of Irish respondents accepted abortion as an option when pregnancy threatened a woman's health. Travel and information amendments involved short additions to Article 40.3.3 on "freedom" to travel from Ireland to other states and "freedom" to access or provide information on "services lawfully available in another state," subject to legislation (Referendum (Amendment) (No 2) Act 1992). Votes on these suggested that there was little stomach for either censorship of information on abortion services outside Ireland or inhibiting women's access to them. Some 68.18 percent of the electorate voted on travel, with 62.39 percent of these in favor of establishing women's freedom to travel. On information, turnout was over 68 percent of registered voters, of whom almost 60 percent voted to permit access to information on abortion (*Elections Ireland* website).

What is striking about the turnout in 1983 and 2002 is that a large proportion of the electorate did not go to the polls in either year. The 1983 referendum was the one that placed in the Constitution the article understood by its proposers to prohibit abortion. The wording put to the people read:

> The State acknowledges the right to life of the unborn and, with due regard to the equal right to life of the mother, guarantees in its laws to respect and, as far as practical, by its law to defend and vindicate that right. (Article 40.3.3)

Despite encouragement from Catholic bishops and clergy, who urged parishioners to support the amendment, the electorate did not overwhelmingly accept the proposal. Only 53.67 percent of those registered went to the polls. While two-thirds of these voted for the constitutional prohibition on abortion and a third voted against, the relatively low turnout meant that endorsement by only 35.9 percent of the electorate was sufficient to vote the Eighth Amendment into place (*Elections Ireland* website). Such a low level of support does not imply national unity in banning abortion. It highlights the shortcoming in a political system in which a vote of just over one-third of "the people" can place an article in the Constitution that has such profound consequences for the lives and health of women citizens.

In 2001, the Fianna Fáil—Progressive Democrat coalition brought forward the Twenty-fifth Amendment of the Constitution (Protection of Human Life in Pregnancy) Bill. The aim was to insert a complex criminal statute in the Constitution, amendable only by referendum. Although similar proposals had been rejected in 1992, the thrust of the measure was to remove risk of suicide as a ground for abortion and strengthen the prohibition on abortion to protect a woman's health. While it would have permitted doctors to provide those medical interventions required when there was a "real and substantial risk" to the life of a woman, for example, from cancer, terminations would be tightly policed with women brought to "approved" centers (designated by the Minister for Health) and they would not be termed "abortions." Up to 12 years' imprisonment was proposed for women having unlawful abortions in Ireland and for anyone who helped them. Although representing a reduction of the possible life sentence under the 1861 legislation, the hypocrisy involved in continuing such criminalization, when so many citizens (19 women each week in 2001) chose to terminate their pregnancies abroad, was focused on by anti-amendment campaigners (*Alliance for a No Vote* leaflets, 2001–2002). On referendum day, in March 2002, only a little more than two in five of those eligible to vote went to the polls (42.9 percent): a turnout that might suggest confusion, lack of interest, or, perhaps, rejection of attempts to use the Constitution in this way. Just under 50 percent of those who did vote supported the Twenty-fifth Amendment while just over 50 percent of voters rejected it (*Elections Ireland* website). It was defeated by 10,548 votes with the result implying some urban–rural divide in attitudes to abortion (Devlin, 2002). Utmost caution is required in analyzing such results and, given that only a minority of those registered went to the polls in the 2002, it can by no means be used as an indicator of a nationally shared position against abortion. Voting figures show only that those who voted were close to evenly divided in support of, or opposition to, the specific proposals put forward by the state and that those opposed to the state's position won narrowly. As in 1983, the 2002 result said nothing about the united will of the nation against permitting abortion. Indeed, that almost 60 percent of the electorate did not vote must call into question the government of the day's assessment of the public appetite for further restrictions, its perception of national values, and its judgment in putting a measure involving complex legislation to the people. Yet, the implication of references to referendum results in political discourse, and before the ECHR, is that a majority of the people proclaimed their adherence to Catholic values and deep opposition to abortion through referenda in 1983, 1992, and 2002. Analysis of the results reveals that only a minority has supported measures to restrict access to abortion and maintain criminalization, while the views of a sizeable proportion of the people remain unknown.

OPPOSITION, APATHY, AND CONFUSION

Why did abortion become a focus in Ireland in the 1980s? After legislation was passed in 1979 legalizing contraceptives (though restricting access to them to married couples), making a stand on abortion offered conservative groups the possibility of regrouping and an opportunity to resist what Girvin summed up as "secularist trends" (like demanding a right to divorce) in a rapidly changing country (Girvin, 1986: 61). Analyzing contemporary discourse, Lisa Smyth's (2005) key study of the period 1983–2002 has demonstrated how, in the early 1980s, a moral panic was constructed with abortion defined as a threat to the nation, one to be staved off by reinforcement of "traditional" and distinctively Catholic values. She suggests that the creators of this panic drew on concepts of republican democracy, particularly that of the political sovereignty of the people, to establish the idea that the people spoke with one unchallengeable, Catholic voice on abortion. In this period, non-Catholic opinion was marginalized and proponents of women's rights virtually silenced. Abortion referendum campaigns have, however, been characterized by opposition and bitter divisions, with the *Irish Times* famously dubbing the 1983 campaign the "Second Partitioning of Ireland" (Editorial, 1983). The Catholic hierarchy has played an important role in each of the abortion referendums, perhaps because, as historian John A. Murphy recalled of the 1970s, certain Catholic bishops "equated democracy with majoritarianism" and demanded the "supportive framework of the State for the Catholic moral code" (Murphy, 2002). In 1981–1982, when prohibition was mooted, the major Protestant churches and Chief Rabbi, whose faiths permitted abortion in some circumstances, issued statements questioning the placing of a prohibition in the Constitution (Arnold and Kirby,

1982: 61–65). Brendan O'Mahony, a Capuchin priest and Professor of Philosophy at University College Cork, applied the term "tyranny of principles" to the unfolding situation in which a group, considering its teachings to be "*infallibly* true," imposed them on fellow citizens regardless of their consent and without considering the implications for their freedoms of religion or conscience (O'Mahony, 1982).

There was a strong anti-amendment campaign, in 1983, in which future President of Ireland, and proponent of women's rights, Mary Robinson played an important role. Its arguments included that the proposal would subordinate women's rights to those of the unborn; that abortion was a legislative rather than a constitutional matter; that current medical practice would be threatened; and that the proposal would "create an atmosphere of fear and intolerance and could encourage a return to the dangerous practice of backstreet abortions" (Hesketh, 1990: 279–285; Smyth, 1983: 58–63). Among many prominent women to speak out against the amendment, Maureen Curtis Black, founder of the Cork Citizens' Advice Bureau, summed up the indifference to women's rights inherent in the pro-amendment campaign, suggesting that "women, especially married women, don't count in Ireland" (Black, 1983). It is important to remember that the nation did not speak as one, and that strong voices opposed the insertion of Article 40.3.3 in the Constitution, as well as that almost half the electorate did not vote in the 1983 referendum. Hug (1999) referred to the apathy and confusion of voters (150), a confusion deepened by an eve of poll warning from the Fine Gael Taoiseach, Garret Fitzgerald, that the wording of the amendment was so ambiguous that even he, its proposer, could not ask the electorate to support it (Anonymous, *Irish Times*, September 6, 1983). If the issue had not had such profound consequences for Irish women and been so divisive, there would be an element of the absurd about the process by which the 1983 amendment was put to the people.

It is suggested earlier in the chapter that the 1992 referendum result is the closest to a measure of the electorate's attitudes to abortion, given that more than two-thirds of registered voters went to the polls. Yet, it cannot be considered an expression of support for a prohibition on abortion since the majority of voters refused to accept further restrictions and endorsed access to information and travel outside the state for abortions. Mahon's (2001: 170) comments on confusion among anti-abortion groups in 1992 on whether the proposed amendment would restrict or extend access are also quoted above. Confusion and conflict about interpretations of every aspect of the state's proposals were also a feature of the 2002 campaign, including whether they would prevent a suicidal child in care from traveling (Kingston, 2001). Again, there were divisions between anti-abortion groups, some of whom believed that supporting the proposal would dilute their position. The Catholic Church gave qualified support to the government's plans; the main opposition parties, the Fine Gael and Labour parties, opposed them but the women's movement may have played a role in defining the outcome of the referendum. As the proposals were designed to control and police women and reflected distrust of their decisions, it is perhaps not surprising that during the planning process, the state failed to consult with women's representative bodies. This proved to be a fatal error. The *Women's Health Council (WHC)*, a statutory body charged with advising the Minister for Health, critiqued the proposals, high-lighting the "adverse health consequences" of being forced to travel for abortions and of women's "falling through the primary care net here at home." Questioning the government's distinction between life and health, it reported members' opinion that "there are health impli-cations related to pregnancy and abortion that must be addressed" (WHC statement, January 2001). Additional concerns included failure of the state to address the issues of nonviable fetuses and pregnancy resulting from rape or incest. National Women's Council of Ireland (NWCI) delegates also voted to campaign against the amendment and a national meeting issued a press release expressing the "overwhelming alarm" of members at the proposal to roll back the X case judgment and their view that "the proposed bill and referendum are an attack on the lives, health and welfare of women." It concluded that members "never again want to see a girl or woman before the High Court with a crisis pregnancy" (NWCI Press Release, February 2, 2002).

This 2002 referendum was more complex than those of 1983 and 1992 in that the electorate was asked to vote on inserting a piece of restrictive legislation into the Constitution. Many had not read it and some found that they could approve certain sections but not others. Ten days before the poll, Mahon argued in an *Irish Times* opinion piece that "the proposed referendum is what sociologists would call an invalid measurement instrument" and that it should therefore not go to the people (Mahon, 2002). The shortcomings of the government's proposals were further exposed, in the closing days of the campaign, when women like Deirdre de Barra, whose babies had been diagnosed with severe fetal abnormalities but whom the legislation would not have permitted to terminate their pregnancies in Ireland, spoke on radio and in print about their experiences (McKay, 2002). A *Sunday Times* post-referendum analysis suggested that their stories were "the defining motif of the campaign" (O'Reilly, 2002).

Political Discourse

It is clear that public dissent has been voiced during all the referendum campaigns and there is little evidence for the claim that they demonstrate that the Irish people exhibit shared cultural and moral values on abortion. Indeed, the outcomes of referenda might be read as suggesting that the majority of those registered to vote had little stomach for further restricting access to abortion. Healey's (2008 and 2009) analysis of how 17 women Dáil deputies and senators (interviewed in 2007) conceptualized the abortion debate, however, confirmed that memories of the divisive 1983 campaign, with its call to stand against abortion to protect a specifically Catholic, rural, Irish identity against an onslaught of foreign, liberalizing forces, still held sway in political circles. The X case and subsequent medicalization of the debate, by bringing home the complexity of the issues, had permitted some of these women to position themselves within a "grey area," in which more nuanced discussion was possible. Some interviewees assumed, despite the evidence of numbers traveling for abortions, that the Irish pro-choice lobby was small and that "abortion on demand" (the term used by antichoice campaigners) was "antithetical to Irish cultural values" and would be resisted by the electorate (Healey, 2008: 71). They believed that politicians were "gatekeepers," charged with preventing legalization of abortion in any circumstances lest permitting it, even in cases of rape and incest, opened the door to women having choice (74). Healey found that those women politicians who recognized the complexity of the issues and the impact of stigmatization felt silenced by "the historical memory of previous, bitter, debates," personal abuse of public representatives, and targeting by militant anti-abortion organizations like *Youth Defence* (79) (a group that in the 1990s used tactics such as picketing the homes of politicians). The atmosphere of stagnation identified by Healey may help explain why a generation of deputies and senators has failed vulnerable Irish women. When those interviews were conducted, women made up less than 14 percent of Dáil deputies and 20 percent of senators and she identified the Irish political arena as a male space, closed to "emotive, sympathetic" discussion of women's needs, a factor inhibiting her interviewees' contributions to political discourse on abortion (82).

During the April 2012 debate on the Medical Treatment (Termination of Pregnancy in Case of Risk to Life of Pregnant Woman) Bill—a private members' bill—there were indicators of some real changes that have occurred in Irish society. For example, John Halligan (Independent) referred to the importing of medical abortifacients, ordered online, and the seizure of 1,216 of these packs by Customs officers: clear evidence that women use the Internet to import abortifacients just as they use it to contact abortion clinics (Dáil Éireann Debate, 2012b). The Bill's co-proposer, Joan Collins (People Before Profit Alliance), read into the record findings in a study of the views of randomly selected general practitioners (GPs), by Dr. Mark Murphy, "a GP with the Sligo general practice training scheme." It says much about changing values. He found that "four out of ten" of those surveyed considered that traveling negatively impacted on women's "health care" and that 52 percent of the "established GPs" who responded considered "abortion should be available to any woman who chose it" (Dáil Éireann Debate, 2012a).

Is there evidence of similar changes in political circles? There were positive and negative signals during the debate. A minimal response to the ECHR Judgement requires the state to do no more than make clear how a woman whose life is threatened may exercise her constitutional right to a termination, already established in 1992. Introducing the Bill, Socialist deputy Clare Daly referred to many reasons why Irish women seek abortions and the message of those speaking from experience that "the pretence and hypocrisy" must end. She made clear, however, that the Bill had been strictly drafted within current constitutional constraints, designed only to legislate for the X case (Dáil Éireann Debate, 2012a). Co-proposer Mick Wallace's (Independent) reference to successive governments' failure to legislate did bring an assurance from Fine Gael Minister for Health James Reilly that the government would act but that its action must be informed by the expert group's report, a position also taken by other government and Fianna Fáil speakers (Dáil Éireann Debate, 2012a). Some of these, like Áine Collins (Fine Gael), did suggest the need for "empathy and understanding" (Dáil Éireann Debate, 2012b). Sinn Fein's Gerry Adams put into words the duty of legislators to do justice to women citizens: that regardless of their personal positions, they must "deal with the dreadful reality, highlighted by pregnant women confronted with life-threatening conditions" (Dáil Éireann Debate, 2012a). Making clear that the party did not support "abortion on demand"—again the nuanced language of antichoice groups—its deputies agreed that "the final decision rests with the woman" when the issue is "rape, incest or sexual abuse, or where a woman's life and mental health is at risk or in grave danger" (Dáil Éireann Debate, 2012a and b). There was also apparent opposition to action. Some speakers, including Tom Barry (Fine Gael) and Mattie McGrath (Independent) feared "opening the floodgates"

(Dáil Éireann Debate, 2012b). Regina Doherty (Fine Gael) was one of those displaying the mistrust of women and doctors that may have influenced the state's failure to legislate over decades. Arguing that the Bill would enable doctors to "provide any form of medical treatment to a woman, despite its consequences for the life of the foetus" she quoted an oft-repeated platitude about Ireland as the "safest place in the world to give birth," as if not comprehending that cases do occur in which women must be protected from death. Private bills rarely succeed and this one was voted down by government parties and Fianna Fáil.

The A, B, and C case hearing, in 2009, and judgment, in 2010, did open up a new space for women to bring home to decision makers the reality of what Smyth summed up in 1992 as the "private anguish" that crisis pregnancy imposes on them and how that is deepened by an enforced and distressing journey outside the jurisdiction. While Healey's research suggested that politicians feared an anti-abortion backlash, the April 2012 Dáil Debates revealed that women who have spoken of their experiences have impacted on political discourse, brought new sensitivity to the debate and some understanding of how state inertia has endangered lives, affected doctor–patient relationships, and criminalized and stigmatized women. The debates also demonstrated that some politicians remain constrained by a folk memory that referenda past reflected a deeply embedded, and still extant, public opposition to abortion. Yet, the assertion that their results or campaigns expressed the will of a majority of citizens must be questioned. The 2012 Dáil discussions did suggest that some deputies may be incapable of moving far enough beyond their strongly held personal views to meet their responsibility, as legislators, to women whose rights to abortion are already protected by the Constitution but who have no clear means of vindicating them.

According to *DFC*, abortion is "the most common gynaecological procedure Irish women undergo" (Favier, 2008: 19). Foot-trailing by politicians means women remain in a legal limbo: forced to continue crisis pregnancies at home or to travel, even in cases meeting the X case test. The state has fought women in the courts instead of guaranteeing their lives, health, and well-being. With politicians fearful of a Catholic backlash, there have been—and perhaps still are—few options for advancing the situation except bringing cases to European and international human rights fora. It is clear that, regardless of what the state's expert group recommends in 2012, the A, B, and C cases were important steps in this longest of Irish journeys: three decades during which women's rights to life, health, and to control their fertility have been subordinated to those of an ill-defined "unborn."

References

All Party Oireachtas Committee on the Constitution Constitutional Review Group Report (1996). Dublin: Stationery Office.

All-Party Oireachtas Committee on the Constitution, Fifth Progress Report: Abortion (2000). Dublin: Stationery Office.

Anonymous (1983) "Taoiseach warns on wording." *Irish Times*, September 6.

Arnold, Mavis and Kirby, Peadar (eds) (1982) *The Abortion Referendum: The Case Against.* Dublin: Anti-Amendment Campaign.

Bacik, Ivana (2004) *Kicking and Screaming: Dragging Ireland into the 21st Century.* Dublin: O'Brien.

Barry, Orla (2010) "Delivering Support to Women in a Crisis Pregnancy." *Irish Examiner*, April 26.

Black, Maureen (1983) "Why I Intend to Vote 'No'." *Cork Examiner*, August 24.

Coulter, Carol (2002) "A Yes Vote Will Protect Doctors." *Irish Times*, February 28.

——— (2010) "No Overall Policy on Operation of Ethics Bodies in HSE Hospitals." *Irish Times*, December 22.

De Barra, Deirdre (2002) "Letter to the Editor." *Irish Times*, February 25.

Devlin, Martina (2002) "Urban Female Vote Helped Save the Day for No Camp." *Irish Independent*, March 8.

——— (2009) "A Woman's Plight Exposes Our Hypocrisy on Abortion." *Irish Independent*, September 10.

Editorial (1983) "The Second Partitioning of Ireland." *Irish Times*, August 30.

——— (2002) "Apathy and Uncertainty over Issue. *Irish Examiner*, February 25.

Favier, Mary (2008) "GPs and the Silence around Abortion." *Forum*, May: 19–20.

Girvin, Brian (1986) "Social Change and Moral Politics: The Irish Constitutional Referendum 1983." *Political Studies*, 34: 61–81.

Green Paper on Abortion (1999). Dublin: Stationery Office.

Healey, Morgan (2008) "'I Don't Want to Get into This, It's Too Controversial.' How Irish Women Politicians Conceptualise the Abortion Debate," in J. Schweppe (ed.), *The Unborn Child, Article 40.3.3° and Abortion in Ireland: 25 Years of Protection?* Dublin: Liffey Press, pp. 65–85.

——— (2009) "The 'Naturalized' Politician: How Irish Women Politicians Construct their Political Subjectivities." Unpublished PhD thesis. University of Limerick.

Hesketh, Tom (1990). *The Second Partitioning of Ireland: The Abortion Referendum of 1983.* Dublin: Brandsma.

Hornsby-Smith, Michael, P., and Whelan, Christopher T. (1994) "Religious and Moral Values," in C. Whelan (ed.), *Values and Social Change in Ireland*. Dublin: Gill and Macmillan.

Hug, Chrystel (1999) *The Politics of Sexual Morality in Ireland*. London: Macmillan.

Human Rights Watch (2010) *A State of Isolation: Access to Abortion for Women in Ireland*. New York: Human Rights Watch.

IFPA (2000) *The Irish Journey: Women's Stories of Abortion*. Dublin: Irish Family Planning Association.

Mahon, Evelyn (2001). "Abortion Debates in Ireland an Ongoing Issue," in D. McBride Stetson (ed.), *Abortion Politics, Women's Movements and the Democratic State*. Oxford: Oxford University Press, pp. 157–179.

——— (2002) "Abortion Referendum as Proposed Is Invalid." *Irish Times*, February 25.

McKay, Susan (2002) " 'Yes' or 'No' Vote, There's Still the Boat." *Sunday Tribune*, March 3.

Murphy, John A. (2002) "Ahern's TV Debate Snub Cost Him Dear." *Sunday Independent*, March 10.

O'Brien, Carl (2008) "Council of Europe Calls on Ireland to Legislate for Abortion." *Irish Times*, April 17.

——— (2010) "Why is Simple Treatment Not Available Even When a Mother's Life Is at Risk?" *Irish Times*, December 21.

O'Mahony, Rev. Brendan (1982) "A Catholic View." *Irish Times*, May 14.

O'Reilly, Emily (2002) "Another Fine Mess." *Sunday Times*, March 10.

Rossiter, Ann (2009) *Ireland's Hidden Diaspora: The "Abortion Trail" and the Making of a London-Irish Underground, 1980–2000*. London: IASC.

Schweppe, Jennifer (2008) "A 'Constitutionally Permissible' Abortion? The Right to Travel, the Role of the Medical Profession and the Duty of the HSE," in J. Schweppe (ed.), *The Unborn Child, Article 40.3.3° and Abortion in Ireland: 25 Years of Protection?* Dublin: Liffey Press, pp. 349–369.

Sheridan, Kathy (2012a) "Stories of Abortion." *Irish Times*, February 25.

——— (2012b) "Stories of Abortion." *Irish Times*, March 24.

Smyth, Ailbhe (1983) *Women's Rights in Ireland*. Dublin: Irish Council for Civil Liberties.

——— (1992) "A Sadistic Farce. Women and Abortion in the Republic of Ireland, 1992," in A. Smyth (ed.), *The Abortion Papers Ireland*. Dublin: Attic Press.

Smyth, Lisa (2005) *Abortion and Nation: The Politics of Reproduction in Contemporary Ireland*. Aldershot: Ashgate.

AUTHOR'S COLLECTION

Alliance for a No Vote (*ANV*) leaflets 2001–2002.
Doctors for Choice in Ireland (*DFC*) leaflet (undated).
NWCI 2002 Consultation document on the proposed referendum.
NWCI Press Release, February 2, 2002.

Websites

25th Amendment of the Constitution (Protection of Human Life in Pregnancy) Bill: www.oireachtas.ie/viewdoc.asp?fn=/documents/bills28 /bills/2001/4801/default.htm, date accessed July 23, 2012.

ABC Case: Statement of Facts, ECHR: www.eclj.org/PDF/081118_ECLJ _StatementofFacts7May2008.pdf, date accessed April 6, 2010.

Action report A, B, and C v. Ireland: Department of Health and Children: www.dohc.ie/publications/pdf/Action_Report.pdf?direct=1, date accessed July 21, 2012.

Action Plan A, B, and C v. Ireland Application no 25579/2005, submitted by the Government of Ireland on June 16, 2011 (press release): www .dohc.ie/press/releases/2011/20110616.html, date accessed July 21, 2012.

Council of Europe Doc. 11576: Committee on Social, Health and Family Affairs report,

Doctors for Choice in Ireland Press Release 2007: http://choiceireland.blogspot .com/2007/05/doctors-for-choice-advocate-safe-and.html, date accessed May 5, 2010.

Dáil Éireann Debate (2012a) Vol. 761, No. 3 (unrevised), April 18: http:// debates.oireachtas.ie/dail/2012/04/18/00025.asp, date accessed 23 July 2012.

Dáil Éireann Debate (2012b) Vol. 762, No. 1 (unrevised), April 19: http:// debates.oireachtas.ie/dail/2012/04/19/00006.asp, date accessed July 23, 2012.

ECHR Judgement: CASE OF A, B, AND C v. Ireland (Application no. 25579 /05), including dissenting opinion, Web: http://cmiskp.echr.coe.int /tkp197/view.asp?item=1&portal=hbkm&action=html&high light=Ireland %20%7C%2025579/05&sessionid=82006301&skin=hudoc-en, date accessed December 16, 2010.

ECHR podcast of A, B and C cases: www.echr.coe.int/ECHR/EN /Header/Press/Multimedia/Webcasts+of+public+he arings/webcastEN _media?&p_url=20091209–1/lang/, date accessed April 10, 2010.

Elections Ireland: http://electionsireland.org/results/referendum/summary .cfm, date accessed April 10, 2010.

European Council Conclusions June 2009: http://europa.eu/rapid/press ReleasesAction.do?reference=DOC/09/2&format=HTML &aged=0&l anguage=EN&guiLanguage=en, date accessed April 10, 2010.

Health Service Executive (*HSE*) Press Release, May 25, 2010: www.irishpress releases.ie/2010/05/25/number-of-women-giving-irish-addresses-at -uk-abortion-clinics-decreases-for-eighth-year-in-a-row-according-to -department-of-health-uk/, date accessed May 29, 2010.

Irish Family Planning Association (IFPAa) Statistics Numbers of Irish Women Having Abortions in (a) the UK 1980–2011 and (b) the Netherlands 2005–2010: www.ifpa.ie/Hot-Topics/Abortion/Statistics, date accessed July 21, 2012.

Irish Family Planning Association (IFPAb) Press Release: www.ifpa.ie/eng
/Media-Info-Centre/News-Events/2009-News-Events/IFPA-Responds
-to-Latest-UK- Abortion-Stats, date accessed May 21, 2009.

Kingston, James (2001), Irish Council for Civil Liberties, Position Paper
(2001) The Need for Abortion Law Reform in Ireland: The Case against
the Twenty-Fifth Amendment of the Constitution Bill, 2001: www
.iccl.ie/the-need-for-abortion-law-reform-in-ireland-the-case-against-the
-twenty-fifth-amendment-of-the-constitution-bill-2001.html, date accessed
August 2, 2012.

Statistical Bulletin, May 2010 "Abortion Statistics, England and Wales:
2009." UK Dept. of Health: www.dh.gov.uk/prod_consum_dh/groups
/dh_digitalassets/documents/digitalass et/dh_116336.pdf, date accessed
June 4, 2010.

Medical Treatment (Termination of Pregnancy in Case of Risk to Life of
Pregnant Woman) Bill 2012 [PMB]: www.oireachtas.ie/viewdoc.asp?fn=
/documents/bills28/bills/2012/1012/b1012d.pdf, date accessed July
23, 2012.

Women's Health Council Statement, January 31, 2001: www.whc.ie
/publications/86, date accessed May 22, 2010.

CHAPTER 4

Irish Migration and Irish Sexuality Scholarship: Queering the Connections

Eithne Luibhéid

Rich histories of Irish migration, and of Irish sexuality, have been set down on paper—frequently without acknowledging one another. What new questions, insights, lines of research, and political possibilities might emerge if we were to put Irish migration and Irish sexuality scholarship into critical conversation? Such a conversation would contribute to "queering" each area of scholarship. "Queering" refers to processes of interrogating epistemological and methodological boundaries that stem from, and further fuel, normalizing regimes of power and violence (Giffney and Hird, 2008; Somerville, 2000). Queer conversations between migration and sexuality scholarship promise to regenerate research agendas and political possibilities.

Critical conversations between migration and sexuality studies have taken root in the United States and elsewhere, under the rubric of queer migration studies. Although significantly focused on gay and lesbian migrants, queer migration studies, following queer theory, is concerned not with identitarian histories but rather with sexuality as a regime of power and governance that *all* migrants must negotiate. Queer migration scholarship particularly analyzes how the interface between sexual regulation and migration controls contributes to racist, heterosexist, colonialist, capitalist, and nationalist processes at multiple scales. Thus, it explores such questions as how migratory and sexual regimes intersect to produce or destabilize constructs of the normative heterosexual, the citizen, the economy, the national, the state, and the global, including in the current moment of capitalist neoliberalization (Luibhéid 2008).

Queer frameworks produced in the United States or the United Kingdom often enter Ireland as colonial knowledge that regulates horizons of possibility while foreclosing alternative histories (Giffney and O'Donnell, 2007). The Republic of Ireland (hereafter Ireland), however, offers a particularly rich site for thinking about sexuality and migration issues together, in ways that promise to expand and transform queer migration studies. In the following section, I sketch some of the interconnections between sexuality and migration in Ireland. The sketch is not intended to be comprehensive but rather to open up further research and dialogue.

Migration and Sexuality

Histories of migration—both emigration and immigration—have been central to the production and ongoing transformation of Irish sexual norms. For example, in the post-Famine period, under British rule, a new social, economic, and sexual order was very much in the making. An economy dependent on the potato, and so-called unrestrained marriage and childbearing, were to be swept away, as the economy was transformed from tillage to livestock (Lyons, 1973). Sexuality would remain organized in reference to marriage, but marriage was now restricted to one son who inherited the land, and one daughter who was dowried. Tom Inglis indicates the connections between transformations in the economy and in sexuality:

> In the supposed cycle of events after the Famine, the segregation of the sexes led to the control of sex. The control of sex helped the control of marriage. The control of marriage helped the control of population and, finally, the control of population helped improve the overall standard of living. (Inglis, 1998)

It was never entirely that neat or simple. Emigration nonetheless emerged as the crucial mechanism for trying to maintain a desired balance among sexuality, population, and economy. For example, Inglis describes that "in most families those sons and daughters not selected for marriage had a choice of remaining sexually inactive, or emigrating" (1998). J. J. Lee is more pointed: "a callously efficient socialisation process postponed marriage and effectively denied the right to a family to a higher proportion of the population than in any other European state…The dispossessed were reconciled to their fate by emigration" (1989).

Jim Mac Laughlin (1997) suggests that Irish nationalists' ability to eventually capture the state from Britain was significantly enabled by post-Famine processes of economic restructuring and mass emigration. We can extend MacLaughlin's analysis, however, to acknowledge that the emerging sexual order was also an important element of the formation of an independent state. That sexual order at once borrowed and differed from its metropolitan counterparts. Clair Wills describes that it prescribed domesticity and sexuality channeled into heterosexual marriage, which were also the standards for the United Kingdom and the United States. Yet, because of Irish-specific conditions, including land war, mass emigration, and the struggle for independence, sexual norms became routed through and used to serve anticolonialist Catholic nationalism.[1] After independence, these ideals became institutionalized including through the 1937 Constitution, which imagined a nation organized through patriarchal heterosexual marriage—one where women were relegated to the roles of wives and childbearers within the privatized home, and there were no same-sex interests or alternative sexualities of any kind. This sexual and gender order entailed class, racial, ethnic, and national logics, too. Poor and working-class families, for example, did not easily fit the model; and white, Catholic, settled people were normed as reproducing the "Irish" family, in a manner that marginalized other racial, ethnic, and cultural groups within the nation state (Helleiner, 2003; Lentin, 1999). Nonetheless, adherence to this sexual order became, as Geraldine Meaney described, "the very substance of what it means to be Irish" (qtd. in Wills, 2001).

The newly independent Irish state never officially promoted emigration. However, it tacitly accepted and came to depend on emigration, not only to sustain the class and economic system but also to sustain the sexual and gender orders. Many individuals resorted to emigration as a way to negotiate the pain and penalties that they faced as a result of these orders. Marella Buckley describes that Irish women internalized an image of emigration to Britain as offering an "escape hatch" in case of reproductive crisis, such as unwanted pregnancy (qtd. in Walter, 2001). The extraordinary history of migration by young women who were pregnant outside of marriage has been well documented (Earner-Byrne, 2004; Ryan, 2002). Numerous writings also describe that until the 1990s, lesbians and gay men understood that they were expected to emigrate if possible, since homosexuality was deemed incompatible with Irishness (Collins, 1995). Íde O'Carroll (1995) has suggested that some women (and no doubt men) who suffered sexual abuse or incest resorted to migration in response. Emigration was also important for those involved in interracial or cross-religious intimate relationships, including as a strategy to nego-tiate racial, religious, and cultural closures around Irishness when children were born (e.g., McCarthy, 2001). Decisions about emi-gration and actual emigration strategies were therefore shaped by sexuality—although sexuality as a factor often remained shrouded in silence or operated as tacit, unspoken knowledge. Even for those who were not consciously pressured by the normative sexual order, sexual-ity was an important dimension of their migration experiences. For example, some people emigrated to experience more "glamorous" forms of heterosexuality associated with the United Kingdom or the United States, while others found by default that emigration threw into disarray their taken-for-granted understandings of sexuality.

Yet, although the state tacitly depended on emigration to stabilize the dominant order, high emigration nonetheless regularly threatened to undermine the dream of a family-centered nation rooted on the land. Sustained emigration by women, and the resulting loss of their childbearing capacities and unpaid labor, generated particular anxi-ety and public commentary. In the 1950s, high emigration, combined with a faltering economy, generated fears that the Irish were becom-ing a "vanishing race." The government accordingly sought to redress the perceived imbalance among low marriage rates, a weak economy, high emigration, and state- and nation-building, including through the work of the Commission on Emigration and Other Population Problems.

In short, emigration has been central to the emergence, consoli-dation, and maintenance of the modern Irish sexual order, in the context of Famine, land struggle, and the drive for independence. The emigration-sexuality nexus was also central to state- and nation-formation processes.

IMMIGRATION AND SEXUALITY

These connections between migration and sexuality would become articulated in new form in the 1990s. At that time, Ireland began to experience significant in-migration, including that as a result of Irish state efforts to reposition the nation more advantageously within the rapidly changing global economy. Ireland became ranked as one of the most globalized countries in the world, and experienced rapid rates of economic growth. At the same time, immigration increased. Claims about the need to control immigration became a means for the government to assert—and in the process to reconstruct—renewed visions and versions of the nation, the people, and the state's role.

Unsurprisingly, these visions further institutionalized neoliberal logics that celebrated the unfettered market and that reconstructed social life using market logics.

Immigration was initially diagnosed as most "out of control" in regard to asylum seeking (i.e., migrants seeking admission because they face persecution). Siobhan Mullally describes that the government's approach to managing asylum was characterized by "a culture of disbelief and a desire to dispense with asylum claims with ever increasing speed" (2003). The practical means that were used to gain control over asylum seekers involved introducing procedures to try to prevent them from ever reaching Ireland to claim asylum, and, when that failed, making sure that their asylum claims were quickly dispatched within a remarkably ungenerous process that generally resulted in refusal. These strategies were congruent with EU approaches.

Beginning in 1997, however, the minister for justice, the media, and sectors of the government and the public began to insist that pregnant migrants were undermining the so-called integrity of the asylum system. At that time, any child born in Ireland was automatically a citizen. Moreover, in 1990, the Supreme Court had ruled that all citizen children were entitled to the company and care of their parents, even if their parents were nonnationals. This meant that when migrants gave birth to a child, they could generally become legal residents of Ireland. The ruling reflected the historic valorization of sexuality channeled into childbearing for the nation state that was codified by the 1937 Constitution. Yet, childbearing and family formation became deemed a serious threat where migrants were concerned. Pregnant migrants became portrayed as spongers, parasites, cynical mothers, helpless victims, and illegal immigrants who threatened the economic miracle. Black migrant women were particularly singled out for racist and heterosexist demonization.

At the same time, growing numbers of asylum seekers waited, often for years, for decisions on their asylum claims. Because of the increasingly restrictive asylum system, even those with strong claims often began to calculate that residency through their citizen child was a better option than persisting with the asylum process. State workers often encouraged migrants to seek residency through their child, though officials now deny this. Routes for legal entry by migrants from outside the European Union, and/or those without "sufficient" human or economic capital, were further reduced, even while migration paths and pressures continued building. These interlocking conditions further pressured migrants to seek residency through a child.

Rather than addressing the underlying factors that drive migration, or adopting an asylum policy that focused on protection rather than deterrence, or crafting a general migration policy that balanced Irish labor needs with other considerations such as shared global responsibility, immigration control was significantly framed as a problem of controlling pregnant migrant women. A 2003 Supreme Court decision ended the practice of granting residency to nonnational parents of citizen children. A 2004 referendum ended the practice of automatic citizenship for any child born in Ireland. Through these and other responses to the figure of the pregnant nonnational migrant woman, we can trace a number of crucial developments in terms of how sexuality and migration have become interconnected in the present.

First, hysterical discourses about pregnant asylum seekers helped to establish a consensus that immigration controls were needed. Yet, immigration controls are never inevitably the state's prerogative; they only become seen as such through political struggle (Mongia, 2007). Through the hysteria about pregnant asylum seekers, the minister for justice significantly expanded state-led immigration controls in many domains, while avoiding critical inquiry about the kind of sovereignty, nation, and citizenry that he sought to foster as a result. Government reports make clear, however, that immigration controls are intended to further, rather than contest, the existing neoliberal economy and neocolonial world system.

Second, the events described earlier have significantly impacted on migrants, who find that their avenues to residency are further closed down, their family forms are often invalidated or unrecognized, their children are preemptively denationalized, and their intimate lives are subjected to increasing state surveillance. This includes for gay, lesbian, and queer individuals and families, who have won some important rights but whose admission nonetheless requires adherence to neoliberal norms of bourgeois domesticity, financial privatization, and cultural "responsibility" (see Simmons, 2008). The controls also racialize migrants. Consider the disparity between the treatment of children born to migrants in Ireland, who are frequently denied citizenship, and the treatment of the children and grandchildren of the largely white Irish diaspora, who remain eligible for Irish citizenship. That disparity, which works through heterosexual reproductivity, rearticulates Irishness as blood and genealogy in the most literally racist way. It also rearticulates global histories and geographies of racism and colonialism that underpin the existence of the Irish diaspora, on one hand, and contemporary immigration into Ireland, on the other.

Third, although migrants are the obvious targets, everyone is affected, as immigration controls have significantly reshaped Irish social life. For example, since phenotypical appearance is increasingly treated as a proxy for national identity and citizenship status (Garner, 2004), many Black Irish women with babies have found themselves reconstructed as targets of anti-immigrant acts and sentiments. Since identities are relational, changes in the status of Black Irish people are directly connected to changes in the status of majority Irish people, some of whom finally get to occupy the status of "truly" white and European, thereby erasing the shame of colonialism (Borneman and Fowler, 1997), but at the expense of others. Heterosexuality as the norm has not been abolished, but rather, redefined to articulate contemporary racial, gender, sexual, cultural, and colonial distinctions.

Fourth, changes in Ireland have drawn on and further fueled a harsh global migration regime. For example, the 2003 Supreme Court decision that ended the practice of granting residency to parents of citizen children drew on US court cases for justification; that Irish decision is now cited by US anti-immigrant groups as evidence that the United States should disenfranchise children born to undocumented parents, while policing Mexican migrant women who have been racialized as "breeders" (see the Federation for American Immigration Reform website).

The outcomes suggest that despite the Catholic Church's diminished status, and tremendous recent social changes, normative Irish sexuality is far from being "liberated." Instead, sexuality is being regulated in new ways, including by the state through immigration controls. Indeed, sexuality remains a point of intense struggle over the continued expansion of immigration control. Struggles over pregnant migrants were followed by struggles to ensure that same-sex couple relationships became recognized as valid for purposes of immigration; to determine which heterosexual marriages and family ties "merit" reunification; and to address trafficking, to name several currently contested intersections between sexual and migration controls. Significant revisions in welfare codes, combined with shifting priorities for migrant admission, have further shaped these struggles.

Queering Migration and Sexuality

I have suggested that emigration in the nineteenth and much of the twentieth century significantly shaped the emergence of a dominant Irish sexual order, and became a crucial means to sustain it. I also suggested that policies for managing contemporary immigration into

Ireland significantly encode, work through, and reconfigure sexual regimes, in ways that affect not just migrants but everyone.[2]

The curious thing is that although sexual concerns are everywhere evident in migration histories and debates, they are rarely explicitly named as such. Instead, they are often subsumed under discussions of gender, family, or culture, which are implicitly organized by heterosexist assumptions. Consequently, the tools and theoretical frameworks offered by critical sexuality studies are rarely mobilized, and scholarship and policy develop accordingly. It is time for migration history, theory, and policy-making to explicitly engage with questions of sexuality, using the tools provided by sexuality and queer migration scholarship. Such an engagement promises to transform key concepts, theories, and methodologies, while leading to a significantly enriched understanding of processes of migration and diaspora, and of the national, transnational, and global connections involved. Such analyses also promise to have significant policy impacts. Equally, I believe that sexuality and queer studies in Ireland will benefit from more deeply engaging with questions of migration, since this is one of the realms where significant transformations in the production and governance of contemporary Irish sexuality are evident and ongoing (and urgently in need of challenge). Attention to migration will particularly highlight the importance of the imperial and of global capitalism in the formation of what we call "Irish sexualities." Moreover, attention to migration underscores the importance of connecting sexuality to questions of gender, race, class, and nationalisms at regional, national, and global scales.

Such work opens up possibilities for comparative projects and transnational collaborations. For example, how might the history of migration by pregnant unmarried women from Mexico compare to, contrast with, or otherwise illuminate the experiences of pregnant unmarried Irish women who migrated (Hirsh, 2003)? Or how might Caribbean histories of "sexile" involving lesbians and gay men who felt forced to emigrate enter into conversation with Irish lesbian and gay migrant experiences? What connections might exist between Ireland and other countries in terms of the handling of same-sex migrant couples, family reunification, sexuality-based asylum, questions of trafficking, issues of abortion, and other such matters? How do policies adopted in one country get taken up, transformed, and used for similar or different ends in another country?

These questions offer grounds for new kinds of research projects and activist coalitions that challenge and rethink migration and sexuality policies, both separately and together, as they travel and become transformed at local, national, and transnational levels. As Ailbhe Smyth suggests, "when power is abused to exclude and deny, it must be contested and overturned" (2000). Irish histories offer particularly rich opportunities for such work, including for rethinking migration and sexuality regimes in relation to logics other than the neoliberal and the neocolonial.

ACKNOWLEDGMENTS

This piece was first presented at the conference, "Neither Here Nor There: Writing the Irish Diaspora," at the University of Limerick on October 30, 2008. Huge thanks to the conference organizers— Tina O'Toole, Kathryn Laing, and Caoilfhionn Ní Bheacháin—for convening such a fabulous event and kindly inviting me to present. Warmest thanks to Breda Gray for hosting me at the University of Limerick, and for her valuable suggestions and questions.

NOTES

1. Domesticity "became deployed in service to Catholic nationalist hegemony," while other aspects of the modern middle-class home, particularly "conjugal love, romance, free choice, were rejected" (Wills, 2001: 46). Rejection "came not only from the Church but also from the economic requirements of small farmers" (46), who relied on matchmaking based not on love, romance, or sexual desire but on strategic calculation to ensure continuity in land settlement and transmission. The Catholic Church's growing monopoly on discourses about sexuality contributed to this configuration. These processes entailed not simply handing over control of sexuality to the Catholic Church; rather, as James M. Smith describes, the state worked in tandem with the Catholic church to "close off internal challenges and contradictions even as they represented society as pure and untainted by external corruption" (3). Thus, the state was "an active agent and willing partner" (47) in the church's regulation of sexuality.
2. This is not to suggest that emigration and immigration are analogous; see Gray (2004) for a brilliant analysis of the pitfalls of such an approach. Nonetheless, emigration and immigration are connected through global capitalism and colonialism.

REFERENCES

Borneman, John and Fowler, Nick (1997) "Europeanization." *Annual Review of Anthropology*, 26: 487–514.

Collins, Eoin (1995) "Editor's Introduction," in I. O'Carroll and E. Collins (eds), *Lesbian and Gay Visions of Ireland: Towards the 21st Century.* London: Cassell., pp. 1–10.

Earner-Byrne, Lindsay (2004) " 'Moral Repatriation': The Response to Irish Unmarried Mothers in Britain, 1920s-1960s," in P. J. Duffy (ed.), *To and From Ireland: Planned Migration Schemes c. 1600–2000.* Dublin: Geography Publications, pp. 155–173.

Federation for American Immigration Reform (n.d.) "Anchor Babies. Part of the Immigration-Related American Lexicon," at www.fairus.org/site /PageServer?pagename=iic_immigrationissuecenters4608.

Garner, Steve (2004) *Racism in the Irish Experience.* London: Pluto Press.

Giffney, Noreen and Hird, Myra J. (2008) "Introduction," in N. Giffney and M. J. Hird (eds), *Queering the Non/Human.* Aldershot: Ashgate Publishing Ltd., 2008, pp. 1–16.

Giffney, Noreen and O' Donnell, Katherine (2007) "Introduction," *Journal of Lesbian Studies,* 11 (1–2): 1–18.

Gray, Breda (2004) "Remembering a 'Multicultural' Future through a History of Emigration: Towards a Feminist Politics of Solidarity across Difference." *Women's Studies International Forum,* 27 (4): 413–429.

Helleiner, Jane (2003) *Irish Travellers: Racism and the Politics of Culture.* Toronto: University of Toronto Press.

Hirsh, Jennifer (2003) *A Courtship after Marriage: Sexuality and Love in Mexican Transnational Families.* Berkeley, CA: University of California Press.

Inglis, Tom (1998) *Lessons in Irish Sexuality.* Dublin: University College Dublin Press.

Lee, J. J. (1989) *Ireland 1912–1985. Politics and Society.* Cambridge: Cambridge University Press.

Lentin, Ronit (1999) "Racializing (Our) Dark Rosaleen: Feminism, Citizenship, Racism, Antisemitism." *Women's Studies Review,* 6: 1–17.

Luibhéid, Eithne (2008) "Queer/Migration. An Unruly Body of Scholarship." *GLQ,* 14 (2–3): 169–190.

Lyons, F. S. L. (1973) *Ireland Since the Famine.* London: Fontana Press.

Mac Laughlin, Jim (1997) "Emigration and the Construction of Nationalist Hegemony in Ireland. The Historical Background to 'New Wave' Irish Emigration," in J. Mac Laughlin (ed), *Location and Dislocation in Contemporary Irish Society.* Cork: Cork University Press, pp. 5–35.

McCarthy, Margaret (2001) *My Eyes Only Look Out. Experiences of Irish People of Mixed Race Parentage.* Dingle, Co. Kerry, Ireland: Brandon.

Mongia, Radhika (2007) "Historicizing State Sovereignty: Inequality and the Form of Equivalence." *Comparative Studies in Society and History,* 49 (2): 384–411.

Mullally, Siobhan (2003) "Too Fast to be Safe? Regular/Irregular Asylum Procedures," in U. Fraser and C. Harvey (eds), *Sanctuary in Ireland. Perspectives on Asylum Law and Policy.* Dublin: Institute for Public Administration, pp. 146–167.

O'Carroll, Ide (1995) "Breaking the Silence from a Distance: Irish Women Speak on Sexual Abuse," in P. J. O'Sullivan (ed.), *Irish Women and Irish Migration*. Leicester: Leicester University Press, pp. 192–200.

Ryan, Louise (2002) "Sexualising Emigration: Discourses of Irish Female Emigration in the 1930s." *Women's Studies International Forum*, 25 (1): 51–65.

Simmons, Tracy (2008) "Sexuality and Immigration: UK Family Reunification Policy and the Regulation of Sexual Citizenship in the European Union." *Political Geography*, 27: 213–230.

Smyth, Ailbhe (2000) " 'Queers March in Dublin, Queers March in Cork, Why Can't Queers March in New York?' The ILGO St. Patrick's Day Protest 2000." *International Feminist Journal of Politics*, 2 (3): 414–423.

Somerville, Siobhan (2000) *Queering the Color Line. Race and the Invention of Homosexuality in American Culture*. Durham: Duke University Press.

Walter, Bronwyn (2001) *Outsiders Inside. Whiteness, Place and Irish Women*. London: Routledge.

Wills, Clair (2001) "Women, Domesticity and the Family: Recent Feminist Work in Irish Cultural Studies." *Cultural Studies*, 15 (1): 33–57.

CHAPTER 5

Affecting Trans-feminist Solidarity

Breda Gray

Last week, it's a verifiable fact,
I was planting polyanthus
A little late in the season
As ever
(Never quite making it into the first bunch of front runners)
Though they'll grow much the same, in my experience,
And thinking—just associatively of course—
That of all the words with poly- at their root
Only one is for a flower
(Though my knowledge is strictly controlled
by contingencies beyond my limits
and univice versa)
Polymeric polynomial polyverse
of polymorphous polytheist polyglots
…
Not grandiose solutions but particular negotiations located, limited,
    inescapably
partial and always personally invested. **Susan Bordo**. *Not dancing in*
    frantic
frenzy to the tuneless theories of disorder and deconstruction. Free, each
    one, to
celebrate her own uncertainties in her own time and place.
Myriad overlapping stories always beginning originating in lived reality
    theory-in the-
flesh politics in the bones.
                    —Polyvalent polygenesis (Smyth, 2005:
                        130/139; emphasis in original)

Ailbhe Smyth's often poetic writing, as well as her re-scriptings and juxtapositioning of the texts of others, defy the linear logics of nationalist and liberal feminist narratives, moving instead between temporal and spatial standpoints to illustrate the complex (re)workings of patriarchal heteronormativity. She proclaims: "I am a *bricoleuse*, still" (2005: 394). Resisting "the rigid anxieties of academic discipline," much of her writing is marked by " 'texturology', rhythm and paroxysm" (ibid.). Transgressing the boundaries of genre and discipline, Smyth's work both strategically reinscribes the two-gender dichotomy and deconstructs it via critical analysis of the gendering and heteronorming practices of state, media, religion, consumer, and popular culture. Another important aspect of her approach for me is the ways in which it keeps the emotional mediation of feminist thought and politics alive, eliciting in the reader contingent (dis)identifications, (mis)recognitions, and affective reactions. For example, in a piece where she examines the dynamics of sexuality and place, Smyth calls for attention, not just to concrete spaces and structures, but also to "the experiential spaces of affect, where identity and desire are variously and diversely formed and played out" (2005: 393).

In the specific context of the Republic of Ireland, Smyth represents feminism as a "resonant challenge to the ideology and politics of our nation-state" thus undermining "the ideological bases of the 'nationness' on which the state was founded" (1995b: 205). While many feminists in the south struggle with the failures of the promise of anticolonial nationalism for women's lives, others (north and south) link feminist politics with ongoing anticolonial nationalist struggles for justice and liberation (Coulter, 1990; Madden and Moane, 2006; Rooney, 1995a and b, 2008; Ryan and Ward, 2004; Speed, 1992; Ward, 2006). Feminism in Ireland has, therefore, a history of transborder negotiations across conflicting political and emotional commitments. For example, Smyth, reflecting on her experiences at a conference in Boston entitled "Reaching Common Ground" in 1994, observed a lack of connection between "the Northern and Southern women" and identified the structured differences and inequalities which she saw as separating these groups of women:

> The Southern group were mainly "public" and professional women from middle-class Dublin backgrounds—the "liberal agenda" incarnate. The Northern women were mostly community activists and working class, from both Protestant and Catholic communities, with a quarter of a century of war behind them, whatever lies ahead. (1995a: 39)

This conference was organized by Elizabeth Shannon, wife of a former US ambassador to Ireland, the late William Vincent Shannon. It brought together 60 women with 20 coming from each of the cities of Belfast, Dublin, and Boston to address how equal rights for women might be secured and gender discrimination removed from laws, institutions, and behavioral patterns. Smyth notes how those from Belfast and Dublin attempted to talk across "dividing lines of class and religion" (1995a: 40), prompting Smyth to observe that "[t]he habits of different histories and experiences are not easily put aside" (1995a: 41). Smyth continues:

> It was a difficult week, full of the wariness and tensions stemming from our complex differences, not least our different experiences of war and peace…"Everybody in Northern Ireland is holding their breath," as one of the Northern women put it, "Peace is not normal," another young woman said. And it is disturbingly unfamiliar…But no women in Southern Ireland have lived in a state of war. Peace and war cannot mean the same things to those who have known only the one, but not (yet) the other. Northern women told us so many times, and in so many ways, that it is a fragile thing, this peace. Unlike war, which is tough, durable, unyielding.
>
> But when we listened, what did we make of
what we heard? (1995a: 40)

But what caused this "atmosphere" of tensions and wariness? There is a sense in which histories of colonialism, anticolonial nationalism, partition, republican and unionist nationalisms, popular and state nationalism of the Republic of Ireland, the Women's Movement, the Civil Rights movement, and "a quarter of a century of war" (among other histories), are condensed in how the "atmosphere" is experienced by Smyth: "It is not just that feelings are 'in tension' but that the tension is located somewhere: in being felt by some bodies, it is attributed as caused by another body" (Ahmed, 2010: 14). It is as if the feelings on both sides in the group are "getting in the way of its organic enjoyment and solidarity" (ibid.). Perhaps, the implications of the war, and class and religious positioning of the northern feminist activists, brought the privileges of class and peace inhabited by the southern feminists into relief? It is also possible that this encounter between working-class northern and middle-class southern feminists unsettled the assumptions that underpinned liberal feminism in the south at the time? It may be that the continuing imperatives of ethno-nationalisms for some of the feminists were difficult to countenance for those who felt their struggle was against the gender and sexual chauvinisms of such nationalisms. Whatever the cause, the feelings of tensions and wariness were probably attributed to different individuals and groups of women at different points during the conference.

Alexander argues that "within the archaeologies of dominance resides the will to divide and separate"; so "reciprocal investments" must be made in order "to cross over into the metaphysics of interdependence" (2005: 6). However, the terms and conditions of "reciprocal investments" and interdependence change over time and from context to context. The Irish Peace Process, uneven secularization, and the embrace of neoliberal globalization by the southern state since the late-twentieth century, have shifted the grounds and scale of the divide between north and south. In 2012, histories of a colonial past and a present marked by a globalized economic crisis are producing new tensions within and between women across the island of Ireland and in relation to the transnational flows of women, cultures, ideas, and capital that shape the spaces of Irish feminist thought and activism.

Balzano et al., commenting on postcolonial Irish criticism, see its repeated appeals to analogies between Ireland and other colonized contexts based on shared experience of colonization as having no "hold in the present, except as an embedded memory" (2007: xviii). However, embedded memory also involves forgetting and raises the important question of which memories and indeed which aspects of the present we choose to align ourselves with. As gendered and racialized migrant labor becomes more deeply inscribed in global capitalist and neoliberal relations in Ireland as elsewhere, feminist tactics must exceed the scope of the national. However, the repositioning of feminist politics alongside and beyond the national, in the spaces of the transnational and the global, involve a rescaling and re-evaluation of the "habits of different histories and experiences" and "embedded memory" in attempting to bring about ethical transnational feminist solidarities.

Although scholarship on intersectional, transversal, and transnational feminisms has proliferated in recent years, "we are still left with a theoretical and political void ... [regarding how] to develop transnational solidarity that takes into account what divides women" (Mendoza, 2002: 304; Gray, 2004). As Smyth noted, class difference, as much as the fragile and anxious boundaries of nationalisms, religion, war, and peace, structured the gap between the Belfast and Dublin women attending the Boston conference. Equally, in the negotiation of solidarity, feminists struggle to develop ethical approaches to engaging "bisexuality, intersexuality, transsexuality, transgender, and other emergent identities that reconfigure both conventional and conventionally feminist under-standings of sex, gender and sexuality" (Heyes, 2003: 1093). How, asks Alexander (2005: 8), can we move away from living "premised in differ-ence to living intersubjectivity premised in relationality and solidarity"? Transnational politics of class, "race," transgender, and multiple-gender expression pose ongoing challenges to the formation of such feminist solidarities. Yet, solidarity is impossible without addressing our mutual implication in the web of intersectional gender relations and a willing-ness to consider "the ethical and affective preconditions of inclusive political ties" (Lyshaug, 2006: 77).

It is the affective conditions of inclusive and ethical political soli-darities that are the focus of this chapter. My aim is to take up Ailbhe Smyth's call to examine the ways in which dividing lines are affectively experienced and constituted and might be ethically transgressed to undo the conventional power hierarchies they inscribe. In doing so, I consider the role of the so-called humanizing emotion of empathy in galvanizing or impeding feminist solidarity among differently posi-tioned feminists. Empathy has rightly come under attack as potentially perpetuating the status quo and/or colonizing the experience of the marginalized (Berlant, 1998; Spelman, 1997). However, I am inter-ested in unravelling the ways in which its promise and anxiety about its failure shape contemporary transnational feminist politics. The aim is to examine whether it is possible to conceive of new "emotional grammars" (McKay, 2007) of empathic (dis)identification that might mobilize "the labor of education, translation, solidarity, dialogue, and self-reflexivity required to forge sustainable [feminist] connections" (Ware, 2006: 530). My concern then is with the political possibili-ties of empathy while keeping its political dangers constantly in mind. What, in the words of Berlant (2004: 5), are "the dynamics of its optimism and exclusions"? I begin with an overview of debates about feminist solidarity followed by a discussion of the potential of empa-thy as a mode of solidaristic relationship. I then reflect on the ethical dynamics of empathy in practice before concluding with a discussion of how such emotional dynamics might be engaged in developing feminist solidarities that do not put aside different histories, presents, and futures.

Feminisms, Solidarities, and the Politics of Emotion

Powerful systems such as imperialism, capitalism, nationalism, mili-tarization, and globalization reproduce conservative gender norms

(Mohanty, 2006). Therefore, the achievement of gender justice requires critical analyses of the social norms that shape gender and self/other relations. To challenge and undermine these systems and norms, Mohanty calls for transnational feminist solidarity. However, such solidarity requires attention to the ways in which we become invested in these norms (Ahmed, 2004a) and the kinds of dividing practices that are the effect of such investments.

Although there is no agreed definition of solidarity, or understanding of how it is secured, grounded, or located, Stean suggests that "[s]olidarity might be founded on the basis of shared principles and/or generated by feelings of empathy towards other members of the group" (2006: 123). Common interests and connection are also important for Mohanty, but she acknowledges that the building of solidarity also involves working with divisions in ways that do not silence, marginalize, or reinforce oppression. She defines solidarity, therefore, as focusing on

> mutuality and common interests across borders, on understanding the historical and experiential particularities and differences as well as the connections between women's lives around the world, and on the connection and division between forms of women's activism and organizing across racial, national, sexual borders. (2006: 17)

Mohanty's account acknowledges the necessity of multiple solidarities working across numerous issues. Moreover, her explicit acknowledgment of women's intersectional, hybrid, and sometimes conflicting interests based on their unequal positioning and multiple differences mean that Eurocentric and global notions of solidarity based on unproblematized notions of "sisterhood" are totally discredited.

While Mohanty's (2003, 2006) work is tenacious in its optimism about forging transnational feminist solidarities, Khanna argues that recognition of "the *complex relationality* between women transnationally" can produce guilt and disengagement on the part of the privileged. Furthermore, she notes that difference has become so reified in feminist debates that "separate ethical universes have been produced with the overarching imperative being that one does not comment on another context" (Khanna, 2001: 102; Gray, 2008). This, Khanna argues, has led to "a kind of paralysis and navel gazing with regard to how to be ethical relating to gender politics outside one's own context" (ibid.). The so-called ethical response is often a nonresponse frequently involving emotions of shame, guilt, or fear and involving patronizing gestures and hasty assumptions of sameness. As such, difference becomes reified through this mode of political invocation which has the effect of producing inactivity as the most ethical response (ibid.). Her question is: How does one respond to another and address conflicts within feminism in ways that allow for feminist action and scholarship? Contemporary transnational feminism is, according to Khanna, haunted by colonialism, those secrets, memories, and traumas from the past that manifest themselves in everyday affective social relations and encounters. These affective hauntings arising from colonialism, nationalism, imperialism, and the (failed) promises of gender justice shape feminist practice and feminist solidarities. Thus, feminist theoretical and political principles have emotional dimensions that are palpably present yet often elided. These emotions shape how feminists inhabit the world with other feminists (Ahmed, 2004b: 28), what is said and done in the name of feminism, and how differences are (re)produced by and between feminists.

Feminists have a long history of critiquing definitions of emotion as simply biological and identifying the shaping of politics by affect (Frye, 1983; Jagger, 1995; Spelman, 1988). Nonetheless, Bartky argues that most feminist theorists, whatever their orientation (anti-racist, post-structuralist, empiricist, Habermasian), identify the misrecognition of the Other "in terms of more and better cognition" (Bartky, 1997: 178). In response to this analysis, Bartky calls for "a knowing that transforms the self who knows, a knowing that brings into being new sympathies, new affects as well as new cognitions and new forms of intersubjectivity. The demand...is for a knowing that has a particular affective taste" (1997: 179). This affective dimension is, she argues, "somehow akin to love...or to the yearning for a more solidary world" (1997: 187). Ahmed moves beyond the individual orientation and cognitive–biological binary that marks this work by arguing for a focus on the "doing" of emotion. Here emotions are not about internal individual experience but circulate and get stuck as they involve different orientations to others and shape both individual and collective bodies. As such, Ahmed investigates "how they stick as well as move" (2004a: 4).

Other feminists have examined how particular emotions enact the social in particular ways, for example, the ways in which feminist or queer communities are created through shared experience and empathy (Probyn, 2005; Sedgwick, 2003). Some of this work has emerged as a reaction against what is seen as the supposed limits of post-structuralist theory and its emphasis on how norms are reproduced through discourse and language as well as the workings of discipline, resistance, and transgression (Hemmings, 2005). Indeed, Hemmings argues that theorists such as Sedgwick and Probyn emphasize the significance of emotion because they see it as potentially shifting the focus from post-structural concerns with power/knowledge to the ontological, intersubjective, and potentially more politically effective domains of experience. Affect and emotion, because they are seen to be *experienced*, are somehow understood as more authentic and thus less susceptible to the influence of theoretical trends. However, Hemmings questions this theory–emotions dichotomy and argues that emotion and affect can only be understood in "the context of social narratives and power relations" (2005: 562), which are also the stuff of theory.

Language, geopolitics, cognition, social categories, and experience cannot be easily separated because they work in and through one another. As Gail Lewis argues, "technologies of the social, in the sense of the ordering and naming of populations into categories based on bodily or cultural variation" as well as economic and class-based divisions, reproduce such social differences and have implications for the everyday performance and experience of social categories (2009: 5). Moreover, the spatial politics of geographical location and the multiple and unequal positionalities occupied by diverse constituencies of women raise questions about "where the centre of 'true' feminism can be said to reside and what kinds of practices can be named as feminist" (ibid.; see also Mohanty, 2006). Indeed, Lewis asks how differently located feminists are to speak to each other and to

> the complex realities of multiple articulations of gender and sexuality; to the varied forms of experiences of womanhood, femininity and masculinity; to the configurations of "race," ethnicity, religiosity and class; to the varieties of ideological and theoretical positions represented across feminist formations? (2009: 7)

Differences are not seen as inhering in individuals or groups but in the technologies of social categories and spatialized political systems that reproduce normative gender and sexual regimes (Lewis, 2009). As such, complex articulations of difference, disadvantage, and privilege have embodied, discursive, cognitive, and emotional effects. For example, in a racist and hetero-sexist world, "the black body carries the weight of…racial affect [and]…the female body caries the burden of the affects that maintain sexual difference" (Hemmings, 2005: 562). Racist and heterosexist encounters are embodied emotional encounters through which "the social" and bodies themselves are defined and redefined (Ahmed, 2004b: 32). So emotion is not random, but operates with "structured precision" and always "in the context of social narratives and power relations" (Hemmings, 2005: 562). Such social narratives, power relations, and embodied emotional encounters are structured by postcolonial spatialized global capitalist relations that can turn Western feminism into a suspect imperialist Euro-American import in some parts of the world (Ware, 2006: 530). This uneven structuring of feminist positions through historical and contemporary geopolitics means that "difficult dialogues" and complex emotional encounters are necessary if "generative conversations about and across all these (and more) fields of difference" are to take place (Lewis, 2009: 9).

The difficulties of forging strategic or provisional solidarities are compounded by these complexities, the perceived inadequacy of any response, dangers of misrecognition, and the potential violence of any gesture. Added to this, particular modes of subjectivization produce embodied forms of attachment, so that we often attach to that which oppresses us. However, it is difficult to identify when such attachments are oppressive, subversive, or transformative.[1] Principles and rights to equality, for example, assume that "affective fulfilment resides in assimilation, inclusion and normalcy" (Cretkovich, 2003: 11), when, in fact, the desire may be to resist the norm, to remain outside. For example, the refusal to take up the offer of same-sex marriage, or to accept the terms of cultural integration on the basis of meeting Western terms of gender equality cannot be read simply in terms of oppression. Similarly, the particular promise of freedom held out by liberal feminism is refused by socialist or nationalist feminists. So, for Mahmood, it is important that feminists "ask of politics a whole series of questions that seemed settled when we first embarked on the inquiry" (2005: 39). In other words, the object of feminist politics is not settled, but continually subject to questioning as "habits of different histories and experiences" come into view and are opened up in new ways.

The domain of feminist politics and scholarship, like most domains, involves the circulation of emotions that produce the effect of collectivities—us/them Western/non-Western feminisms. Ahmed argues that

> emotions do not inhabit *anybody* or *anything*, meaning that "the subject" is simply one nodal point in the economy, rather than its origin and destination...it suggests that the sideways and backwards movement of emotions...is not contained within the contours of the subject. (2004a: 46)

However, specific emotions, whether anger, guilt, shame, or empathy, "circulate through 'sticky' associations between signs, figures and objects" (Ahmed, 2004a: 45) and so cannot be apprehended in and of themselves, but must be located within a specific economy of emotions to understand their operation and solidaristic potential. Following Ahmed then, I consider in the following section how "emotions do things" (2004b: 26);[2] how empathy, in particular, as an emotionally inflected mode of relationship, "does things" with regard to feminist solidarity and politics.

EMPATHY AND ITS POTENTIAL FAILURE— A MODE OF SOLIDARISTIC RELATIONSHIP?

Empathy is a modern term translated in the early twentieth century from the term *Einfühlung*, which dates from 1897 (Garber, 2004). The term *Einfühlung*/empathy did not exist then until the end of the nineteenth century and is seen as signaling particular aspects of the modern self. For example, appeals to empathy are linked to the post-Enlightenment emotional regime of sympathy, which was deemed a crucial component of the enlightened self (Dean, 2004: 2). Indeed, from the seventeenth to the nineteenth centuries, the cognate emotions of sympathy and compassion were viewed by British moralists and writers of sentimental fiction as the basis of ethics central to the development of morality and justice (Chabot Davis, 2004; Moyn, 2006). Empathy suggests identification or "perspective-taking" because it involves "imaginatively experiencing the feelings, thoughts and situation of another" (Chabot Davis, 2004: 403). It can be provoked in many ways, for example, by witnessing another's emotional state, by hearing about the condition of another, by reading, or by viewing a film or television program.

Relationships based on empathy are easily read as always already hierarchical with the empathizer having the power to act or turn away. As such, empathy circulates a part of a gift economy, as what one gives to the other where the one and the other remain positioned within conventional hierarchical demarcations of power. Here, the emotion that moves us to question may involve fixing others (Ahmed, 2004b), as for example, in Western feminist calls for the liberation of the Islamic veiled woman. The very call for her liberation fixes her as oppressed, while those making the call claim to be moved to make such "feminist" declarations by her oppression. In a similar way, feminists concerned with the failures of postcolonial nation-state building in the Republic of Ireland may foreclose the feminist potential that inheres in the specific context of Northern Ireland in transition.

The assumed logics of empathy constitute some as in need of inclusion or support and others as potentially empathic, cosmopolitan, and inclusive citizen-subjects, or "enlightened" feminists. This kind of empathic or compassion-based politics is very close to old-fashioned charitable relations. However, although some theorists focus on the limits of empathy and how it lines up with charity and conservative compassion (Woodward, 2004), others see it as basic to human experience, central to progressive public education, and integral to the search of social justice (Nussbaum, 2001). My aim is not to make a strong claim for empathy but rather to identify the "moments" of political possibility opened up by the possibilities of empathic identification, or its refusal. However, before doing so, I want to attend to how empathy is constituted (i.e., how it comes into being as an emotion) by its potential failure. Put differently, empathic identification cannot be understood without reference to disidentification or dissociation, because empathy is a precarious sentiment. The very idea that one should respond empathetically to the pains or traumas of another came to the fore as sentimental humanitarianism came to be the moral horizon of modern times (Moyn, 2006: 402). In turn, a failure to respond came to be seen as deplorable (ibid.). We might ask then how we are trained in empathy, and also in distancing, dissociation, withholding empathy, and turning away. This question haunts debates about empathy and its failure.

Empathy or feeling-with cannot, according to Bartky, "go forward without the parallel construction of its opposites: feeling too little for others or feeling nothing at all," so questions of "despondency, excessive privatization, or indifference" are all integral to questions of feeling-with (1997: 193). Indeed, the sentimentalists of the eighteenth century were concerned that sympathy might be trumped by self-interest, or that it might fail as a result of exhaustion with witnessing suffering. Sympathy, as Moyn (2006) argues, has always been haunted by its fragility and its potential to fail. He notes that David Hume and Adam Smith made sympathy a *countervailing force* against Hobbes's emotion of envy rather than a replacement for envy, thus revealing the assumption that envy is inevitable, while sympathy has to be worked at to be achieved. Rousseau, who saw sympathy as core to human nature, was also aware of its fragility and potential failure (ibid.). The production of good citizens was seen as involving the cultivation of moral emotions by the state, or the promulgation of what Rousseau called "civil religion", that is, sentiments of sociability that were understood to be integral to good citizenship. Similar concerns about the failure of empathy and waning of affect circulate today but these are different insofar as they are less focused on how to overcome this failure than identifying with a state of numbness; being overwhelmed to the point of exhaustion—"worn out" (Berlant, 2007: 434). For example, Carolyn Dean sees numbness as a form of self-protective dissociation and suggests that "it is arguably a new, highly self-conscious narrative about the collective constriction of moral availability if not empathy" (2004: 5). As such, an incapacity to feel for others is naturalized as a feature of contemporary culture.

ETHICAL GROUNDS FOR FEMINIST SOLIDARITY

Because empathic relationships involve "feeling with," there may be a tendency, as already noted, to search for experience in common, that is, to make her like me. It is important, therefore, to distinguish between modes of empathy that assimilate the other into the self and empathic relationships that maintain the distance between the self and the other (Bartky, 1997; Scheler, 2008). For example, the often-invoked comparison between female genital cutting (FGC) and body modification by Western feminists tends to be framed either by analogy or along a continuum in attempts to produce empathic identifications that are ethical (Pedwell, 2007). However, the consequent reduction of these practices purely to gender relations obscures other axes of power (e.g., imperialism, "race," and nation), thus reproducing stereotyped relationships among "race," nation, and gender that are a product of "a 'western' empathic gaze" (2007: 45). As Pedwell argues, such attempts to produce cross-cultural empathy through similarity emphasize identification and conceal the "continuing operation of geo-political relations of power and privilege" (ibid.). Similarly, in Smyth's description (1995a) of the encounter between feminists from north and south of the Irish border at a conference in Boston, the continuing operation of geopolitical relations of power and privilege arising from their locations on either side of the border and the different class, religious, and national(ist) locations can either serve to reproduce stereotyped relationships among nation, gender, class, and religion, or open up spaces for strategic solidarity beginning from an acknowledgment of how these axes of power positioned these feminists in relation to one another.

The politics of identification at stake in feminist theorizations of empathetic relationships are examined by Kaja Silverman (1996) who identifies two main forms of empathic identification; *idiopathic* identification and *heteropathic* identification. She suggests that the seeing of the self in the image of the other, or, indeed, the other in the image of the self, leads to idiopathic identification. This form of identification takes place along a trajectory of incorporation because it involves assimilating the other to the self; that is, the experience of the other is interpreted only with reference to one's own prior experience (Bennett, 2003). The effect is the annihilation of the other because she is deprived of her specificity, her unique existence and character (Silverman, 1996). The experience and subjectivity of the other are domesticated or made like one's own (Bennett, 2003) when experiences are assimilated to that of individual or collective idiopathic identification, thereby excluding the potential of other experiences and narratives (LaCapra, 2001).

Silverman's (1996) notion of heteropathic identification is helpful for my purposes because it is a mode of identificatory relationship that keeps difference at the heart of identification. This form of empathic identification maintains openness to radical difference that may not be easily recognizable and to experience beyond what is known by the self. In a related discussion, Sara Ahmed warns against attempts to achieve an account of embodied specificity—to make the other knowable in specific ways, because such an aim presumes that the specificity of another can be accessed. She calls for thinking particularity in terms of modes of encounter, that is, "the particularity of modes of encountering others" (Ahmed, 2002: 561). Here, the particularity of others is not to be found on their bodies, but in "the history that the encounter reopens as well as the future that it might open up" (2002: 568). Thus, difference and particularity emerge as a result of namings in the meetings and encounters (ibid.). Particularity apprehended in this way potentially reveals the processes of differentiation between others (ibid.). This mode of identification involves the constitution and negotiation of difference at the level of the encounter. In the case of the Boston conference referred to by Smyth, the structured differences that separated the women from north and south of the border (as well as within both groups) might be both acknowledged and engaged with via provisional moments of heteropathic identification. As such, questions might be raised about which women come to represent feminism in each case. Northern Irish feminism is represented at the conference Smyth refers to by working-class activists and feminism south of the border by middle-class liberal feminists; these categories and the categories and histories they instantiate are also structured by absences (e.g., of working-class southern feminists and of middle-class northern feminists) and the feelings that such absences both prohibit and promote.

All encounters involve relationships among the past, present, and future and are inflected by the regulation of citizenship, work, bodies, and spaces (Ahmed, 2002). However, efforts to forge solidarity pose the ethical question of how to develop "ways of encountering others that are *better*" (2002: 562: emphasis in original). Marianne Hirsch's (1999) work adds another dimension to this discussion by suggesting that heteropathic identification or ethical modes of empathy can best be achieved via strategies of distanciation and displacement. Hirsch calls for an engagement with past experiences from different perspectives. For example, by locating experiences in different contexts, she suggests that they are brought to memory in different ways that potentially open up new interpretive frameworks and prevent over-identification or fixed identifications. So, for example, by rethinking Irish Catholic/Protestant feminist encounters at a different period such as during the Suffrage movement or the war of independence new interpretive frameworks might be opened up that would unsettle the emotional grammar of contemporary Irish feminist politics. Here Hirsh discusses empathy not as an abstract emotion, but a cognitive and emotional practice that contributes to judgment based on an assessment of contextual and perspectival factors.

However, Hirsch's strategies of displacement and distanciation do not go far enough for Susannah Radstone (2001) whose aim is to complicate the assumed workings of empathic identification by shifting it away from often implicit calls to identify with victimhood. I see her intervention as helpful because it shifts the assumed object of empathy away from pain and suffering toward the complexities of affect, desire, interests, and aspiration. Radstone calls for engagement with the ambiguity, unsettlement, and multiplicity of identification, which partly arises out of its combined psychic and social dimensions. Noting Hirsch's focus on identification with victimhood, she calls for a reading against the grain of identification with pure victimhood. Situations that include the exercise of power and authority, according to Radstone, may "prompt a particular identification *with* the wielder of that power, as well as with the object upon whom it is exercised" (2001: 65: emphasis in original). These power-invested webs of identification constitute aspects of personal and public fantasy and, of course, the domain of feminist politics. Radstone challenges the tendency in everyday life to reproduce an absolute distinction between good and evil by foregrounding potential identifications with perpetration as well as with victimhood (ibid.). In this way, according to Radstone, the self-righteousness and silencing that accompanies a dualistic good/evil culture (and by extension a progressive/backward culture dualism) might be unsettled and come into question.

Radstone's argument is most helpful in locating the potential of ethical empathic identification within a spectrum of experience rather than in the witness–victim relationship. Suffering cannot be assumed to produce a straightforward empathic identification but has a darker side, what Radstone, after Primo Levi (1989) calls "an ethical 'gray zone' " (2001: 61). For the Irish feminists at the conference described by Smyth, the lines of emphatic refusal or identification may be contradictory extending beyond the membership of the group: for example, the middle-class liberal feminists may aspire toward equal status with men in powerful social or political positions (identifying with such men) and/or may desire the grounded politics of working-class northern feminist activists. As Radstone argues, the position of witness is a complex one "that can exceed an empathic identification with victimhood to include identifications with other positions especially those of perpetration" (ibid.).

For LaCapra, empathy, instead of being caught in the binary logic of identity and difference, "should…be understood in terms of an affective relation, rapport, or bond with the other recognised and respected as other" (2001: 212–213). Empathy is activated through a process of "empathic unsettlement" what he describes as "a kind of virtual experience through which one puts oneself in the other's position while recognizing the difference of that position and hence not taking the other's place" (2001: 78). The aim is a greater reflexivity or self-understanding such that "a sensitivity or openness to responses that generate necessary tensions in one's account" is opened up (2001: 105). Thus, LaCapra suggests empathy without identification, or the pulling to likeness and that demands self-reflexivity.

Bearing witness to the more complex, difficult, and equivocal identifications that constitute the unrealized potential of empathy would mean struggling to read it in "the gray zone": It would complicate the workings of Irish and Global North/South feminist dichotomies, identify interconnections/dependencies, and acknowledge the potential for domination and exclusions that all feminist encounters represent. Such complex identifications could move politics onto new ground where solidarities involve the negotiation of unequal positionings, difference, and exclusions in ways that enable the affective hauntings of colonialism, imperialism, capitalism, and feminism to be acknowledged and reflexively engaged rather than denied and foreclosed.

CONCLUSION

Empathy can be seen as a mode of being that is "about how we respond to a situation of being with someone whose situation is not one that we are in: this being with, but not in, requires that we take care, that we be careful" (Ahmed, 2010: 1). However, there are times, as Ahmed notes, when there is no time to reflect and accepted social/political grammars of emotion including empathy prevail and give rise to responses that enact conventional demarcations of power. In this context, the demand of the other is less to feel what it is like to be in her situation and experienced more as a "naturalized" social demand to respond in a way that adheres to the "feeling rules" of the situation.

As Khanna (2001), Phillips (2007), Woodward (2004), and others argue, we live in a time when globalizing neoliberal capitalism and associated processes of individualization, localization, and privatization contribute to a sense of social numbness, a perceived failure of empathy, and a disavowal of the need for solidarity. However, the circulation of the idea that empathy and solidarity are exhausted, or no longer possible, serves to naturalize the idea that persistent and powerful local and transnational injustices cannot be changed. However, solidarities are not pre-political, but "are recurrently remade by political efforts" (Calhoun, 2003: 23), "difficult dialogues" (Lewis, 2009), complex emotional encounters (Ahmed, 2002) and in the "gray zone" between and across perpetration and victimhood (Radstone, 2001). In a world where "the most salient inequalities are intersocietally global" (Calhoun, 2003: 5), gender justice, and feminist and queer politics must be multiscalar. But globally structured inequalities can lead to the endless division of feminisms and other politics into internally bound identity politics that hinder transnational and transgender solidarities and (re)produce "naturalized" and depoliticized apathy.

Despite its potential narcissism, defensiveness, impulse toward redemption, and normative effects, it may be possible to mobilize empathic impulses in ways that enact the political in more progressive ways. For example, a reflexive and progressive mobilization of empathy as a process of emotion and imagination could contribute to catalyzing politically progressive thought and action. Such intersubjective relationships would not always be structured by victimhood but involve addressing socially unexpected or unacceptable empathic identifications in both directions. This is not about bonding with another or assuming "that one shares the other's actual interests, it does not provide encouragement to the self to deny the ways in which one might be implicated in another's suffering" (Lyshaug, 2006: 97). Instead, it is by moving empathy outside the gift economy and reposing it as a question of the *affective politics of feminist solidarity* that potential lies. For, solidarity, however provisional or strategic, cannot "be grounded in ur-languages of feminism" but can "only ensue within the uncertain, at times opaque, conditions of intimate and uncomfortable encounters in all their eventuality" (Mahmood, 2005: 198–199).

Returning to Ailbhe Smyth's references to the tensions and wariness between differently positioned Irish feminists, her "refusal of indifference" and willingness to stay proximate to the tensions and wariness "*however*" she might be affected (Ahmed, 2010: 16; emphasis in original) bring the complex feminist politics of empathy to the fore. However, the apparent failure of empathic identification she identifies can be turned into a point of departure rather than wariness, paralysis, or numbness. Although together as a group of Irish feminists, with their own pragmatic interests and agendas, the wariness and tensions "stemming from [their] complex differences" demand a feminist politics that engages such affect (Smyth, 1995a: 40). Critical attention to the grounds for and complex operation of empathy in feminist politics has the potential to contribute to the forging sustainable feminist connections beyond the "bounds of a liberal progressive imaginary" (Mahmood, 2005: 155). Learning to look out for the absences and listen for silences is, as Rooney (2008) argues, another important tactic in deconstructing received categories and frameworks of understanding. However, in the progressive imaginary of the feminist project (in most of its guises), "moments of difference" tend to be insistently "subsumed within a teleological process of improvement" (Mahmood, 2005: 198), and the affective politics that are at work in all politics and that keep inequalities and injustices in place, are overlooked. Ailbhe Smyth's work, through its deep commitment to and simultaneous critique of feminism and queering of the academic field, stages affective and intellectual opportunities for feminist heteropathic identification and solidarities. As such, one of Smyth's many contributions to feminist and queer scholarship is to keep open the spaces in which to continuously ask of feminism those questions that seem settled.

Uninscribed place of the future. This is what we must remember.
"Wildish things these
little newbreed Irish girls, scarce

**parented, not to be grooved into
rectangular requisite"**
Eithne Strong, "Identity," *My Darling Neighbour*
. . .
Uncertain, risky, feeling inappropriate because, place of passage,
of becoming, beyond (mis)appropriation. Evolving, open,
spacial, unfixed.
*A floozie, forsaking their jacuzzi,
must always feel like this.*
"I won't to back to it"
Evan Boland, "MiseÉire," The journey
"Ciúnas!, Quiet! Listen!"
(Smyth, 1991: 26/28; emphasis in original)

Acknowledgments

Thanks to Sara Ahmed, Eilish Rooney, and Margrit Shildrick for their most helpful comments on earlier versions of this chapter.

Notes

1. See Scott (2007) and Mahmood (2005) in relation to liberal feminist assumptions relating to veiling.
2. See also Ahmed (2008) and (2009).

References

Ahmed, Sara (2002) "The Other and Other Others." *Economy and Society*, 31 (4): 558– 572.
——— (2004a) *The Cultural Politics of Emotion.* Edinburgh: Edinburgh University Press.
——— (2004b) "Collective Feelings or, the Impressions Left by Others." *Theory, Culture and Society*, 21 (2): 25–42.
——— (2008) "Multiculturalism and the Promise of Happiness." *New Formations*, 63: 121–137.
——— (2010) "Becoming Unsympathetic: Living Outside the Happiness Care." Paper delivered at *Affecting Feminism: The Cultural Politics of Care, Compassion and Empathy* Symposium, University of Newcastle, Gender Research Group (GRG), May 7.
Alexander, M. Jacqui (2005) *Pedagogies of Crossing. Meditations on Feminism, Sexual Politics, Memory and the Sacred.* Durham: Duke University Press.
Balzano, Wanda, Anne Mulhall, and Moynagh Sullivan (2007) "Introduction," in W. Balzano, A. Mulhall, and M. Sullivan (eds), *Irish Postmodernisms and Popular Culture.* Basingstoke: Palgrave Macmillan, pp. xiii–xix.

Bartky, Sandra Lee (1997) "Sympathy and Solidarity: On a Tightrope with Scheler," in D. T. Meyers (ed.), *Feminists Rethink the Self.* Boulder, CO: Westview Press, pp. 177–196.

Bennett, Jill (2003) "Tenebrae after September 11. Art, Empathy, and the Global Politics of Belonging," in J. Bennett, and R. Kennedy (ed.), *World Memory. Personal Trajectories in Global Time.* Basingstoke: Palgrave, pp. 177–194.

Berlant, Lauren (1998) "Poor Eliza." *American Literature,* 70 (3): 635–668.

——— (2004) "Introduction," in L. Berlant (ed.), *Compassion.* Chicago, IL/New York: Routledge, pp. 1–13.

——— (2007) "Starved." *South Atlantic Quarterly,* 106 (3): 433–444.

Calhoun, Craig (2003) "The Elusive Cosmopolitan Ideal." *Berkeley Journal of Sociology,* 47: 3–26.

Chabot Davis, Kimberly (2004) "Oprah's Book Club and the Politics of Cross-racial Empathy." *International Journal of Cultural Studies,* 7 (4): 399–419.

Coulter, Carol (1990) *Ireland. Between the First and Third Worlds.* Dublin: Attic Press (Lip Series).

Cretkovich, Ann (2003) *An Archive of Feelings. Trauma, Sexuality, and Lesbian Public Cultures.* Durham: Duke University Press.

Dean, Carolyn J. (2004) *The Fragility of Empathy after the Holocaust.* New York: Cornell University Press.

Frye, Marilyn (1983) *The Politics of Reality: Essays in Feminist Theory.* Trumansburg, NY: The Crossing Press.

Garber, Marjorie (2004) "Compassion," in L. Berlant (ed.), *Compassion. The Culture and Politics of an Emotion.* New York: Routledge, pp. 15–28.

Gray, Breda (2004) "Remembering a 'Multicultural' Future through a History of Emigration: Towards a Feminist Politics of Solidarity across Difference." *Women's Studies International Forum,* 27 (4): 413–429.

——— (2008) "Putting Emotion and Reflexivity to Work in Researching Migration." *Sociology,* 42 (4): 919–936.

Hemmings, Clare (2005) "Invoking Affect. Cultural Theory and the Ontological Turn." *Cultural Studies,* 19 (5): 548–567.

Heyes, Cressida J. (2003) "Feminist Solidarity after Queer Theory: The Case of Transgender." *Signs,* 28 (4): 1093–1120.

Hirsch, Marianne (1999) "Projected Memory: Holocaust Photographs in Personal and Public Fantasy," in M. Bal, J. Crew, and L. Spitzer (ed.), *Acts of Memory. Cultural Recall in the Present.* Hanover: University Press of New England, pp. 3–23.

Jagger, Alison (1995) "Caring as a Feminist Practice of Moral Reason," in *Virginia Held* (ed.), *Justice and Care: Essential Readings in Virginia Held. Feminist Ethics.* Boulder, CO: Westview Press.

Khanna, Ranjana (2001) "Ethical Ambiguities and Specters of Colonialism: Futures of Transnational Feminism," in E. Bronfen and M. Kavka (ed.), *Feminist Consequences. Theory for the New Century.* New York: Columbia University Press, pp. 101–125.

LaCapra, Dominick (2001) *Writing History, Writing Trauma*. Baltimore: The Johns Hopkins University Press.

Levi, Primo (1989) *The Drowned and the Saved*. London: Abacus.

Lewis, Gail (2009) "Editorial: 'Difficult Dialogues' Once Again." *European Journal of Women's Studies*, 16 (1): 5–10.

Lyshaug, Brenda (2006) "Solidarity without 'Sisterhood'? Feminism and the Ethics of Coalition Building." *Politics and Gender*, 2: 77–100.

Madden, Siobhan and Moane, Ger (2006) "Critical Psychologies in Ireland. Transforming Contexts and Political Possibilities." *Annual Review of Critical Psychology*, 5: 281–304.

Mahmood, Saba (2005) *Politics of Piety: The Islamic Revival and the Feminist Subject*, Princeton, NJ.: Princeton University Press.

McKay, Deirdre (2007) " 'Sending Dollars Shows Feeling'—Emotions and Economics in Filipino Migration." *Mobilities*, 2 (2): 175–194.

Mendoza, Breny (2002) "Transnational Feminisms in Question." *Feminist Theory* 3 (3): 295–314.

Mohanty, Chandra Talpade (2003) *Feminism without Borders. Declonizing Theory and Practicing Solidarity*. Durham: Duke University Press.

——— (2006) "US Empire and the Project of Women's Studies: Stories of Citizenship, Complicity and Dissent." *Gender, Place and Culture*, 13 (1): 7–20.

Moyn, Samuel (2006) "Empathy in History, Empathising with Humanity." *History and Theory* 45: 397–415.

Nussbaum, Martha C. 2001. *Upheavals of Thought: The Intelligence of Emotions*. Cambridge: Cambridge University Press.

Pedwell, Carolyn (2007) "Theorizing 'African' Female Genital Cutting and 'Western' Body Modifications: A Critique of the Continuum and Analogue Approaches." *Feminist Review*, 86: 45–66.

Phillips, Anne (2007) *Multiculturalism without Culture*. Princeton and Oxford: Princeton University Press.

Probyn, Elspeth (2005) *Blush: Faces of Shame*, Minneapolis: University of Minnesota Press

Radstone, Susannah (2001) "Social Bonds and Psychical Order: Testimonies." *Cultural Values*, 5 (1): 59–77.

Rooney, Eilish (1995a) "Women and Political Conflict." *Race & Class*, 37 (1): 51–56.

——— (1995b) "Political Division, Practical Alliance: Problems for Women in Conflict." *Journal of Women's History*, 6, 4 and 7 (1): 13–39.

——— (2008) "Critical Reflections: Documenting Gender and Memory." *Women's Studies International Forum*, 31 (4): 457–463.

Ryan, Louise and Ward, Margaret (2004) *Irish Women and Nationalism: Soldiers, New Women and Wicked Hags*. Dublin: Irish Academic Press.

Scheler, Max (2008) [1970]. *The Nature of Sympathy*, trans. Peter Heath. New Brunswick: Transaction Publishers.

Sedgwick, Eve Kosofsky (2003) *Touching Feeling. Affect, Pedagogy, Performativity*. Durham: Duke University Press.

Silverman, Kaja (1996) *The Threshold of the Visible World*. New York: Routledge.

Smyth, Ailbhe (1991) "The Floozie in the Jacuzzi." *Feminist Studies*, 17 (1): 7–28.

——— (1995a) "Paying Our Disrespects to the Bloody States We're In: Women, Violence, Culture and the State." *Journal of Women's History*, 6 (7), 4 (1): 190–215.

——— (2005) "A Reading from the Book of Beginnings, or the End of the Line." *Estudios Irlandeses: Journal of Irish Studies*, 1: 127–140.

Speed, Anne (1992) "The Struggle for Reproductive Rights. A Brief History in its Political Context," in A. Smyth (ed.), *The Abortion Papers Ireland*. Dublin: Attic Press, pp. 85–98.

Spelman, Elizabeth V. (1988) *Inessential Woman. Problems of Exclusion in Feminist Thought*. London: The Women's Press.

———(1997) *Fruits of Sorrow: Framing Our Attention to Suffering*. Boston: Beacon Press.

Stean, Jill (2006) *Gender and International Relations*. Cambridge: Polity.

Ward, Margaret (2006) "Gender, Citizenship, and the Future of the Northern Ireland Peace Process." *Éire-Ireland*, 41 (1 and 2): 262–283.

Ware, Vron (2006) "Info-war and the Politics of Feminist Curiosity." *Cultural Studies*, 20 (6): 526–551.

Woodward, Kathleen (2004) "Calculating Compassion," in L. Berlant (ed.), *Compassion. The Culture and Politics of an Emotion*. New York: Routledge, pp. 59–86.

CHAPTER 6

Wonderful Documents and Male Begrudgery: Postconflict Reconstruction in Northern Ireland

Margaret Ward

Ten years ago, when Elizabeth Rehn and Ellen Johnson Sirleaf traveled around the world's major conflict zones interviewing women on the impact of war on their lives, they found women repeatedly describing the "wonderful documents that had been created and signed—and the failure to implement most of what has been promised" (Porter, 2005: 5). Northern Ireland is no stranger to lack of implementation of signed promises. Fifteen years have elapsed since our peace agreement was signed, and it seems an appropriate moment to reflect upon our "wonderful document"—the Good Friday Agreement of 1998—to assess where women now stand. Are we stuck in a Gramscian moment where "the old is dying and the new cannot be born" (Gramsci, 1971: 176)? Ni Aolain and Rooney have demonstrated how "absence of gender awareness in the transitional context" results in the "under-enforcement of negotiated equality commitments" (ni Aoláin and Rooney, 2007: 342). Continued gender-based inequalities therefore symbolize a wider failure to achieve a society based upon a commitment to social justice, equality, and inclusion.

How do we measure progress for women? Is it a begrudging head-count, or is it informed by a transformative vision? Mary Robinson has identified the problem as a reluctance to give any meaningful consideration to what equality should entail. In her view, the account of progress toward women's equality "is recorded less through deep and generous shifts in established thinking and more by listing laws or doing a number count of the women in public positions" (Robinson, 1992). Ireland, north and south, has significant similarities when it comes to considering women's long journey toward emancipation, not least in a shared begrudgery regarding women's struggle for liberation. Although the 1916 Proclamation promised equal citizenship to women, it was followed 20 years later by a constitution that pledged women's natural place to be in the home. In the years since the signing of the Good Friday Agreement, we can see clear signs of a process of retrenchment in the north of the island.

Could it have been different? Two years before the Agreement came into being, women from the community and voluntary sector and from academia mobilized against "the audacity of men sitting around a table planning the future of N Ireland without women" (Hinds, 2009). In challenging political parties who were prepared to negotiate peace without any inclusion of women's voices, they had to make a "mental shift" to move from informal networking to contemplating the taking of formal power. The outcome was that women's signatures *were* included within that international peace agreement. Easter 1998 in Belfast was a historic moment, with women's signatures included for the first time in an international peace agreement.

The particular qualities brought to the negotiating table in the 1990s by the Northern Ireland Women's Coalition exemplified all that is best in what might be considered as "womanly" abilities regarding negotiation and conciliation. In part, this stemmed from their very different approach to problem solving and their awareness of the gendered nature of political life. A few years previously, South African negotiators had demonstrated their understanding of the importance of including women in negotiations to achieve a political settlement. Cheryl Carolus, an African National Congress (ANC) representative and negotiator, believed that if women had not been so heavily involved, "(t)he talks would have suffered from what I call 'testosterone poisoning'. Women are used to dealing with conflicts, in the family, in the community. When they find an obstacle, they find a way to overcome it" (*Irish Times*). Although the Women's Coalition had a small team compared with the resources of other political parties, Fionnuala ni Aoláin's analysis of peace agreements concludes: "While numerically small and politically untested their impact on the negotiation process and its outcomes was to be substantive" (ni Aoláin, 2003: 4).

This does not mean that essentialist conclusions need to be drawn attributing to women automatic peacemaking abilities. Those abilities are developed out of the lived realities of our lives. The process of peacemaking has many stages, from mediation through to negotiation, and the social production of gender roles can give women an edge when it comes to such processes. After all, women spend more time than most men in sustaining domestic life; in doing so, they develop particular skills, for example, in encouraging compromises to maintain harmony within the family. Women also predominate in service and caring work. It is undoubtedly the case that women in Northern Ireland, like women in many other conflict zones, were engaged in informal processes of peace-building through working on behalf of their children, their families, and for their own needs. The Kvinna Till Kvinna Foundation is one of many organizations to acknowledge their contribution to the maintenance of civic society:

> Women were actively building bridges between the Catholics and Protestants long before the official peace negotiations began. Instead of focusing on old injustices they discussed solutions and strategies for healthcare and education etc. The women developed a common cause that in time influenced public opinion. By cooperating they became a peaceful alternative which showed that coexistence is possible despite a bloody history. (Kvinna Till Kvinna, 2004: 15)

However, women in conflict zones do more than concentrate on issues aimed at improving services for their communities; living in the midst of violence also has profound consequences in terms of understanding the connections among violence, militarism, and certain masculine cultures. It is this gender-differentiated experience that, as Cockburn argues, helps to explain why women are less likely to support war (Cockburn, 1999: 2). This understanding certainly helps to precipitate women toward the urgency of peacemaking. Arguably, the Women's Coalition went beyond that stage, or attempted to do so, because the task of reconstruction needs more than enhanced understanding of the other. Without feminism, as an explicit understanding of gender power and of the male-dominated gender order, a compelling vision of the future cannot be developed.

Within the negotiations, the women emphasized active listening, the importance of body language, pressing for a seating arrangement that did not emphasize tribal loyalties. As a Coalition, membership included nationalists and unionists and well-known feminists, as well as women who did not identify with feminism. What they agreed upon was the importance of basing all policy decisions on the key principles of human rights, inclusion, and equality. Their attitude toward problem solving was rooted in the skills that women can bring to the process and a determination to change the culture of negotiations so that all parties engaged with each other; they "blew apart the mystique" of what politics was about (Hinds, 2009; Ward, 2006: 274–275). In doing this, they succeeded in bringing issues to the table that would not otherwise have been included: victims, integrated housing and schooling, the rights of women, and the future involvement of civic society. Crucially, the lack of any mechanism to implement the hard-won pledge to promote "the right of women to full and equal political participation" means that we still have unacceptably small numbers of women in political life: 20 out of 108 Assembly members and 22 percent of councillors in local government. The experience of the Northern Ireland Women's Coalition therefore demonstrates most vividly both the necessity of including women in peacemaking and also the dire consequences of excluding women from the longer-term project of peace-building.

Christine Chinkin's analysis of gender dynamics within present-day conflicts stresses the importance of a social transformation that includes the transformation of gender relations. While UN Security Council Resolution 1325 (2000) on "Women, Peace and Security" emphasizes the importance of women's participation in peacemaking, much of the rationale behind this is based on what Chinkin perceives as essentialist assumptions regarding women's abilities as peacemakers. While welcoming Resolution 1325 as an important stage in the recognition of the importance of women in areas of conflict, Chinkin argues that more is required so that the role of women as agents of social change is acknowledged. This would ensure that women were also involved in the ongoing process of reconstruction and nation-building. Too often, there is a gendered vision of a reconstructed state that assumes male subjects, a rule of law based on male premises about law and governance, and a failure to deliver on the promises made to women in the early stages of peacemaking (Chinkin, 2004: 12–13).

When women's voices grow silent and the "wonderful document" fails to live up to its promise to grant women the right "to full and equal political participation" or to advance women in public life, we find ourselves entering that patriarchal backlash identified so precisely by Cockburn:

> the civil society rebuilt after war or tyranny seldom reflects women's visions or rewards their energies. The space that momentarily opens up for change is not often used to secure genuine and lasting gender transformations. Effort may be put into healing enmity by reshaping

> ethnic and national relations, but gender and class relations are usually allowed to revert to the status quo ante... Instead of the skills and confidence forged by some women by the furnace of war being turned to advantage, the old sexual division of labour is reconstituted, in the family, in the labour force. (Cockburn, 1999: 17)

South Africa provided the model for our peace process and was instrumental in coaxing it along the way. However, since the euphoria of the "rainbow nation," it too has suffered from a lack of fulfillment of those initial high hopes. While women's representation in the formal political sphere in South Africa remains high and policies on paper hold out the promise of gender equality, sexual violence against women remains at worryingly high levels and women's organizations face the withdrawal of international donors, a breakdown in coalitions and networks, a dilution of issues, increased competition for resources, and the re-emergence of old divisions (Artz, 2009; Hamber et al., 2006). All of this is now being experienced in Northern Ireland. Are we emulating this downward trajectory, with lack of political and economic progress now to be exacerbated by economic crisis?

As the authors of the *Global Monitoring Checklist on Women, Peace and Security* have noted, women in Northern Ireland:

> continue to face major inequalities, such as... having very little access to formal politics, with women under-represented in the judiciary and public office. Extremely significantly, despite being in a post-conflict and reconstruction phase, Northern Ireland is not covered in the UK National Action Plan (NAP) (2006) on women, peace and security, in which the UK government committed to promoting gender perspectives and supporting women in post-conflict situations. (Gender Action for Peace and Security UK, 2009: 102)

Hegarty, in evaluating cross-community work undertaken by the women's voluntary sector, argues that analyses of security threats are still "biased towards men and their concerns—the dialogue is about 'putting weapons beyond use' and 'dissident threats', whilst 'domestic violence' and sexual violence are on the increase" (Hegarty, 2010: 21). What kind of discourses would we have on how we deal with the past if gender-based concerns were included? Would we include "difficult" issues in terms of the relationships between women and men? What models of masculinity exist when a society emerges from conflict? If there is a "warrior-type masculinity," how does that impact on the lives of women and the levels of violence they might experience? Is it accidental that such societies experience increased levels of gender-based violence and should that be a cause for concern? Donald Steinburg, who helped to negotiate the Angolan Peace Accord, has spoken of the frustration of male ex-combatants exploding into "an epidemic of alcoholism, drug abuse, divorce, rape and domestic violence. In effect the end of civil war unleashed a new era of violence against women" (Steinburg, 2009).

In Northern Ireland, there were more recorded crimes with a domestic motivation in 2007/8 than the combined total of nearly all other crimes (Women's Aid Federation Northern Ireland, 2009).[1] Recent qualitative research in Northern Ireland has demonstrated that some women experiencing violence have partners from paramilitary organizations and the police, to an extent that would not be the case in countries not making a transition out of conflict (McMurray, 2010). Female use of prescription drugs is twice the male rate and particularly high in the 55- to 64-year age range. That needs to be understood, along with greater understanding of the many reasons for high rates of male suicide.

The urgent need for a gendered perspective becomes apparent when we consider the range of crucial issues currently on the political agenda, all of which require gender-specific responses and actions. The *Report of the Consultative Group on the Past*, for example, fails to acknowledge any gender-specific experiences. There is one reference to people experiencing "alcohol or drug dependency, depression or domestic abuse" (Consultative Group on the Past, 2009: 87). The lack of any gendered dimension means that the identities and needs of perpetrators and victims are jumbled together, concealing the continuing disadvantages experienced by women. There is also the reality that women have been combatants and participants in conflict. One in 20 of those imprisoned for politically related offences were women (Hillyard et al., 2006: 56), yet nowhere in the report is there any acknowledgment of the needs of female ex-prisoners. As a consequence, no specific provision seems likely to be made for the inclusion of women in all the many aspects involved in dealing with the past. Neglect of socioeconomic issues is discriminatory against women and serves to undermine initiatives to deal with the past. Any effort therefore to deal with the past has to acknowledge and redress the conflict's socioeconomic consequences, and the particular toll of poverty on women (Hillyard et al., 2005: 145).

There is a danger that the future will see women's position in the labor force, in public life, and in the community being threatened. Increasing rates of unemployment and cuts in services due to economic decline, the inability of many ex-prisoners to obtain employment, and reforms to our system of public administration that threaten the already limited numbers of women in local government, are some of the challenges we are facing. The exclusion of women from the decision-making process affects other rights, particularly reproductive rights. Abortion remains a criminal offence, regarded not as a health issue but as part of the criminal justice system. Although justice and policing have been devolved to the Assembly, there has been no change in responsibility for abortion reform and Northern Irish politicians have twice voted against having any progressive future change. Louise Vincent, considering the South African experience, warns that resisting ideologies that assert women's "proper role" to be primarily domestic remains an important issue in a period of social reconstruction, when "both women and men struggle to identify and consolidate new identities and roles." As "struggles of identity and status are often mixed with battles over resources and power, the reconstitution of gender is potentially conflictual" (Vincent, 2001: 15–30). Hamber goes even further, arguing that social stability in South Africa—because of the failure of the transitional process to address either women's experiences or the socioeconomic harm caused by apartheid—"has involved the reassertion of power and advantage by those elites who benefited most from the apartheid regime" (ni Aoláin and Rooney, 2007: 348).

A key issue still to be agreed within Northern Ireland is that of a Bill of Rights. A Bill of Rights was central to the Agreement, but resistance remains, particularly regarding the inclusion of socioeconomic rights. Conflict over the "reconstitution of gender" underlays much of the proceedings of the Bill of Rights Forum. As the convenor of the working group on women for the Forum (on which equal numbers of politicians and members of civic society were represented), I experienced that potential for conflict during the 15 months of its life, particularly when the women's report was presented at a plenary session of the Forum. Unsurprisingly, reproductive rights and the full implementation of the Good Friday Agreement promise of "full and equal political participation" proved extremely contentious (Bill of Rights Forum Women's Report). Reproductive rights have been omitted from the advice given to the Secretary of State by the Northern Ireland Human Rights Commission (NIHRC). In turn, the Secretary of State has chosen to ignore the entirety of the Commission's advice in drawing up proposals for consultation on the issue (Northern Ireland Office, 2009).

Gender parity in representation remains a fraught issue. In relation to the 2011 elections, the Centre for the Advancement of Women in Politics at Queen's University commented "the low overall representation of women in Stormont is a matter of concern for democratic decision-making" (Centre for the Advancement of Women in Politics, 2011). In local government, female representation is likely to decline as a result of local government reform. Transition Committees intended to oversee the establishment of "super councils" to replace the current 26 councils were established, consisting of members drawn from existing councilors. While the politicians were scrupulous in ensuring parity regarding nationalist/unionist representation, they admitted, when challenged, that gender parity had not been a consideration. In consequence, some Transition Committees were all-male and women's representation never exceeded more than 15 percent overall. Women's sector organizations made vigorous responses to a consultation on the establishment of the Transition Committees and continued to lobby politicians and the minister for the environment. They received the unhelpful reply that the proposals were "gender neutral" and would have "neither a negative impact…nor a positive impact" (Murphy, 2009).

The struggle to convince a male-dominated polity of the importance of women's agency, of their role "as active citizens whose contribution to improving relations has an important impact on reducing intolerance" (Hegarty, 2010: 25), remains an uphill one. Yet, women's involvement in the continuing work of peace-building, which includes community-based women as well as women in other areas of public and political life, has to be sustained and the commitment of the Agreement to ensure "equal opportunity in all social and economic activity" must be lived up to if we are ever to move beyond mere possession of a "wonderful document" and achieve progress based on a commitment to transform lives.

Notes

1. The Women's Aid Federation analysis of official police figures shows the situation for 2008/9 as follows: there were more domestic-related crimes (9,211) than the following crimes combined (9,155 in total):
   - Sexual offences (All): 1,943
   - Armed Robbery: 508
   - Robbery: 650
   - Hijacking: 125
   - Theft or unauthorized taking of a motor vehicle: 2,954
   - Arson: 2002
   - Dangerous driving: 746
   - Handling stolen goods: 220
   - Offenses under antiterrorism legislation 7

References

Artz, Lilly (2009) "Presentation to AGM of Women's Aid Federation NI," Gender Health and Justice Unit, University of Capetown, South Africa. Belfast.

Centre for the Advancement of Women in Politics, Queen's University of Belfast. "Elections." Available at www.qub.ac.uk/cawp/UKhtmls/election NIMarch07.htm

Chinkin, Christine (2004) "Peace Processes, Post-Conflict Security and Women's Human Rights: The International Context Considered," 9th Torkel Opsahl Memorial Lecture, Belfast. www.wrda.net/wrdanews /data/upimages/Opsahllecture041.pdf

Cockburn, Cynthia (1999) "Gender, Armed Conflict and Political Violence," background paper prepared for the World Bank, Washington, DC, June 10/11, 1999. (A later version of this paper can be found in Caroline Moser and Fiona Clark, eds (2001) *Victims, Perpetrators or Actors? Gender, Armed Conflict and Political Violence.* London: Zed Books.)

Gender Action for Peace and Security UK (2009) *Global Monitoring Checklist on Women, Peace and Security.* London: GAPS UK.

Gramsci, Antonio (1971) Q. Hoare, and G. Nowell-Smith (eds.), *Selections from the Prison Notebooks of Antonio Gramsci.* London: Lawrence & Wishart.

Hamber, Brandon, Hillyard, Paddy, Maguire, Amy, McWilliams, Monica, Robinson, Gillian, Russell, David, and Ward, Margaret (2006) "Discourses in Transition: Re-imagining Women's Security." *International Relations,* 20 (4): 487–502.

Hegarty, Angela (2010) *Review of the WRDA's Good Relations Project.* Belfast: Women's Resource and Development Agency.

Hillyard, Paddy, McWilliams, Monica, and Ward, Margaret (2006) *Gender Audit for Northern Ireland.* Available at. auditardywww.wrda.net/wrda news/data/upimages/genderaudit1.pdf

Hillyard, Paddy, Rolston, Bill, and Tomlinson, Mike (2005) *Poverty and Conflict in Ireland: An International Perspective.* Dublin: IPA/CPA.

Hinds, Bronagh (2009) "Lessons on Peacebuilding from Ireland." Address to Hanna's House Seminar, *Feminism and Peacebuilding: Why Women Matter.* Galway. Available at www.hannashouse.ie/index.php?option=com_content &task=view&id=4&Itemid *Irish Times,* March 5, 2001.

Kvinna Till Kvinna (2004) *Rethink! A Handbook for Sustainable Peace.* Sweden.

McMurray, Anne (2010) *Women's Experience of Violence: Mapping Experiences and Responses. A Pilot Study.* Belfast: Women's Centres Regional Partnership.

Murphy, John (2009) Letter to Women's Ad hoc Policy Group, December 3, 2009, Department of the Environment.

ni Aoláin, Fionnuala (2003) "Peace Agreements as a Means for Promoting Gender Equality and Ensuring Participation of Women," Expert Group

Meeting on *Peace Agreements as a Means for Promoting Gender Equality and Ensuring Participation of Women—A Framework of Model Provisions.* UNDAW: Ottawa, Canada. Available at www.un.org/womenwatch /daw/egm/peace2003/reports/EP4NiAolain.PDF.

ni Aoláin, Fionnuala and Rooney, Eilish (2007) "Underenforcment and Intersectionality: Gendered Aspects of Transition for Women." *The International Journal of Transitional Justice,* 1 (3): 338–374.

Northern Ireland Human Rights Commission (2008) *A Bill of Rights for Northern Ireland. Advice to the Secretary of State for Northern Ireland.* Belfast: NIHRC.

Northern Ireland Office (2009) *Consultation Paper. A Bill of Rights for Northern Ireland. Next Steps.* London: NIO.

Porter, Elisabeth (2005) "Women and Security: 'You Cannot Dance if You Cannot Stand.'" www.opendemocracy.net/taxonomy/term/820/0/feed.

Consultative Group on the Past (2009) *Report of the Consultative Group on the Past, Presented to the Secretary of State for Northern Ireland Belfast.*

Robinson, Mary (1992) "Striking a Balance," Allen Lane Foundation Lecture, quoted in *The Field Day Anthology of Irish Writing* Vol. 5. Irish Women's Writings and Traditions. Cork: Cork University Press, 2002, p. 285.

Steinburg, Donald (2009) "Beyond Victimhood: Protection and Participation of Women in the Pursuit of Peace." Testimony for U.S. Senate Foreign Relations Committee. Available at http://foreign.senate.gov/testimony /2009/SteinbergTestimony091001p.pdf.

Women' s Aid Federation Northern Ireland (2009) Internal document, courtesy of Annie Campbell, Director. *Women's Aid Federation NI Annual Analysis of the PSNI Figures.*

Vincent, Louise (2001) "Engendering Peace in Africa: A Critical Enquiry into Some Current Thinking on the Role of African Women in Peace-Building." *Africa Journal in Conflict Resolution* 1. Available at www.accord.org.za /web.nsf

Ward, Margaret (2006), "Gender, Citizenship, and the Future of the Northern Ireland Peace Process." Eire-Ireland, 41 (1 & 2), Spring/Summer 2006: 262–283.

CHAPTER 7

Pride, Politics, and the Right to Perform

Fintan Walsh

Following the annual Dublin Pride parade on June 27, 2009, certain voices within the Irish media heavily criticized the performance of the Lesbian, Gay, Bisexual, Trans, Queer (LGBTQ) community involved. In particular, writing for the *Sunday Times*, journalist and barrister Brenda Power used the occasion to argue against the provision of marital and adoptive rights to same-sex couples, following the publication of the government's proposed Civil Partnership Bill the previous month.[1] The debates that subsequently played across radio stations, newspapers, blogs, and social networking sites, in addition to the demonstrations that took place on the streets, were not only sparked off by a mass cultural performance, but they also followed a week of theater and performance events programmed by Calipo and THISISPOPBABY theater companies as part of the extended Pride festival. Although Civil Partnership legislation would eventually take effect in Ireland in 2011, this critical, contentious turning point provides an opportunity for reflecting upon the relationship among LGBTQ people, politics, and performance in contemporary Ireland.

This chapter considers how Power's condemnation of an important queer cultural performance provoked the mobilization of accelerated performative protests in the form of written, spoken, and virtual acts of resistance, as well as embodied intervention in the shape of public marches, street protests, and sustained activism. I maintain that while LGBTQ community politics had suffered from relative complacency in preceding years, events surrounding this period occasioned the unification of an otherwise diverse and frequently divided group of people, and the emergence of what the philosopher Jacques Rancière has described as "a dramaturgy of politics" (Rancière, 2009: 120). This was significant not only, and perhaps not even, because of the legal stakes involved, but also because these debates were fought over and alongside the right to perform.

PRIDE

Dublin's first recognizable Pride parade (programmed as 'Gay Rights Protest March') took place on Saturday, June 25, 1983.[2] While Pride parades around the world have grown to commemorate the Stonewall riots, and serve as a form of activism in the present, Dublin's first event was initially spurred on by more immediate concerns. On March 19 of the same year, a group passed from the city center to Fairview Park on the north side of the city, to protest against increasing levels of violence against gay men and women in the city. More specifically, the occasion was sparked off when suspended sentences of manslaughter were issued to a gang of men for the homophobia motivated murder of 31-year-old gay man Declan Flynn the previous year. Carried by this local spirit of commemoration and protest, the first parade was organized by the National Lesbian and Gay Federation (NGLF), and it moved from Saint Stephen's Green Park to the General Post Office on O'Connell Street.

In its 29-year run, Pride (which has since expanded into a full-length festival, marked in other cities and towns across the country) has endeavored to respond to the changing interests and concerns of LGBTQ people. This focus is enshrined in the festival's commitment to celebrating diversity, promoting inclusiveness, and increasing visibility and mutual respect.[3] Moreover, this is reflected in the fact that the organization plans each festival according to a relevant theme, as is the case with some other locations too. In 2008, for example, "Always the Bridesmaid, Never the Bride" was chosen to highlight the lack of legal recognition for same-sex couples under Irish law following the proposed partnership legislation, and in 2009, the interrogative "Pride and Prejudice?" sought to celebrate achievements within the LGBTQ community while provoking questions about persistent exclusions.[4]

2009 was an especially significant year in Ireland insofar as heightened discussions surrounding the Civil Partnership Bill forced a frequently disparate group of people to reckon with the symbolic and legal status of their relationships in a way many people had not done since the decriminalization of male homosexual acts in 1993. While many lesbian and gay people remain at odds with the specific terms of partnership, marriage, and associated concerns surrounding adoption, the swell of national interest that rose in 2009 made it virtually impossible to ignore the issue.[5]

Most interesting of these developments was the rapid establishment of a number of volunteer organizations that sought to raise awareness, give advice, and promote the recognition of same-sex unions. While groups supporting lesbian and gay interest have been around for some time, such as the NGLF (founded in 1979 to work for the rights of and the elimination of discrimination against lesbian, gay, bisexual, and transgendered people) and the Gay and Lesbian Equality Network (GLEN, founded in 1988 to secure legislative changes and bring about equality for the LGB population in Ireland), the number of similar groups increased since 2007.

Noise, for instance, was established in November 2007 in response to the Irish government's decision to vote down the Civil Union Bill in March of that year, and its refusal to introduce legislation that would grant civil marriage equality to same-sex people. Similarly, Marriage Equality was founded in February 2008 to lobby for equal martial rights for lesbian and gay couples, and it developed from an initiative introduced to support the high-profile legal case taken by Katherine Zappone and Ann Louise Gilligan to have their Canadian marriage recognized in Ireland.[6] In both instances, these activist initiatives were notable for the performative tenor to their approaches, which variously involved initiating Internet viral campaigns, protests, and parades, and linking with professional performers, musicians, and filmmakers to mobilize action. A notable example includes the short film *Sinead's Hand* (2009), which was specifically made to promote the legalization of same-sex marriage, and was circulated virally across the Internet. Directed by Peter Murphy, the film shows an ostensibly straight man ask a range of people for permission to marry his girlfriend, in a bid to highlight the absurdity of what gay people were effectively being forced to do.

In Ireland, as elsewhere, LGBTQ culture has been both constituted and sustained by a variety of performance modalities. In *Queer Political Performance and Protest* (2009), Benjamin Shepard argues that queer social movements often involve a lot of enjoyable as well as angered performances: "To a great degree, social movement protests are constructions of countless performances. The aim of such a performative protest is to represent the idea that another world is possible and to do it with panache" (Shepard, 2009: 12). Perhaps it comes as little surprise, then, that in the interim between the government's publication of the proposed partnership Bill and its planned discussion within the Oireachtas (Parliament) in Autumn 2009, performance asserted itself as a central means through which the legislation's terms and implications would be negotiated. Significantly, however, these varied performances were politically inflected and invested in ways not typical of recent trends in Irish queer culture. Throughout the Celtic Tiger years, for example, homosexuality seemed more visible in mainstream and popular culture than ever before, especially male homosexuality. Despite this apparent saturation, however, LGBTQ issues became seemingly depoliticized, arguably through an overreliance on the architecture of neoliberalism for recognition. The symbiotic relationship between gay culture and consumerism is not confined to Ireland, of course, but rapid economic expansion in the late 1990s, so soon after the decriminalization of male homosexual sex acts, created the illusory gloss of social and political equality. In 2009, when gay rights came under the spotlight in the middle of a world recession, a more politically focused response took shape. Propelling this intervention was a wide variety of aesthetic and social performance practices. Quite often, the distinction between performance and politics became so blurred that the right to perform appeared just as important as the right to marry or indeed adopt.

PERFORMANCE

In addition to the formally organized activist groups that I have already described, Dublin Pride 2009 also revealed a heightened focus on performance events. While Pride is likely the LGBTQ community's most established and wide-ranging cultural expression, the 2009 festival foregrounded performance events in a way it had not done before. There were the usual workshops, sports activities, remembrance ceremonies, and club nights, but with the newly programmed Arts and Cultural events section also included an art exhibition, a short-film competition, and a literary and poetry night. The festival also included Queer Notions—a week of theater and performance events curated by THISISPOPBABY.

Queer Notions featured a number of theater and performance pieces drawn from local and international talent. While international artists included London-based performers David Hoyle and neo-cabaret duo Bourgeois & Maurice, homegrown work included Phillip McMahon's *All Over Town*, a play about a young Irish man coming out in Australia; Úna McKevitt's devised work *Victor and Gord*, which focused on the real-life relationships of a group of straight and gay friends; *Dancing at the Crossroads: Glamour Rooted in Despair*, a performance/lecture on the history of Ireland's longest-running queer beauty pageant, the Alternative Miss Ireland; and a work-in-progress production of *A Woman in Progress*, a theater piece written and performed by one of Ireland's most well-known drag queens Panti (Rory O'Neill), which was later staged in full at the Ulster Bank Dublin Theatre Festival.

While many of the performances explored issues surrounding LGBTQ rights, queer relationships and history, *A Woman in Progress* proved to be the most topical in terms of its treatment of partnership legislation, and also in its exploration of the relationship among religion, cultural memory, and sexuality in Irish culture. Furthermore, the performance was most explicit in its appeal to politicize the LGBTQ community in the service of legal amendment. Much of the solo performance by Panti involved recalling significant moments in the development of her character, juxtaposed against influential national events, beginning with the Pope's visit to Ireland in 1979. Toward the end of the performance, Panti used the opportunity to critique what she saw as the death of the queer culture that once saved her, and taught her to question widely accepted truths and normative culture more generally. Targeting what she referred to as the complacency of the "baby gays," Panti admonished a young generation of LGBTQ identifying individuals for being more interested in teen pop star Miley Ray Cyrus than equal rights and social and political change.

Since the 1990s, Panti and her alter ego O'Neill have been central in the development of Ireland's queer social, political, and performance scenes. Following a number of years in Tokyo, where she performed as part of the drag duo CandiPanti, Panti launched her career in Dublin in 1996 as host of the Alternative Miss Ireland. Conceived in the mind of art graduate O'Neill as a mid-Atlantic aunt returned home, Panti accrued popularity by making astute, satirical observations of the culture in which she found herself. While Panti may have been an imaginary construction, the social and political dynamics she indexed were real. For instance, Panti was not the only person coming home at this time. Following mass immigration during the 1980s, many people were similarly returning to Ireland to enjoy the benefits occasioned by the country's financial boom. Three years after the decriminalization of homosexuality, Ireland was about to experience its greatest period of economic expansion in history, and an unprecedented level of cultural cross-fertilization. Panti started performing at this rich intersection, and became a central figure in Ireland's emergent queer culture.

The Alternative Miss Ireland, which concluded its 18-year run in 2012, represented a rich meeting point of pleasure and politics in the

Irish queer calendar. Modeled on Andrew Logan's *Alternative Miss World*, the pageant staged an irreverent take on the sanitized depictions of gender and sexuality typical of normative beauty pageants worldwide, while also dialoging with specifically Irish ideas about gender and sexuality, not least of which include those cultivated by contests such as The Rose of Tralee and Miss Ireland.[7] In this, the performance existed as an important community-driven political forum dedicated to both celebration and activism.[8] Drawing on Pantomime's tradition of playing highly current politics in humorous but no less committed terms, the event also known as Gay Christmas quickly became an important arena through which Panti began to deploy drag as a vehicle for activism while encouraging similar modes of intervention among others.

This particular approach to queer sociality and politics found further progression in collaborative partnerships to emerge from AMI. Working with producers, promoters, and artists that included individuals such as Trish Brennan, Niall Sweeney, and Tonie Walsh, Panti proceeded to appear at a number of performance-based pub and club nights throughout the 1990s such as Gag, Powderbubble, HAM, Gristle, in addition to leading Dublin's Pride parades and running the long-standing Casting Couch Karaoke night at the Front Lounge pub on Parliament Street. Most recently, Panti has extended her remit by staging a trilogy of retrospective theater pieces—*In These Shoes* (2007), *All Dolled Up* (2007), and most recently *A Woman in Progress*—that conspired to narrate recent Irish history from a distinctly queer perspective.

The criticism of certain strands of contemporary LGBTQ culture that Panti articulated in *A Woman in Progress* followed on from remarks posted on her very popular blog "Pantiblog" in which she berated people for not turning out to a Noise marriage rally on February 14, 2009. In the entry entitled "No More Mr. Nice Gay," Panti complained that only about 150 people turned out to the Noise event, and that it was time for people to become more politically involved. In a lengthy post, Panti derided the LGBTQ community for trading in political awareness for consumerism and pop culture:

> But 150 people? That's pathetic…When Alexandra and a bunch of other people you'd never heard of a few weeks earlier, make it to the *X Factor* final, you won't leave the house and no one can get through to you because you're furiously text voting, but when you're told you're a second class citizen and your relationships aren't *real* relationships, you can't be arsed walking over to Dame St from H&M because the cute assistant has just gone to check if they have that cute jacket in your size. Where the *FUCK* is your righteous anger? (Pantibar Blog, 2009)

Arguably as a direct result of Panti's post, which was widely spread across the Internet and social media sites, when Noise staged another rally on Sunday, April 19, 2009, outside the Central Bank in Dublin, over 1,000 people were in attendance.

One week after *A Woman in Progress* was staged as part of "Queer Notions," Panti reiterated many of these sentiments again while acting as emcee for the post-Pride celebrations at the Civic Offices of Dublin City Council. During this gathering, partnership legislation was once again highly topical, and this concern was performed though a mixture of banners, chants, and costumes by the estimated 12,000 strong group in attendance. The numerous half-constructed tuxedos and bridal gowns on show signified the feeling that partnership was less than marriage, while many invited speakers addressed the issue explicitly. Grand Marshall Ailbhe Smyth compared the Bill to an "apartheid system" in her speech, adding: "We are not to be insulted and humiliated, we want marriage for lesbians and gays, our goal is equality." Representing Noise, Anna McCarthy ripped up a copy of the Bill to widespread applause, while saying "Civil partnership will officially make us second class citizens in the eyes of the law and in the eyes of society." But it was Panti's speech that proved to be the most powerful on the day, and the most provocative in the weeks that lay ahead.

Addressing those gathered, the performer acknowledged divisions in the LGBTQ community surrounding the proposed legislation, while adding that these differences needed to be respected in the interest of attaining other shared goals: "Some think it is a stepping stone to full equality, some disagree and think full equality is the only thing that we can accept, all agree that the proposed Bill does not go far enough," she said. Reiterating ideas from her blog, and those articulated in *A Work in Progress*, Panti urged those present to get political and mobilize action. Speaking to a cheering crowd, she emotively charged: "Anyone can get married in this country except you, any soccer hooligan, any gay basher, any fascist, any murderer, any sex offender can get married, but you cannot."

Writing on protests, demonstrations, and parades, Paul Allain and Jen Harvie suggest that these performative forms often stage a challenge to authority in ways that radically destabilize the status quo:

> These are forms of mass group performance that generally take place in public spaces in order to influence public opinion by occupying and exploiting the power of those sites…protests and demonstrations occupy public space in ways intended to challenge authority, claim freedom of movement and expression, consolidate a sense of

counter-cultural group identity, and reclaim a sense of democratic agency for the people rather than the State. (Allain and Harvie, 2006: 194–195)

Sally Munt and Katherine O'Donnell caution that while performances of queer sexuality might indeed threaten the status quo, heteronormativity is often rigorously enforced and reproduced in public performance. In "Pride and Prejudice: Legalizing Compulsory Heterosexuality in New York's Annual St. Patrick's Day Parades" (2007), the authors discuss the exclusion of gay and lesbian people at the New York City St. Patrick's Parade by the Ancient Order of the Hibernians, the Irish Catholic fraternal organization that run the parade. They highlight how queerness and nationalism are uneasy bedfellows, and maintain that this tension is thrown into relief in the negotiation of public space. In national parades, they propose, " 'Sameness' is highly regulated: Routes, music, dress, and the order of participation must remain unchanged." In queer parades such as Pride, however, sameness is challenged in public, "as embodied notions of subjectivity are sold, enacted, transgressed, and debated." This negotiation of space often raises other questions about social propriety and symbolic centrality. "In the heat of the Pride parade," Munt and O'Donnell argue:

> The history and materiality of homosexual oppression and resistance rubs against regulated spaces subject to planning controls and state intervention. As such, parades are often subject to public debate about which space they may occupy and what kind of displays are deemed appropriate. (Munt and O'Donnell, 2007: 100)

Although Dublin Pride has passed without controversy in recent years, this was not the case in June 2009. Even though Panti's speech was received with resounding applause on the day in question by those present, and featured on the national news station that evening, and in the press the following day, not all reactions were supportive. Most notably, in her opinion column in the *Sunday Times*, Brenda Power responded to the event and its coverage to make a case against the provision of partnership and adoptive rights to gay people. Deploying crude culinary metaphors, she wrote:

> Marriage is a legal and religious union between a man and a woman. That's a definition, in the same way as Irish stew is a dish made with lamb, spuds and turnips. You can, of course, substitute wild boar, aubergines and pilau rice, and you will have a perfectly delightful meal that will satisfy more sophisticated palates. But it won't be Irish stew.

Change the ingredients, and you change the institution. A legal, civil and religious union between a same-sex couple may well be new and wonderful, or sacrilegious and distasteful, depending on your point of view, but it's not a marriage. (*Sunday Times*, July 5, 2009)

Metaphors aside, what is perhaps most interesting about Power's article is that she seemed to be more affronted by the idea of Pride as a performance, than equality or the possibility of legal recognition itself. In fact, she was so outraged by the performance that she used its carnivalesque tenor as evidence of a depraved homosexual lifestyle:

Homosexuals insist that their nature is an inherent, essential reality, and not a lifestyle choice. But if we were to judge by the get-up and carry-on of some of those in the Pride march last week, that's hard to believe. Some are definitely choosing to pursue a way of life that is quite alien to the majority of married heterosexual parents in this country, indeed deliberately and defiantly so...While the gay community in this country chooses to express itself in the manner of last week's Pride march, deliberately provoking reaction and comment, keen to shock and primed to take umbrage if the wrong pronoun is applied to a bloke in a dress, there's not much chance of that. (*Sunday Times*, July 5, 2009)

Moreover, Power seemed appalled by the appearance of Panti, undermining her speech by virtue of the fact that she was a cross-dressed performer:

It is not easy for a man to make a serious political point on the shortcomings of the new Civil Partnership Bill while he is wearing half a wedding dress and calling himself Miss Panti. Last weekend Panti was the parade host for the annual Pride rally, now officially the LGBTQ Pride Festival, with the abbreviation used to include the entire lesbian, gay, bisexual, transgender and queer community. (*Sunday Times*, July 5, 2009)

As soon as the article was published online, it was posted on Panti's Blog under the heading "Apparently I'd better shut my big Gay Trannie Mouth." Immediately, comments of support and protest were posted on these pages, and the *Sunday Times* was inundated with criticism over the article. Many people who would not necessarily attend Pride complained, while a small minority, some of whom were gay, supported Power. The overwhelming feeling, however, was that a large majority were very offended by Power's article, not only because of her politics but because she seemed to be objecting to a popular performer, and the LGBTQ community's right to perform. Throughout this discussion, the suggestion that Pride was the gay community's version of St. Patrick's Day appeared more than once.

Ironically enough, when Panti spoke a week previously about the inertia of the gay community, an event like this was exactly what was needed to reinvigorate people. Writing on her blog, and speaking on *The Last Word* radio program on Today FM as Rory O'Neill with Matt Cooper, the performer celebrated the fact that this kind of bigotry would motivate more people to take action. With a number of weeks to go before the next Noise rally, Panti encouraged the LGBTQ community to take to the streets.

One week after Power's article was published, and following heated debates in the print media, radio, and across the Internet, the columnist published a follow-up article entitled "I Must Not Offend Gay People," in which she defended her position. She challenged the militancy of the reaction to her article, calling it misogynistic and undemocratic:

> Within a community that expects and demands so much tolerance, there appears to be a vocal, militant and markedly misogynistic element that is reluctant to show tolerance for any opinions that don't accord precisely with its own. No democratic society can afford to indulge groups who seek to punish and silence those who dare disagree with them. (*Sunday Times*, July 12, 2009)

Power seemed particularly affronted by the whole concept of queer performance as having anything to do with political action. Elaborating her defence, she wrote:

> I have no time for the Ali G school of debate ... if you are arguing that you should have the right to be considered as a mature, responsible adult competent to provide a balanced, regular, appropriate upbringing to a stranger's vulnerable child, it's probably best, for the moment, not to do so while wearing fancy dress and a fright wig. That's neither a fact nor an opinion—it's just my advice. (*Sunday Times*, July 12, 2009)

What we see in Power's follow-up article, then, is an elaboration of the bias that homosexuality is fine as long as it does not interfere with normative culture or indeed public space. I would even go so far as to suggest that while same-sex civil partnership or marriage might indeed be acceptable to many people insofar as it builds upon a preestablished model of sociality; queer performance, and the possibility that queer families might perform themselves differently, poses a greater affective threat to many. Power's article reveals not only an anxiety around queer performance, but a lack of awareness that for LGBTQ social and political movements, performance, pleasure, and politics have always been intimately connected. As Shepard remarks: "cultural resistance functions as creative support, not merely a reactive force. Chock-full of hopeful celebration, camp, and humor, many such performances inject a resilient dose of creative play into struggles against social and cultural oblivion" (Shepard, 2009: 12).

Politics

In *Radical Street Performance* (1998), Jan Cohen-Cruz maintains that street protest "draws people who comprise a contested reality into what its creators hope will be a changing script" (Cohen-Cruz, 1998: 1). Furthermore, Cohen-Cruz claims that performances of this kind tend to take place in periods of social flux, "during or just after a shift in the status quo" (Cohen-Cruz, 1998: 1). She continues: "When one needs most to disturb the peace, street performance creates visions of what society might be, and arguments against what it is. Street performance is porous, inviting participation of all who pass" (Cohen-Cruz, 1998: 1).

Following on, it is perhaps no surprise that in the weeks that followed the initial controversy sparked off by Panti's Pride speech, a record number of people turned out to the subsequent Noise marriage rally on August 9, 2009. This time, gay and lesbian people were not the only groups encouraged to attend, but their families who were also implicated: "Do your straight friends and family think you are equal? Now is their chance to show it!" the group's campaign urged.

On the afternoon of the 9th, people from all around the country gathered on Dame Street to march to the Department of Justice, Equality and Law reform on St. Stephen's Green. While Panti stayed out of the limelight on this occasion, apart from encouraging people through her blog and weekly performances, the event featured a range of other performers and speakers including Niall Crowley (former CEO of the Equality Authority), Patricia Prendeville (former executive director of the International Lesbian, Gay, Bisexual, Trans and Intersex Association, Europe), and Brendan Courtney (broadcaster and entertainer). With a conservative estimate of 5,000 people

in attendance, the march attracted greater numbers and media attention than previous events of its kind.

Addressing an animated crowed outside the Department of Justice,
Equality and Law Reform, Crowley claimed that the legislation was
part of a "backlash" against the equality agenda that had seen some
notable gains in recent years, particularly over legislation on incite-
ment to racial hatred. He maintained that the civil partnership legislation would do nothing for equality, because it did not value diversity
but merely tolerated it.

In addition to overt political commentary, personal stories were
shared with the crowd. Individuals, gay couples, straight couples,
and parents of gay children spoke about their experiences, while live
music balanced the tone between protest and cheerful celebration.
Encouraged by the turn out, the organizers of the event said that they
planned to continue their campaign to lift the ban against same-sex
marriage, as they have continued to do.

While the event received positive coverage in certain strands of the
media, writing for the *Irish Independent*, broadcaster and columnist
Kevin Myers used the opportunity to belittle the cause, by mocking some of the people who addressed the crowd. In particular, he
sneered at a lesbian couple who introduced themselves by their first
names, using the opportunity to infantilize the entire agenda: "Two
of the people who addressed the rally were a lesbian couple who were
introduced just as Mia and Shani. Sorry, girls, only children are introduced by their first names." (*Irish Independent*, August 12, 2009).
Discussing the girls' description of the difficult, demeaning process
of applying for residency, Myers commented:

> Did lickul Mia shed a lickul tear at this point? Stamp her lickul foot?
> Listen, dear, a rudimentary understanding of our immigration laws
> would reveal that even marriage alone does not secure an uncondi-
> tional right for a foreigner to live in Ireland. As for same-sex mar-
> riages: are you, gentle reader, in favour, with all the legal rights that
> ensue? You are? Good. So, do you think that married homosexuals
> should have precisely the same right to adopt children as heterosexual
> couples? (*Irish Independent*, August 12, 2009)

This kind of patronizing reaction found further resonance in an article penned by John Waters in which he wrote:

> Marriage, a contract between a man and a woman, is an institution
> maintained by society for reasons having little or nothing to do with

"love." All men and all women have a right to marry, provided they wish to marry members of the opposite sex to whom they are not closely related by blood. Heterosexuals, like homosexuals, are prohibited from marrying people of their own sex. It is no more valid to allege wrongful discrimination in this context against gays than to argue that cycle lanes "discriminate" wrongfully against wheelbarrows. (*Irish Times*, July 31, 2009)

The rhetorical strategies used in both Myers's and Waters's articles are remarkably similar to those deployed by Power. In all cases, the writers attempt to deprive the events, and the contexts in which they took place, of any political agency by infantilizing and patronizing those involved, ultimately dismissing demands for legal recognition as nothing less than childish. Depicted as immature, not least of all because of a propensity for performance, the LGBTQ community is thus figured as ill prepared for partnership, marriage, and parenting. However, this approach can barely conceal the anxiety that undergirds it: the suspicion that queer performance has real potential to agitate the status quo and produce change.

The Right to Perform

The fully developed version of *A Woman in Progress* was staged in the Project Arts Centre as part of the Ulster Bank Dublin Theatre Festival in 2009.[9] In the weeks leading up to the production, Panti reiterated her thoughts about gay culture and partnership legislation in a range of press interviews. While the performance itself contained many pointed references to these matters, more importantly, the production became a platform through which these issues could be circulated through a variety of mainstream and marginal, public and counterpublic spaces (Figure 7.1).

Unlike the work in development, the final version of *A Woman in Progress* contained a new scene devoted to the Brenda Power debacle. In the scene in question, Panti claimed that even though she had not been particularly interested in fighting for gay marriage on a national level, she was virtually forced into it by people who wanted her to be their spokesperson. While uncomfortable with this role initially, she saw in it the opportunity to pluck people from commercialist and consumerist self-interest, and to encourage them to engage in political activity. Using the opportunity to destabilize some of Power's most heinous comments on *The Last Word*, Panti satirically reenacted

Figure 7.1 Panti performing in *A Woman in Progress* at Project Arts Centre as part of the Ulster Bank Dublin Theatre Festival, 2009. Photo by Fiona Morgan.

a section in which she said that a woman was more likely to choose abortion over adopting her child to a gay couple:

> The optimum social condition in which to bring up a child. You know Matt, we've a great difficulty in this country persuading young women not to have abortions but give their children up for adoption. I have to say, I suspect, that if you were pregnant, and uncertain, and you knew that there was a possibility that your baby could go to Miss Panti and his boyfriend, you would think again about an adoption. (*Today FM*, July 9, 2009)

In the August edition of *Attitude* (gay men's lifestyle magazine), editor of Dublin-based magazine *Gay Community News* Brian Finnegan published an article in which he celebrated Panti's role in mobilizing the LGBTQ community to political awareness and action in the lead up to the marriage marches, and the government's discussion of the Bill:

> The recent political outpourings of Miss Panti have galvanized the gay rights movement in Ireland like never before. Since she, and her alter-ego Rory O'Neill, began to speak about the differences between the Irish government's proposed legislation for same-sex couples and the actual right to civil marriage, a whole wave of newly politicized gay men and lesbians ranging in ages from teens to thirties have emerged on to the streets, shouting out loud for equality. (Finnegan, 2009: 38)

In Finnegan's assessment, Panti vitalized an inert political consciousness and mobilized activity through using her widespread appeal to connect with people, especially a younger generation who never experienced being gay while it was illegal. Panti reinvigorated the campaign though exploiting her popular cross-dressing persona as a vehicle for political debate and action. Of course, no single performer is the beginning or end point of LGBTQ interests and politics in Ireland or elsewhere. However, I think that because the LGBTQ community was so divided on the question of partnership or marriage, and many did not want to jeopardize whatever legislation the government was prepared to pass, no coherent voice or singular drive emerged during this time, as had happened during decriminalization. However, Panti's intervention at this time created an important space in which LGBTQ people were compelled to recognize that the debates were at least relevant to their lives. In the time period in question, Panti effectively demonstrated how performance and politics entertain a synergetic role in LGBTQ culture, while illustrating how performance can be harnessed to ignite people's imagination and potentially provoke change. Since the first controversial Noise demonstration, there have been significant developments in partnership legislation in Ireland. On January 1, 2011, The Civil Partnership Act came into effect, and Noise has continued to lobby for Civil Marriage legislation, armed with the statistic that 73 percent of Irish people are reported to support Civil Marriage, with marches in 2010 and 2011 reported to include up to 5,000 people.[10]

This chapter has explored the relationship between queer performance and politics as played out in events relating to same-sex civil partnership legislation in Ireland, revealing how both pleasurable and dissenting performance participated in mobilizing LGBTQ social and political action. What was most interesting about this period,

I suggest, was not strictly the demand for partnership or marriage rights but, perhaps queerer still, the eventing of an impulse among the LGBTQ community to mobilize and maintain what Rancière terms scenes of "dissensus"; enacting what Judith Butler refers to as "a sensate democracy…aesthetic articulation within the political sphere" (Butler and Spivak, 2007: 62–63). Now that same-sex couples all over the country are being legally recognized, and civil marriage is likely to be ratified at some point in the future, the challenge for LGBTQ identifying individuals, and Irish society more broadly, is to stay attuned to the complex ways in which power is not simply legislated for or against the most marginal people in society, but to the increasingly complex ways in which it is aesthetically and affectively regulated and distributed.

NOTES

1. The Bill was published by Dermot Ahern on June 26, 2009. It can be viewed on www.justice.ie/en/JELR/General%20Scheme%20of%20 Civil%20Partnership%20Bill.pdf/Files/General%20Scheme%20 of%20Civil%20Partnership%20Bill.pdf

2. Although the 1983 event most closely resembled a recognizable Pride protest march or parade, it built upon a number of important, earlier public interventions. For example, the first ever public gay demonstration in Ireland took place in Dublin on Saturday, June 27, 1974. On Gay Pride Day, as it was then termed, a small group protested outside the Department of Justice and the British Embassy. In 1979 the city hosted the first Gay Pride Week. In 1980, a dozen activists took to the streets of Dublin with armfuls of pink carnations and leaflets explaining the history of Stonewall, while informing shoppers that "Gay Rights Are Simply Human Rights" and "Gay Rights Are Your Rights."

3. These three core values are enshrined in the organization's ethos. View at www.dublinpride.org

4. Even though I accede to the enormous positive impact Pride has had on the development of LGBTQ rights and culture in Ireland, I think it is worth mentioning that it seems to feel increasingly more homogenized and commercialized, and an outlet for corporate sponsorship and advertising. Of course, this has to do with the machinery of neoliberalism, and also with an unclear sense of what the LGBTQ community's shared social and political goals might be, particularly now that partnership legislation has passed.

5. The Partnership Bill grants nearly the same legal rights to same-sex unions as marriage, with the exception of adoption rights. Furthermore, some people feel that the semantic difference is discriminatory. While many young gay people may not be so concerned with adoption, many

older gay people are, especially those who already have children and seek their legal recognition and protection. In being popular with so many young people and active on the LGBTQ scene, Panti was instrumental in bridging generations over this concern.

6. Katherine Zappone and Ann Louise Gilligan married in Canada in 2003, but their marriage is not recognized in Ireland. In 2006, they took a case against the state for not recognizing their filing of joint tax returns. Although they lost their case, they are currently awaiting their Supreme Court appeal.

7. The first Alterntive Miss Ireland took place in Sides nightclub, Dublin, in 1987. It did not take place again until 1996, after which it became an annual event at the Olympia theatre, Dublin. The final Alternative Miss Ireland took place on March 18, 2012.

8. Here, I do not presume "community" to be monolithic or homogeneous, of course, but I use the term to strategically denote a group of people who are (however provisionally) united on the basis of some kind of a shared interest or identification.

9. It is worth mentioning that the festival program in 2009 was particularly queer. In addition to Panti's performance, Dublin-based Broken Talkers theater company staged *Silver Stars*, a documentary-style song cycle developed from interviews with older gay Irish men, while London-based physical theater company DV8 brought *To Be Straight with You*, another documentary-style production that explored the relationship between homosexuality and religious fundamentalism across the globe drawing on interviews with people affected.

10. The Red C poll for *Sunday Times*, March 6, 2011, found that 73 percent of all people surveyed agreed that same-sex couples should be allowed to marry.

REFERENCES

Allain, Paul and Harvie, Jen (2006) *The Routledge Companion to Theatre and Performance*. London and New York: Routledge.

Butler, Judith and Spivak, Gayatri (2007) *Who Sings the Nation-State?* London: Seagull Books.

Cohen-Cruz, Jan (ed.) (1998) *Radical Street Performance* London and New York: Routledge.

Finnegan, Brian (2009) "Civil War," in *Attitude*, August 2009.

Munt, Sally R. and O' Donnell, Katherine (2007) "Pride and Prejudice: Legalizing Compulsory Heterosexuality in New York's Annual St. Patrick's Day Parades." *Space and Culture*, 10 (1): 97–114.

Myers, Kevin (2009) "Dogmatic Liberalism Insists that Tolerance isn't Enough." *Irish Independent*, August 12.

Panti (2009) "No More Mr Nice Gay." *Pantibar* Blog, posted February 15, 2009. Available at www.pantibar.com/blog.aspx?month=February%20 2009&pageno=6. Accessed on August 20, 2011.

Power, Brenda (2009a) "You Can't Trample over the Wedding Cake and Eat it." *Sunday Times*, July 5.

——(2009b) "I Must Not Offend Gay People." *Sunday Times*, July 12.

Rancière, Jacques (2009) "A Few Remarks on the Method of Jacques Rancière." *Parallax*, 15 (3): 114–23.

Shepard, Benjamin (2009) *Queer Political Performance and Protest*, London and New York: Routledge.

Waters, John (2009) "Gay Lobby Mangles Meaning of Marriage." *Irish Times*, July 31.

PART II

Culture

CHAPTER 8

Race, Sex, and Nation: Virgin Mother Ireland

Gerardine Meaney

FEMINISMS AND NATIONALISMS

If "all nationalisms are gendered" (McClintock, 1993: 61), the Mother Ireland trope merely indicates the operation of a fundamental structuring principle recognizable in both official and insurgent nationalisms. It is one instance of the structural interdependence of gender and national identities. "The hegemonic process of constructing a nationalist ideology depends upon distinguishing between self and other, us and them, in the creation of a common (shared) identity; women as symbol, men as agents of the nation, colonized space as feminine, colonial power as masculine" (Feldman, 1999: 177–178). Miroslav Hroch argued in the 1990s with regard to resurgent European nationalisms and to nineteenth-century nationalisms that:

> Identification with the national group…includes…the construction of a personalized image of the nation. The glorious past of this personality comes to be lived as part of the individual memory of each citizen, its defeats resented as failures that still touch them. One result of such personalization is that people will regard their nation—that is, themselves—as a single body in a more than metaphorical sense. If any distress befalls a small part of the nation, it can be felt throughout it, and if any branch of the ethnic group—even one living far from the "mother-nation"—is threatened with assimilation, the members of the personalized nation may treat it as an amputation of the national body. (Hroch, 1993: 15)

If the nation is experienced as "a body," then the body in Western culture is primarily figured as and through the female body. The systematic violation of individual women's bodies in a way which understood itself as destroying both an organic community and an abstract nation was an horrific validation of Hroch's analysis of the new nationalisms in this respect. According to Anne McClintock:

> All too often in male nationalisms, *gender difference* between women and men serves to symbolically define the limits of national difference and power between *men*. Excluded from direct action as national citizens, women are subsumed symbolically into the national body politic as its boundary and metaphoric limit. (1993: 62)

Women are obviously crucial to national expansion and consolidation in their role as biological reproducers of the members of national collectivities, but something more complex than the desire to see the nation's population expand is at stake. Peggy Watson offers an explanation that would indicate why certain nationalisms seem more and some less prone to obsession with control of women through and as mediums of reproduction. Watson offers an example with striking parallels to Ireland. She recounts a response from an unnamed member of the postcommunist Polish senate that:

> The reason for concentrating on the abortion issue at the expense of other pressing problems was simply because it was regarded as something which *could* be done...the regulation of women was seen as an area which required action, but also one where power could readily be exercised, whereas the economy engendered feelings of powerlessness...Attempting to legislate against the right to abortion in effect serves both to institutionalize the power of men, and to legitimate this power by providing a platform for new, more radical and "modernized" definitions of women as *exclusively* grounded in domesticity. (Watson, 1993: 75)

A range of legislative measures to promote just such ends occurred in newly independent southern Ireland after 1922, culminating in the delineation of women's social function within the home in Article 41.2 of the 1937 Constitution. The elision of women's role as activists into idealized passivity and symbolic status is again characteristic of the transition from national movement to state authority internationally. (The analogy with Poland is another reminder that the conjunction of white faces and histories of colonization and migration is not nearly as unusual as Irish cultural theory has sometimes made it seem.) Gender resurfaced as an area where reassurance could be sought against political violence, mass unemployment, and rapid social change in the 1980s, a decade characterized in the Republic of Ireland by bitter constitutional campaigns to control the domain of reproduction and the family and ferocious divisions over sexual, familial, and religious values.[1]

It might be assumed that the emergence of a prosperous post–Celtic Tiger Ireland would have eliminated the need for this kind of policing of the internal border constituted by women's bodies. In some regards, that was the case. In most important respects, however, the work of national scapegoat was simply outsourced, as was so much other domestic labor, onto immigrant women. The ease with which popular hysteria about pregnant migrants "flooding" Irish maternity hospitals with their nonnational babies could be translated into 80 percent electoral support in 2004 for a constitutional amendment limiting Irish citizenship on the basis of ethnicity and affiliations of kinship and blood indicates that racism was never a marginal factor in Irish political life nor a specific historical response to the numbers of actual migrants arriving in Ireland in the late 1990s. It was, and is now constitutionally enshrined as, a structural principle in national identity. Liberal appeals for Irish sympathy with immigrants on the basis that previous generations of Irish emigrants shared their experience ignore the extent to which the Irish cultivated, traded in, and still exploit the valuable commodity of their white identity both abroad and at home. Kingsley's cry of horror that Irish white chimpanzees were so much worse than black African ones is perhaps too much quoted for a reason. It obscures the extent to which subsequent generations of Irish have been able to trade on their difference from the Africans with whom Kingsley's racist perceptions were more comfortable. The Victorian parlor game that Luke Gibbons so influentially described halted, like Kingsley, at the one point in the map of the British Empire where the natives were white (Gibbons, 1996: 149). Far from subverting racial hierarchies, the existence of liminally white groups has always been a functioning part of the racist system. Colonized or ethnically distinct whites such as the Irish and Scottish provided the British Empire with a highly expendable soldiery and an army of civil servants to deploy around the empire in the nineteenth century. As the Irish immigrated to the United States, they progressively "became white"[2] without at all disconcerting racist structures. (The way in which certain kinds of white ethnicities such as Irish and Polish function in the construction and control of working-class identity in the United States is an increasing area of study.)[3] Long overdue, as studies of Irish emigration develop, is a thorough analysis of the way in which the experience of Irish emigrants abroad had an impact on how the Irish who remained at home viewed themselves, particularly in relation to race. It is certainly the case that a highly racialized and rigidly gendered identity was promulgated by both Church and State in Ireland as true Irishness.

GENDER AND THE CONSTRUCTION OF WHITENESS

Without rehearsing in detail well-known arguments, it may be useful to summarize. The psychodynamic of colonial and postcolonial identity often produces in the formerly colonized a desire to assert a rigid and confined masculine identity, against the colonizers' stereotype of their subjects as feminine, wild, ungovernable. This masculine identity then emerges at state level as a regulation of "our" women, an imposition of a very definite feminine identity as guarantor to the precarious masculinity of the new state. The specific role of the Irish Catholic Church in this maelstrom of economic, political, social, and psychological forces is rather more than one among a number of regulatory institutions. It is after all sometimes very difficult to ascertain where church began and state ended in regard to the institutionalization of individuals, public health, and education, for example. The fissure between whiteness and the colonial (not typically white) historical experience of Ireland was traditionally concealed by radiant images of Ireland itself in terms of what Richard Dyer calls "the supreme exemplar of…feminine whiteness," the Virgin Mary (Dyer, 1997: 74).

Dyer's work on whiteness is very suggestive in the Irish context, though his own analysis is primarily of whiteness in imperial and postimperial cultures. Dyer's work on the function of white women in colonial culture and of liminally white groups and the porous boundaries of white identity are particularly relevant. I want to put forward an argument here that the centrality of Mariology in Irish Catholicism and the extent to which issues of reproduction and sexuality dominated public debates and anxieties around modernization while sharing many of the general characteristics of the gendering of national identity outlined earlier are in the Irish case also powerfully linked to residual anxieties around race and Ireland's postcolonial position as a white European nation.

National identities are structured by the binary of them and us, insiders and outsiders, natives and foreigners. Irish nationalism may have had within it the potential for all kinds of hybrid, liberation-ist, adulterated, and inclusive versions of Irish identity. However, the dominant ideology of state and nation was for most of the twentieth century extraordinarily narrow and exclusive. Bryan Fanning has doc-umented the "othering" of Protestants, Jews, and Travellers as part of the process of state nationalism in the Republic of Ireland (Fanning, 2002). The dominance of the postcolonial-revisionist debate in the formation of Irish Studies and the analyses it produced of Irish nation-alism have long outlived their usefulness. Both sides of the debate have obscured the role of whiteness in the construction of Irish identity as well as the relationship between gender and race in that construction.

Postcolonial theory offered feminist critique in Ireland a vital way of understanding sexual conservatism, the relationship of the Catholic Church and the state and the gendering of national identity as elements that it shared with a wide variety of postcolonial cultures. Postcolonialism remains part of the context in which "non-national women were made central to the racial configuration of 21st cen-tury global Ireland, illustrating not only orchestrated moral panics about 'floods of refugees,' but also the positioning of sexually active women as a danger to the state and 'the nation' " (Lentin, 2005: 7). However, as the sociologist and theorist of race, Ronit Lentin pointed out, during the economic boom theory failed to keep pace with the transition from emigration to immigration in Ireland:

> To date, theorizing Irishness as white privilege has been hampered by legacies of racialisation of Irishness as structured by anti-Irish racism in Ireland and abroad. However, Ireland's new position as topping the Globalisation Index, its status symbol as the locus of "cool" cul-ture, and its privileged position within an ever-expanding European Community calls for the understanding of Irishness as white suprem-acy. Whiteness works best when it remains a hidden part of the norma-tive social order. (9)

The emerging field of "whiteness" studies offers a necessary develop-ment that illuminates the extent to which race performed a key func-tion in the construction and policing of Irish identity throughout the twentieth century and of the origins of contemporary social and institutional racism in Ireland. It is vital to deconstruct the binary of colonizer and colonized, agency and victimization, pure and hybrid, and acknowledge the extent to which complex processes of accom-modation, resistance, and opportunism have shaped the concept of "Irishness."

The promulgation of the image of the Virgin Mary as "Queen of Ireland" (Turpin, 2003: 72) is on one level just another permutation of the Virgin–Whore dichotomy at the heart of Western culture's representation of women. That dichotomy acquired a very particular paranoid intensity in twentieth-century Ireland, however, which is linked to both the history of colonialism and the compensatory urge to promote an essential Irishness which was purer—in effect whiter—than other European races. In this context, the relationship between images of the Blessed Virgin and Mother Ireland is important, not least because the veneration of the former was shadowed by disappointment in the later. Tracing the evolution of "visual Marianism" in Ireland, art historian John Turpin has argued that "Marianism was a badge of national identity" sponsored by the postindependence southern state as well as the Catholic Church (70). The influence of French Catholicism on the development of Marian devotion in Ireland is well documented; in effect, the image of the Virgin Mother imported from France in the nineteenth century was already highly politicized, an anti-Marianne, and an instrument of anti-enlightenment, counter-revolutionary propaganda. Ultimately highly compatible with romantic nationalism, the cross-fertilization of this image with that of "Mother Ireland" helped dislocate the traditions of radical republicanism from insurgent nationalism in nineteenth-century Ireland. In the post-independence southern state, this fusion of national and religious iconography became a lynchpin of the ideology of race and gender.

THE DISEMBODIED MOTHER

A highly racialized discourse of nationality was prevalent in popular Catholic devotional literature in twentieth-century Ireland, which promulgated the idea of a special link between Ireland and the Virgin Mother. Most existing histories of Mariology focus on high art. For example, Kristeva suggests that in the Renaissance figures of the Madonna and child, we see the emergence of a secular humanist sensibility, the new ego-centered, rational, masculine subject consecrated in the Christ child but also grounded in his very human relationship with his adoring mother (Kristeva, 1986). This is not the type of image of the Virgin Mary that predominated in popular Mariology in twentieth-century Ireland. The images that appear to have been most popular were, in statue form, Mary as apparition, with raised hands, sometimes standing on the stars, sometimes crushing the serpent and, particularly, the picture of the Immaculate Heart of Mary juxtaposed with the Sacred Heart of Jesus. This latter image is preserved in the names of numerous churches and religious institutions including a religious order in both Ireland and the United States. The conflation of images of Mother Ireland and Virgin Mary in Irish populist Catholic nationalism deployed the Virgin Mother's status as epitome of whiteness as a guarantee of Irish (racial) purity. This function could only be performed if the maternal body was idealized out of existence, or at least out of representation. The peculiar stillness and singularly unmaternal figures of the Virgin Mary, which predominate in Irish churches and grottoes, only become apparent by contrast with the expressive faces and rounded bodies prevalent in Andalucian ones, for example. The refusal to countenance any representation of the mother's body as origin of life was paralleled by the predominance of images of the Virgin Mary as mother of an adult son, usually Jesus in the mode of the Sacred Heart, and in general in visions, icons, and statues that represented her after her Assumption, that is to say after her disembodiment.

Yeats in the cultural nationalist journal, *Samhain*, identified the trend toward curiously lifeless images and the centrality of the images of an impersonal Virgin in this process as early as 1905, which would indicate that it was already implicit in Catholic nationalism in the late nineteenth century.

> A Galway convent a little time ago refused a fine design for stained glass sent from Miss Sarah Purser's studio, because of the personal life in the faces and in the attitudes, which seemed to them ugly, perhaps even impious. They sent to Miss Purser an insipid German chromo-lithograph, full of faces without expression or dignity, and gestures without personal distinction, and Miss Purser, doubtless because her enterprise was too new, too anxious for success, to reject any order, has carried out this ignoble design in glass of beautiful color and quality. Let us suppose that Meister Stefan were to paint in Ireland to-day that exquisite Madonna of his, with her lattice of roses; a great deal that is said of our plays would be said of that picture. Why select for his model a little girl selling newspapers in the streets, why slander with that miserable little body the Mother of God? (Yeats, 1905)

Irish censorship was extraordinarily sensitive in excising all references to childbirth from the films it cut, including even comic scenes of fathers pacing hospital waiting rooms. Even the liberal journal, *The Bell*, found itself at the center of a storm of controversy when it published Freda Laughton's poem, "The Woman with Child" in 1945:

> And like the moon I mellow to the round
> Full circle of my being, till I too
> Am ripe with living and my fruit is grown.
> Then break the shell of life. (Laughton, 1945: 289)

The Bell's editorial view of Laughton was overwhelmingly positive: It announced in the same issue that she had won the competition for the best poem published in *The Bell* in 1944 for "When You Were with Me" (Laughton, 1944: 287). A short article by Valentin Iremonger praised, "the exactness of her visual imagination" (1945: 249–250). "Whatever sort of building she eventually raises, the foundations are being well laid…her verse has a sensuous and imaginative quality that raises it above the level of realism" (249). Iremonger was in no doubt about Laughton's canonical potential, comparing her to Spinoza and Pope, as well as Tennyson and Arnold. "How far or in what direction she is likely to develop it is yet too early to say. Certainly she is one of the few poets today who are worth watching, who have a strong individual talent, and a distinct flavor of their own. Her ultimate importance will depend on whether what are as yet barely opinions will crystallise into an attitude to life. In the meantime, I look forward with more than usual interest to her first book" (250). Laughton's work insists that her gender is part of her poetic identity, but this is regarded as a strength: "Like most female good poets, she shows a strong intellectual bent but still does not forget that 'there is danger in utterly forgetting / The setting of fine jewels, / The subtle arrangement of the perfumed bouquet, / The studied mosaic of the harem'" (250).

This appraisal of Laughton did not go unchallenged. The "Public Opinion" section of *The Bell* some months later, in August 1945, included a long letter from a Patricia K. Harrison that criticized Laughton's work for her alliteration and her use of metaphor, but above all for being "sensuous": "In these poems there is sensuousness for the sake of sensuousness, and not real imagination; compare 'Mary, his espoused wife, being great with child,' with 'Like the moon I mellow to the round Full circle of my being'" (Harrison, 1945: 446). Unusually (but not uniquely), this particular public opinion was felt to require an editorial answer provided by poetry editor, Geoffrey Taylor. Taylor replies in considerable detail to Miss Harrison's "dogmatic and capricious" technical statements about poetry, then concludes "But what Miss Harrison seems most to object to is 'sensuousness.' Let her remember Milton and Keats." This storm among the teacups of Irish literature's back pages neatly illustrates the difficulties of this terrain for the woman poet: Laughton is attacked for her implied impropriety on the one hand, but even when lavishly praised for the sensuousness of her work, admonished to beware her "intellectual bent" on the other. More than that, however, Harrison's odd letter indicates how immediately any representation of pregnancy provoked mariological analogy. The contrast between the mother as active subject, "I mellow," and passive vessel, "being great," is crude but instructive. Presumably, Patricia Harrison could not bear to quote the lines in full: Her quotation excises the pagan connotation of "And like the moon I mellow to the round/Full circle of my being" (Laughton, 1945: 289). *The Bell*'s championship of Laughton's work indicates it understood feminine self-representation as part of its modernizing project even if it sometimes characterized that self-representation in terms of jewels, bouquets, and harems. The controversy marks one of a number of points where the self-conscious project of cultural change in *The Bell* coalesced with an eruption of the female body into mainstream literary discourse (see also, for example, O'Horan 1948).

THE VIRGIN MARY, QUEEN OF IRELAND

At the zenith of Catholic influence in the southern Irish state, Pope Pius XI's address to the Eucharistic Congess of 1932 spoke of the "The Virgin Mary, Queen of Ireland." A survey of mariological devotional literature, religious souvenirs, and Episcopal pronouncements indicates that Pope Pius was not indulging in metaphorical flourishes. The concept of a special relationship between Ireland and the Virgin Mary was heavily promoted in the early decades of southern independence. Rev. James Cassidy was a notable contributor to the genre of quasi-historical mariological literature. In his book on *The Old Love of the Blessed Virgin Mary, Queen of Ireland*, he remarks on the prevalence of pictures of the Holy Family in Irish households of the time. In this devotion, he finds "an echo of what must have been a marked devotion of ancient Ireland, devotion of the family to the Mother of the Holy family." Cassidy's reasons for assuming such a devotion "must have been" widespread echo rather chillingly over the intervening decades: "To such a devotion, Ireland would naturally lend itself, for the constant tribal scrutiny of family life encouraged the preservation of those domestic virtues which are the fundamental props of wholesome nationhood." The naturalization of tribal surveillance over the family is essential for Cassidy to "the preservation of moral beauty," but it is also an intrinsic part of Irish identity. The modernity of the dogma of the immaculate conception does not at all trouble Cassidy's identification of Mary's immaculacy with ancient, pure Irish identity: He suggests that a version of the doctrine could be found in the eighth-century writings of St. Colgu. The circularity of Cassidy's myth making is an object lesson in the promulgation of ideology. Praising a "typically Celtic tribute to Mary," Cassidy remarks:

> The rugged humility of the tribesman and the chivalry of the holy war-rior seek hand in hand the protection and ideal leadership of a great Queen in whom they see a fount of spiritual fortitude and a mighty inspiration. Its note of child-like familiarity and trustfulness tell of the ease with which the Irish have always lived in the world of the super-natural. What race could express to Mary the desire for eternal life in words of more trusting and loving simplicity than the writer uses here. Heaven for him meant the "visit" of a child to its Mother. Of that "visit" he felt assured, just because she was such a Mother and he had such a vivid sense of his child-like right to her maternal solicitude.

A twentieth-century theological construction of Mary is rendered timeless by reference to an ancient Celtic past and the purity and con-tinuity of the Irish nation validated by the attribution to it of devotion to a changeless icon of feminine purity. Cassidy's book is indicative of a strong trend in Irish Catholic publications where purported his-tories of devotion to Mary are also politically charged appropriations of Celticism for Catholic nationalism. "The Irish people, too, have always seemed dowered with a genius for domesticity. In ancient Ireland, as in the Ireland of today, all roads seemed to lead to the hearth and the home. The result was an exceptionally wholesome family life that leavened the entire nation. This devotion to the prin-ciples of home life explains the unusual moral rectitude of Irish maid-enhood." In this formulation, Ireland was a nation that defined itself primarily in terms of its women precisely because they were scarcely there, immaterial, "the true Gael saw a more fundamental support of national life in the luminous ideal of womanhood than in the more material service of the country's manhood."

Cassidy ends his book by calling Mary "great Queen of Eire," "the greatest queen Ireland ever knew, or ever can know, the Immaculate Mother of God." Not all accounts of mariological devotion in ancient Ireland were quite so haphazard with historical fact as Cassidy. Concannon's *The Queen of Ireland: An Historical Account of Ireland's*

Devotion to the Blessed Virgin, for example, praises the Irish role in the promulgation of the doctrine of the Immaculate Conception, thus at least acknowledging that both the doctrine and the Irish have a history that intervened between ancient Celts and 1922.

While the pictures of the disembodied mother as ideal may have disappeared, her cultural impact has not. An echo of this arose in the controversy over the European Union (EU)-wide advertising campaign to promote voting in the last European Parliamentary elections. The advertisement naturalized the EU by embodying it as a nurturing woman, the good white mother offering herself freely (as opposed to impregnable Fortress Europe). The EU's attempt to produce a transnational form of identity resorted to ideological devices typical of nation building in order to attract affiliation. The opening image of a baby trying to choose between its mother's bare breasts was apparently considered offensive only by Ireland and Britain. The British response was to airbrush out the nipples, the Irish initially at least to simply not show the ad. (Irish exclusion of the maternal body in this instance reduced the English response to mere eccentricity.)

The popular reaction overrode civil-service squeamishness through sheer derision—though the laughter might have been more convincing did Ireland not have one of the lowest rates of breast-feeding in the world. The EU advertisement controversy and the low rates of breast-feeding are both indicative of residual unease around the maternal body in action. Indeed, the willingness of women from other cultures to breast-feed at least in front of other women has been constructed as an intercultural "problem," particularly in rural Ireland. The problem of the maternal body as a body has a very specific history in the construction of white, gendered, Irish identity.

The contemporary perception of Catholicism as an atavism that Ireland has outgrown ignores its specifically modernizing project in Ireland, promulgating regulation, bureaucracy, and integration within the global/universal church. This is modernization that understood itself in terms of achievement of an essential and ancient national destiny and identity, but fully utilized twentieth-century industrial and media production to promulgate that identity. John Turpin's work on visual marianism in Ireland points out the importance of mass manufacture of objects of devotion in its popularization. The material culture of popular Catholic devotion in Ireland was a point of intersection with the modern marketplace, not its antithesis. This is not so very different from the alliance of the Gaelic Athletic Association, Guinness, Bank of Ireland, and ancient Irish myth in a series of twenty first century sponsorship deals (Cronin 2007). The ensuing advertisment campaigns prove the endless plasticity of Cuchulainn in their promotion of the Celtic Tiger's trinity of questionable banking practice, beer, and competitive sport in the holy spirit of high-end technical innovation as expressions of true Irish identity. The combination of the Giant's Causeway and Computer Generated Imagery is the contemporary correlative of the industrialization of devotion. And both produce images of Ireland that are both racial and gendered.

ARE WE POST-POSTCOLONIAL YET?

Irish critics sometimes react in hurt and bewilderment at the skepticism about Ireland's postcolonial status expressed by critics for whom the conjunction of postcolonial and white is highly suspect. The extent of Irish filiation to the late Edward Said's foundational model of postcolonial critique is in part accounted for by his understanding of Yeats and Joyce as paradigmatically postcolonial modernists. Vincent Cheng gives a highly illuminating account of the antipathy he experienced in the American academy for his work on a dead white male, no matter how colonized the Dublin of Joyce's upbringing. Cheng's use of Joyce as an emblem of inauthenticity and a useful resource for the construction of all sorts of cosmopolitan, migrant, hyphenated, and intercultural identities, is a highly attractive alternative to those elements in Irish cultural criticism that regard Irishness as some sort of privileged category for the understanding of Joyce's project. Cheng's warning that "the search for genuine and authentic native voices will serve only to provide us with a feel-good liberal and multicultural glow—while in actuality merely recycling tokenism and nostalgia" (Cheng, 2004: 27) is salutary. Cheng's analysis draws heavily on Declan Kiberd's *Inventing Ireland*. Yet, Kiberd's speculation, "who is to say that the latest group of arriving Nigerians might not" become "more Irish than the Irish themselves" (Kiberd, 2005: 303) is predicated on the kind of "authenticity without risk" that Cheng critiques. Kiberd is very much to be commended for addressing the issue of racism directly in his recent work. However, there are limitations implicit in a paradigm where there still exists something called "a people," which must be "secure in its national philosophy" before it can deal confidently and fairly with others. Kiberd's essay lauds hybridity, not least because it assumes Irishness as the ultimate hybrid identity, infinitely capacious, assimilative, and already so postcolonial that it need never be challenged and changed by the experience of Nigerian immigrants. The identification of Nigerian immigrants and Norman invaders hardly needs to be deconstructed: The sense of a foreign threat the nation must contain seriously threatens the liberal impulse. Kiberd's recruitment of the legacy of Irish missionaries and Bob Geldof to the argument (that argument again) that Ireland is not racist obfuscates completely the extent to which the discourse of missionary Ireland mimicked colonial stereotypes, this time casting the Irish as the bringers of civilization and salvation to the barbarian "black babies." (The assimilation of the lyricist of "Banana Republic" to the postcolonial nation as inheritor of that tradition would, if it were tenable, certainly add weight to the argument that the "Make Poverty History" campaign was more about assuaging the affluent world's guilt than solving Africa's problems.)

The danger to postcolonial critique now in Ireland is that it will be co-opted to a discourse of the authentic and native, sometimes called shared history. In short, the danger is that the history of the nation will once again become an alibi for the depredations of the state. The relationship between nation and state is an unresolved tension within Irish postcolonial theory. As Colin Graham acutely observes, the case made by David Lloyd and Carol Coulter for an affiliation between nationalism and feminism in the Irish context depends on the elimination of the hyphenated relation of the nation state (Graham, 2001: 109–110). The economic disjunction between the two parts of the island of Ireland became the elephant in postcolonial theory's sitting room during the economic boom. In Sean O' Reilly's *The Swing of Things* (2004), the released republican prisoner and his Russian neighbor are (almost) equally marginal to contemporary Dublin. They sit silently over a pint, not talking about their past. Their status is of course different. One has an unquestioned right to stay, the possibility of a Trinity degree, and of access to insider status, even if his history ultimately precludes these achievements. The Derry laborers in the city's construction industry living like the other migrants in hostels, the "wife and wains" back home, are a closer parallel. O'Reilly's novel is interesting in that it marks one of the very few attempts to write a contemporary Dublin novel within the paradigms of Irish post-modernist fiction and it posits its northern protagonist (an odd amalgam of Leopold Bloom and Stephen Dedalus) as an insider/outsider. It is a position that might usefully be explored in contemporary theory, lest the north become the south's token of authentic historical trauma, another alibi.

The Postcolonial Girl

Of course, the position of the insider/outsider, of the bifurcated other within, is one that is already well articulated in Irish cultural theory.

It is the position of feminist analysis, of queer theory, of groups whose marginality is romanticized into silence. Postcolonial theory in Ireland has been highly resistant to being "differenced" from within. Declan Kiberd's *The Irish Writer and the World* quotes extensively from Julia Kristeva's *Strangers to Ourselves* in its concluding essay on multiculturalism, but includes no extended engagement with any Irish women writers. There are interesting parallels in the first issue of the *Field Day Review*, which reads almost as an elegy for the critical paradigms with which the key contributors to it have changed the face of Irish Studies in the last two decades. (The history of racism features fairly obliquely here in Cormac O'Grada's article on "Dublin's Jewish Immigrants of a Century Ago.") The text of the review essays is relatively familiar to anyone working on Irish Studies, with many essays based on lectures delivered to the Notre Dame summer seminar. It is significant that the only real paradigm affecting piece is an elegy, Seamus Deane's essay on Edward Said, and that this is the only place where the radical shifts in cultural theory post 9/11 and the Afghan and Iraq invasions surface, however fleetingly.

As in *The Irish Writer and the World*, the literary writing of Irish women is absent, though there are a couple of scholarly essays by women. Images of women are not absent, however, and the inclusion of (one) woman artist's work is of particular significance. It is on the visual dimension of the volume that I want to concentrate, for it suggests the challenges that Irish Studies glimpses at its windows. The high production values of the review mark it as a product of a particularly well-endowed corner of the global academic marketplace. The first thing to strike the casual flicker through the review is the contrasting preponderance of photographic images of past poverty. There is an emigrant narrative inscribed here, but it is too easy to dismiss it as an Irish-American narrative of sepia rags to well-designed riches. For the volume visually disrupts its own coordinates and it does so through the construction of a feminine gaze directed beyond its project. The front cover is folded over, with only one figure from Bert Hardy's[4] original picture of Willie Cullen and his family apparent. This figure is a little girl, her back to the photographer, who is looking out of the window. When the cover is fully extended, her younger sister becomes the center of the composition, looking up at her father who returns her look with great affection. The caption tells us that this is a picture of Willie Cullen playing with his children, but it is only the smaller child who plays back. On the cover, the disengaged little girl is central but unreadable, her face turned in the opposite direction to our scrutiny.

The design offers the possibility of two overlapping interpretations. The most overt plane of meaning is that the new review, while representing the past, is conscious of an other subject position, one oriented toward the future, the outside, the world beyond the little Cullen girl's window. This future-oriented Irish subject is constructed by the cover as feminine, nascent, yet to mature, and still resistant to engagement and interpretation. It is the central enigma of the subject and critical perspective that this review celebrates and institutionalizes. The folding over of the photograph implies a further and autocritical impulse. The complete picture would place this feminine future within the framework of the domestic and the family. The design hides this possibility away, turning the picture of the nurturing father and the affectionate child into the lining of a carapace of feminine refusal. The review wears its unconscious on its sleeve, intensely desirous of an encounter with a feminine subject, insistent that such engagement is beyond its reach. But the little girls in the photograph would be women in their fifties now, women with lived lives beyond the photographic frame, their own mature perspective on the world beyond the window. The girls in the picture might be readable in terms of the definition of a (feminized) subaltern that Deane commends in Gayatri Spivak's writing, "populations below the horizon for whom everything, even their liberation, had been already so spoken for that the effort was to enable these people—mostly women—to begin to speak and thereby create an alternative form of power to that which had silenced them" (Deane, 2005: 199). But what of the women the girls became and the generation they represent? Didn't they begin to speak, find their own alternative form of power? They belong to the generation of civil rights, women's liberation, of articulate women in all walks of life who engaged in a wide variety of political and artistic practices. They are far more than silent potential.

The rest of Bert Hardy's photographs of women, including a number where women and girls face the camera directly, form part of a sequence in the volume where they are heavily outnumbered by images of men engaged in work and politics. The female gaze continues to trouble the frame(work), however. Margaret Corcoran's series of paintings, *An Enquiry*, takes its title from Edmund Burke's *An Enquiry into the Origins of the Ideas of the Sublime and the Beautiful*. Two paintings from the series are included, both within the pages of Benedict Anderson's essay on globalization. The painting that figured prominently in Luke Gibbon's essay on the series, "Engendering the Sublime: Margaret Corcoran's *An Enquiry*," *An Enquiry VIII*, is

included in a small format. *An Enquiry VIII* rhymes with the front-cover
illustration, showing a woman again with her back to us, her attention turned to the painting in front of her (George Barret's painting
of Powerscourt Waterfall). The full page and dominant illustration
of Corcoran's work is *An Enquiry I*, which features a young woman
looking toward the viewer, turned away from Thomas Hickey's orien-
talist painting of an Indian woman. All the paintings in *An Enquiry*
are set in the Milltown Rooms of the National Gallery. These rooms
contain the late eighteenth- and early nineteenth-century paintings
of the Irish School so that Corcoran's series is an interrogation of a
canon of Irish painting as well as an exploration of Burke's aesthetics. Gibbons's reading of Corcoran's work in *Circa* (2004) effectively
reads it as a feminist extension of Burke's project, even suggesting that
Burke's emphasis on anticipation and identification as elements of the
sublime aesthetic experience prefigures Laura Mulvey's analysis of the
gendered nature of spectatorship in cinema. Corcoran's identification
of her painting technique with Degas and Monet certainly supports
Gibbons's reading of her work in terms of modernist self-reflexive use
of both framing and the gallery space. Yet, this neat recruitment of
An Enquiry to both Burkean aesthetics and modernist interrogations
of tradition is undercut by *An Enquiry 1*. The feminine subject here
is not a good daughter who plays the game, nor simply a recalcitrant
one who refuses to be read. Moreover, the differencing of the gaze
in Corcoran's work exceeds the category of singular feminine intervention into an artistic practice and critical discourse conducted in
exclusively masculine terms. The modern young woman who looks
back at us from *An Enquiry 1* does not block our gaze at the objectified "oriental" woman behind her, but she does interrupt it. She
looks back, challenging our secure spectatorship position, blocking
the secure binary identifications of active gaze and agency on the one
hand and object of gaze and passivity on the other. In this painting
to-be-looked-at is to challenge that look, at least if you are the white
woman in the foreground of the canvas, not the "other" woman in
the background. The intervention of the female gazer poses a question before Hickey's portrait, "what do you think you are looking
at?" This painting is much harder than *An Enquiry VIII* to read as
straightforwardly Burkean for it insists on a pause before the onward
rush of paint and emotion, forcing an internal dislocation in the
position of subject and object rather than a synthesis of the two. *An
Enquiry 1* differentiates the roles of painter and spectator and in the
process differentiates itself from the Burkean sublime. There is a definite satirical edge to the portrayal of the female figure as art student,

the painter framing her own position as copyist of the (minor) masters within the narrative of the series. That narrative is of course beyond the scope of selective reproductions to reproduce. However, it is worth noting that what gets lost in the transposition is the sense of movement that all commentators (including Gibbons) have identified as a major component of Corcoran's technique. The foregrounding of *An Enquiry 1* precludes any simplistic reading of this in terms of a transition from object to subject of painting, because the contemporary female figure is remarkably still and sharp while it is the framed portrait behind which seems to promise movement and life.

In this respect, it echoes another woman's painting, one that thematically bears comparison with Corcoran's series. Moira Barry's *Self-Portrait in the Artist's Studio* (1920) is set within the privacy of the artist's studio rather than the national/public space of the National Gallery, but it also features a woman looking away from a variety of canvasses, over her shoulder, directly at the onlooker, in a pose which is uncannily close to the foreground young woman in *An Enquiry I*. The canvasses behind Barry are, however, blank with one exception (which appears to be a still life) and only one is framed. Again the paintings are more fluid than the woman in front of them. Barry's self-portrait is a highly stylized work in a very traditional form, but it also uses the modernist techniques whose influence Corcoran acknowledges. *Self-Portrait in the Artist's Studio* is, like the paintings by Barrett and Hickey, owned by the National Gallery, but not part of the canon configured by the Milltown rooms. It was, however, exhibited as part of the 1987 exhibition of Irish Women Artists at the gallery and featured prominently in the published catalog of that exhibition. Juxtaposing the two paintings suggests a genealogy of women artists' relationship with both modernist and postmodernist painting. Both challenge the opposition of subject–object, inside–outside, and framed–framing. The woman in Barry's *Self-Portrait* is an artist surrounded by the potentiality of her own painting, the blank canvasses yet to be filled. She reminds us that women have not only been part of the history of art, but have an artistic history of speaking, looking, and painting "for themselves." In *An Enquiry I*, there are two women, one an acute observer of a tradition of painting, which leaves her below its framed horizon, overshadowed by a beautiful image of female otherness. The second woman seems almost to be flowing out of focus, her gaze directed at an object we cannot identify. The double framing of her image—within Corcoran's painting of Hickey's painting—in important respects demystifies her. She becomes less a token of the exotic unknowable to be exchanged for the authenticity of the sublime and more a reminder of the structural limitations of the aesthetic.

An Enquiry suggests that the postmodern, feminist artist can keep on moving through and beyond the limitations of a national and patriarchal culture, but will never have the luxurious fiction of really blank canvasses to be filled. The Irish tradition behind her produces sublime and beautiful images of romantic landscape and racial stereotype—and Corcoran's series links the two in a way that exceeds Gibbon's description of its presentation of "the image itself as an enquiry into its own making" (2004). The positioning of Corcoran's paintings in *Field Day Review* is highly significant, for it both cordons them off from the textual analysis of Ireland, which dominates the volume, and identifies them with the investigation of globalization in Benedict Anderson's essay. Irish Studies has been heavily invested in its particularity, a particularity that seeks exception from the global system that produces it. Ireland is produced in turn by this discourse as a beautiful and disturbing original, rather in the manner of a modernist work of art. Irish literary criticism has a brilliant history—brilliant in the mode of a moving searchlight, providing blindingly clear illuminations of particular texts and times without ever offering the larger view that would show where exactly it is itself positioned. The inclusion of Corcoran's painting hints at a nascent awareness that race and gender will reconfigure the field. Perhaps, it glimpses outside the window a landscape that includes Moira Barry, the adult women the Cullen girls became, the books written out there, the cultural maps the new immigrants will produce, the possibility of a very differenced Ireland in the world.

NOTES

1. Contributors to the 1999 special issue of *Interventions* 2 (1) consistently remarked on the process whereby, in the Indian context, relatively liberated women in the 1980s and 1990s became metaphors for secularism and modernity and a constituency to be targeted by the religious right.
2. For an account of this process in the context of US immigration history, see Ignatieve (1997).
3. See, for example, Negra (2006).
4. The volume includes an excellent contextualizing essay on Hardy by Sarah Smith (2005).

REFERENCES

Cassidy, James F. (1933) *The Old Love of the Blessed Virgin Mary, Queen of Ireland.* Dublin: Gill.

Cheng, Vincent (2004) *Inauthentic: The Anxiety over Culture and Identity.* New Brunswick, New Jersey, and London: Rutgers University Press.

Cronin, Michael (2007) "'Is it for the glamour?': Masculinity, Nationhood and Amateurism in Contemporary Representations of the Gaelic Athletic Association," in *Postmodernism and Irish Popular Culture*, (eds.) Wanda Balzano, Anne Mulhall, Moynagh Sullivan. Palgrave Macmillan.

Deane, Seamus (2005) "Edward Said (1935–2003): A Late Style of Humanism." *Field Day Review*, 1 (1): 189–202, Spring.

Dyer, Richard (1997) *White.* London, New York: Routledge.

Fanning, Bryan (2002) *Racism and Social Change in the Republic of Ireland.* Manchester and New York: Manchester University Press.

Feldman, Shelley (1999) "Feminist Interruptions: The Silence of East Bengal in the Story of Partition." *Interventions: International Journal of Postcolonial Studies*,1 (2): 167–82.

Gibbons, Luke (1996) *Transformations in Irish Culture.* Cork: Cork University Press.

——— (2004) "Engendering the Sublime: Margaret Corcoran's *An Enquiry.*" *Circa*, 107: 32–38, Spring.

Graham, Colin (2001) *Deconstructing Ireland: Identity, Theory, Culture.* Edinburgh: Edinburgh University Press.

Harrison, Patricia (1945) "Letter to the Editor." *The Bell* (August): 446.

Hroch, Miroslav (1993) "From National Movement to the Fully Formed Nation: The Nation-Building Process in Europe." *New Left Review*, 198 (March/April): 15.

Ignatieve, Noel (1997) *How the Irish Became White.* New York and London: Routledge.

Iremonger, Valentin (1945) "The Poems of Freda Laughton." *The Bell*, 9 (4) (January): 249–250.

Kiberd, Declan (2005) *The Irish Writer and the World.* Cambridge: Cambridge University Press.

Kristeva, Julia (1986) "Stabat Mater," in Toril Moi (ed.), *The Kristeva Reader.* Oxford: Blackwell.

Laughton, Freda (1944) "When You Were With Me." *The Bell*, (August): 287.

——— (1945) "The Woman with Child." *The Bell*, 9 (4) (January): 289.

Lentin, Ronit (2005) "Black Bodies and Headless Hookers: Alternative Global Narratives for 21st Century Ireland." *Irish Review*, 33: 1–12, Spring.

McClintock, Anne (1993) "Family Feuds: Gender, Nationalism and the Family." *Feminist Review*, 44: 61–79, Summer.

Negra, Diane, ed. (2006) *The Irish in US.* Durham, NC: Duke University Press.

O'Horan, Eily (1948) "The Rustle of Spring." *The Bell*, 13 (5) (February): 28–39.

O'Reilly, Sean (2004) *The Swing of Things.* London: Faber.

Smith, Sarah (2005) "Ireland in the 1940s and 1950s: The Photographs of Bert Hardy." *Field Day Review*, 1: 133–156.

Turpin John (2003) "Visual Marianism and National Identity in Ireland: 1920–1960," in Tricia Cusack and Sighle Bhreathnach-Lynch (eds),

Art, Nation and Gender: Ethnic Landscapes, Myths and Mother-Figures. Aldershot, Hampshire; Burlington VT: Ashgate.

Watson, Peggy (1993) "The Rise of Masculinism in Eastern Europe." *New Left Review*, 198 (March/April): 75.

Yeats, W. B. (1905) *Samhain: An Occasional Review.* Maunsel and Co. and AH Bullen, November.

CHAPTER 9

Outside-in and the Places In-between: Feminist Community Higher Education

Aideen Quilty

Introduction

In a very literal sense, since its inception, the interdisciplinary field of Women's Studies had to "make room"[1] for itself and its students "within" the academy. It has for decades been creating, contesting, resisting, and celebrating its various spatial contexts including, though by no means limited to, disciplinary, institutional, conceptual, aesthetic, political, and pedagogic. In carving out spaces of feminist knowledges, practices, and pedagogies within the academy, it has been challenging the history of women's exclusion from the "formal" knowledge-making arena while simultaneously contesting the terms of knowledge construction and legitimization (Macdona, 2001).

A particular contribution of Irish Women's Studies has been the determination to "make room" for other sorts of students, students other than those traditionally deemed "suitable" for inclusion within higher education (HE) resulting in the development of a dynamic university/community partnership approach to HE provision based on a model of feminist community education. Delivered nationally since 1997, the Women's Studies community HE program targets women, largely in designated areas of disadvantage, for whom first or previous experiences of education were in the main negatively defined. On the one hand, courses are accredited and subject to academic examination, however, with considerable scope in the context of Women's Studies for innovation in pedagogy and assessment. On the other hand, courses are developed and delivered in community locations with participants who come from the local community and, unlike most participants in academic settings, have some degree of shared life experiences and opportunities for community involvement as well as considerable diversity in age, ethnicity, and other background factors (Moane and Quilty, 2012).

This short essay poses the question how we might contextualize this feminist community HE project. Foregrounding its exploration within the context of the "spatial turn," and more specifically the concept of "place," I make four observations as follows: first, how learning places might have significance beyond their physical architecture; second, how these feminist learning places embrace an approach to knowledge construction as situated, as coming from somewhere; third, how our subjective experiences take on a constitutive and pedagogic role within feminist learning place; fourth, how feminist community HE highlights a process of dynamic intervention and agency by community groups as they strive to reimagine HE place.

"Turning" to Place

More than ever before, scholars working in other disciplines in the humanities are thinking and writing in explicitly spatial terms, most notably in terms of imaginative geographies and the multiple and contested spaces of identity, which are often articulated through spatial images such as mobility, location, borderlands, exile, home. (Blunt, 2007: 75–76)

The not insignificant attraction of the spatial within the human sciences, particularly since the 1990s, and the renewed interest in recent years, has resulted in volumes of work being generated on how the spatial might be interpreted in an informed manner beyond the discipline of geography. Such thinking can be seen to reflect a broader "spatial turn" (Hubbard et al., 2005; McDowell, 1999) as "social thought appeared to be increasingly smitten with a geographical idiom of margins, spaces and borders" (Crang and Thrift, 2003: xi). Within this context, "place," one of geography's core concepts, has experienced significant interest. Nevertheless, place is conceptually problematic and has been variously understood and contested over the course of its life. As Castree comments, "the semantic elusiveness [of place] is compounded by the fact that human geographers have used it in a variety of ways throughout the discipline's history" (2003: 167). The linguistic familiarity of place as a word used in everyday parlance renders it both attractive as a term and simultaneously generates serious challenges as it is used in multiple contexts often with different meanings and purposes: There is no place like home; to be put in one's place; a place for everything and everything in its place, rendering it one of the most multilayered and multipurpose words in our language (Harvey, 1993: 4). This poses challenges for the development of theoretical concepts of place. Yet, in terms of feminist learning places, this layering of meaning that "reflects the way that places are socially constructed, given different meanings for different purposes" (Knox and Pinch, 2006: 194) suggests an educational place landscape open to interpretation and dynamic possibility.

It is thus perhaps unsurprising that the spatial lens has been so attractive to me in my desire to capture something of this university/community feminist project. The fact that the outreach locations have over the years represented an eclectic range of places seems too obvious a starting point to ignore: a meeting backroom in a midlands rural town adjoining the Catholic Church and containing a portable altar should we require the same; a resource center in a flat up three flights of stairs in a council tower block; a convent community center in a Dublin city suburb where a feminist Sister, literally, welcomes us in; a classroom in a kitchen in a sprawling west Dublin housing estate; an action project housed in a reclaimed cinema in south Dublin. These are just some of the outreach places that have become the Women's Studies outreach program over the past 15 years. And they are significant. Yet, these dynamic feminist learning places are so much more beyond these places. Here, I concur with Pallasmaa who suggests that "the ultimate meaning of any building is beyond architecture; it directs our consciousness back to the world and towards our sense of self and being" (2007: 11).

Viewing place in this way reflects a post-positivist tradition that envisions space relationally, that sees it as a product of cultural, social, political, and economic relations and where, crucially, the space "prioritizes analysis of how space is constituted and given meaning through human endeavor" (Hubbard et al., 2005: 13). Our educational places are thus, in this sense, relational. These buildings, these places of learning and knowledge, are critically important because they are constituted through the human endeavor of people, their emotions, feelings, ideas, visions, and realities. This spatial interpretation of educational place differs significantly from the previous "essential" or absolute consideration of space, which, in geographical analysis up to the 1970s, viewed space as geometric, neutral, and abstract (Hubbard et al., 2005) and which led to multiple exclusions of various social groups, including women, and social constructs such as gender, from theorizing and disciplinary knowledge creation. While this situation has been challenged by feminist scholars from multiple disciplinary fields, educational exclusions persist. In this light, Felicity Armstrong's call for a sustained intellectual relationship with geography as a way toward understanding and challenging the persistent exclusionary forces within education is instructive:

> The contribution of ideas from social geography and, in particular, a geography which itself is open and seeking out perspectives from other disciplines, highlights what a great deal of work we have to do in terms of exploring and decoding the deep movements and multiple dimensions and spaces of exclusionary forces. (Armstrong, 2010: 108)

Knowing Place

According to Puwar, the persistent exclusions or underrepresentation of some social groups in HE can be seen through the "cultures of exclusion," which operate within "contested social spaces as universities" (Puwar, 2004: 51, cited in Leathwood and Francis, 2006: 147). Reflecting the Irish HE landscape, Kathleen Lynch makes a strong statement about the spatialized university, one of boundaries and procedures, impacting not only on who enters but on what is valued:

> They practised exclusion, not only through their selection procedures for students and staff, but also by maintaining rigorous boundary maintenance procedures within and between disciplines, and between what is defined as legitimate and what is not. (Lynch, 2006: 73)

It remains the case that the academy is one of the most valorized and legitimized locations of knowledge generation. Doreen Massey, in a call for scrutiny of such locations, says:

> And one thing which might immediately occur to us there is the need to ponder the elitist, exclusivist, enclosures within so much of the production of what is defined as legitimate knowledge still goes on. (2006: 75)

Conscious of the university as "elitist, exclusivist, enclosures," feminist scholars, attempting to counter their invisibility and exclusion from masculinist knowledge-making arenas and to articulate their situation in the world, strove to give women a central place within philosophizing and theorizing (Massey, 1999, 2004, 2006, 2007; McDowell, 1997, 1999; Valentine, 2001). They developed methods of listening to women's socially situated narratives and of co-constructing knowledges with women as a way to challenge their invisibility not just within academia, but within the processes of the very construction of knowledge (Hesse-Biber and Leavy, 2006), a process Barr captures in the following:

> Women's education as it developed in adult education thus challenged, in concrete, practical ways, the notion of disembodied knowledge, recognising that knowledge, is not neutral but always socially situated: there is no "God's eye view, no 'knowledge from nowhere'." (Barr, 1999: 40)

This pedagogic approach, in striving to develop dynamic, inclusive learning environments, critically positions knowledge as "situated" (Haraway, 1991). In this sense, knowledge is "not simply out there waiting to be collected and processed, but rather is made by actors that are situated within particular contexts" (Hubbard et al., 2005: 8).

By viewing knowledge as being in place, the centrality of experience to feminist pedagogy becomes clear. Stake and Hoffman (2000) point out that descriptions of feminist pedagogy have been "remarkably consistent" including personal experience as valid source of knowledge and that this validation increases self-confidence. Yet, experience should not be viewed as some sort of pedagogic panacea. We can learn much from "feminist poststructural perspectives of 'experience' (which) have illuminated the theoretical limitations and simplifications entangled in unproblematic notions of experience" (Burke, 2002; Davies et al., 2004; Pereira, 2012). So too are Jean Barr's cautionary comments on the need to move beyond simply recounting our experiences as she states "starting from where people are at is an excellent starting point but a lousy finishing point! It can too often leave people there" (1999: 91). Despite these limitations, when seen as diverse, multiple, contradictory, complex, and socially constructed, experience can be a valuable educational and teaching resource (Burke, 2002: 42). Thus, if we are to take these limitations seriously and yet hold the centrality of experience within the feminist classroom, then we must strive for learning environments that embrace pedagogy and research methodology, which is related to people's lived experiences and feelings but which also develops critical thinking so that new thoughts and new ideas can be generated.

EXPERIENCE IN PLACE

Creswell observes that the majority of writing on place focuses on the realm of meaning and experience, on how we experience the world and make it meaningful (2004: 12). In this way, once again, place extends beyond architecture, beyond the physical structures that delineate it, and crucially becomes both a way of knowing, and of being in, the world.

> Different theories of place lead different writers to look at different aspects of the world. In other words place is not simply something to be observed, researched and written about but is itself part of the way we see, research and write. (Cresswell, 2004: 15)

As an educationalist, I am particularly drawn to this idea of educational place as something that offers both epistemological and ontological insights into how we view and understand the world. In other words, it encourages us to view educational places as being at once about how we are, how we think, feel, see, experience, and understand ourselves and the world. Such a position also confers huge responsibility as it demands that we acknowledge how our differences, our multiple and fluid identities, impact on the various and layered ways we experience learning environments as teacher and student.

All those positioned within the learning environment are "entrenched in the historical, geographical, political, personal, economic, psychological and social dynamics of the moment" and clearly such dynamics "shape both 'teacher' and the students' interpretations, perceptions and ways of knowing" (Burke, 2002: 40). Acknowledging this is important as Moane and Quilty observe:

> The learning journey of students and tutors can challenge the basis of what we might know, or come to know, as women in communities, as feminists, where class, race/ethnicity, and sexuality come under the spotlight: This epistemological and ontological journey is also an explicit feminist journey where there is an acknowledgement that gender affects how we use, access, and convey our understanding of the world and thus how we come to see, know, and act. (2012: 148)

Both an epistemological and ontological place as seen earlier, the feminist classroom is also a political place where not only are the "kinds of questions it asks and of whom, what is considered 'knowable' and how we can know things" saturated with politics but furthermore "that the practitioners of a discipline are not coincidental to the dominant forms of knowledge that are produced within the discipline" (McKittrick and Peake, 2005: 42). "Practitioners" thus cannot be understood as neutral participants within the educational process (Apple, 1982, 1996; Armstrong, 2003; Burke, 2002; Freire, 1979; Greene, 2005; Pinar, 2004). Rather, our being in place is intimately connected to race, class, sexuality, and other axes of power. Accepting this, Cousin calls on us to acknowledge our subjective positioning, stating that "our knowledge of the world is always mediated and interpreted from a particular stance and an available language, and that we should own up to this in explicit ways" (2010: 10). Recognizing my situatedness in the world as a woman, feminist, lesbian, and the like demands ownership and acknowledgment of my role within this knowledge-construction process. For example, it demands that I question the ways in which my sexuality, my sexual politics, influence my teaching. Discussed at length elsewhere (Quilty, 2010), the important point to make here is that these subjective knowledges, my body knowledges, all speak to and inform how I teach and thus should be acknowledged within the learning process. In this sense, I agree with Burke and Jackson who suggest that not doing so can result in "distorted knowledges when those who produce knowledge fail to recognise their own social/cultural/historic locations" (2007: 113).

OUTSIDE-IN AND THE PLACES IN-BETWEEN

The subjective experience of students and place is equally important. Let us consider for a moment the notion of "out of placeness," something experienced by so many adults within HE. The "keeping someone in one's place" or "putting someone in their place" suggests a connection between "geographical place and assumptions about normative behaviours" (Cresswell, 2004: 103). We are all familiar with the idea of "feeling out of place," indicating a level of discomfort, a dissonance between the place in which one finds oneself and one's comfort zone. This notion of out-of-place-ness is excellently captured through Bourdieu's (1991) idea of the "fish in/out of water," where our habitus and our zones of familiarity are linked directly to our cachet of social and cultural capital. As Thompson notes:

> Through a myriad of mundane processes and training…the individual acquires a set of dispositions which literally mould the body and become second nature. The dispositions produced thereby are also structured in the sense that they unavoidably reflect the social conditions within which they were acquired. (1991: 12)

Clearly, difficulties and challenges emerge for the student when there is a lack of congruence between the habitus and the field, for example, a "non-traditional"[2] student within a third-level educational institution, wherein "an individual may not know how to act and may literally be lost for words" (Bourdieu, 1991: 17). The impact of these cultural collisions can be significant for students, which Fleming and Murphy (2002) discuss in terms of "common versus college" knowledge. Let us also consider Lynch's argument that nontraditional students can at once be seen as the outsiders within, where hitherto nontraditional students have been regarded as some kind of exception in college: She states, "they come, but they are not fully expected; very often they are not fully accommodated" (2006: 89). This can be understood as a failure of the system, the place of the university, to fully understand and embrace the reality of promoting diversity where, as Lynch highlights, students end up in a between space, "as 'outsiders within' both in college and their communities" (2006: 90). This suggests that there is more than a little ambiguity about the sense of being in place, an ambiguity we might explore through notions of the simultaneity of some educational places.

Different individuals and groups can experience the same place differently at the same time, "they can simultaneously be experienced by different people as places of belonging and of frightening exclusion" (Holloway and Hubbard, 2001: 107). We can be both comfortable and ill at ease at once in the same place, for example, being present or in place physically yet psychologically be elsewhere, in another world. As Cresswell importantly observes, "the creation of place by necessity involves the definition of what lies outside. To put it another way the "outside" plays a crucial role in the definition of the "inside" (2004: 102) or as Clarke et al. remind us "there is no inside without an outside" (2002: 293). Importantly, "outsider" should not automatically be conflated with an assumption of "out of placeness" or as negatively defined "outside." While the inside–outside dichotomy might resonate within a history and tradition of a class-based education within Ireland, it is important that we do not close ourselves off from the possibility of the outside as a dynamic place.

I posit that the resistive strategies employed by returning adults and students on mature grounds reflect a dynamism, resourcefulness, and confidence in negotiating this double pathway, not as limiting, rather as liberating. It suggests a capacity to navigate both in and out, through and across, in a way that can be potentially empowering (Quinn, 2003; RANLHE, 2009). We can develop the in–out relationship in more dialectical terms through Rose's (1993) conceptualization of paradoxical space, which she posited almost 20 years ago as an opposition to the limiting masculinist tradition of binary distinction, based on rational/emotional or male/female distinction or indeed in/out distinction. Paradoxical space refers to a sense of being out of place within place where there is a coextensive experience of being inside/outside, where one must paradoxically be out in order to be in or vice versa.[3] This paradoxical simultaneity is really useful for our consideration of feminist community HE.

Drawing on my professional experience within the Women's Studies outreach education program, I have seen the positive impacts of acknowledging this inside-out paradoxical relationship where these outreach students are strategically and purposefully outside the campus in order that they can be inside, or within, HE. These, predominantly women, learners actively set out to address their educational exclusion by creating their own learning environments within their communities exploiting the advantages of outreach provision. Responding to their own needs and sociocultural realities and specifically the persistent barriers of childcare, eldercare, finance, travel, and time (WERRC, 1999), such education opportunities, existing on the "outside" of traditional delivery, might be seen to represent the most appropriate and expedient education opportunity for these learners. In tandem, reflecting these women's desires for a formal level of accreditation, they sought strategic partnerships with those "inside" institutions of HE, in this case with Women's Studies and its underpinning feminist pedagogy. By creating these feminist places of learning on the "outside" of the university, they at once make institutional place for themselves on the "inside," through their registration, student cards, formal accreditation, and ultimately graduation. In order to be "in" the university in this way, they drew on the capacity of the outside and in so doing, forced the redrawing of the boundaries of both.

Conclusions

> Your context—your location in the world—shapes your view of the world and therefore what you see as important, as worth knowing; context shapes the theories/stories you concoct of the world to describe and explain it. (Hanson, 1992: 573, cited in Hubbard et al., 2005: 9)

Feminist education programs can represent a dynamic place on the HE landscape. Viewed through the particular lens of the spatial, and drawing on my experience as director of the University College Dublin (UCD) Women's Studies outreach program and of feminist pedagogy, I made a number of observations about how we might contextualize these programs. I argued that we might view such places as organic places of learning that impact on students' way of looking at, and politics of being in, the world. Carrying ontological, epistemological, and political significance, these education places are anything but neutral. Rather, such places reflect the idea of being in place, an experienced place beyond architecture, which, to recall Pallasmaa, may "direct our consciousness back to the world and towards our sense of self and being." In this context, the significance of place becomes clear. Indeed, my efforts to pay attention to place, one of geography's core concepts, within feminist education speaks to Castree's argument that "the renewed study of place is too important to be left to geographers alone" (2005: 182): an idea shared, perhaps, by our community partners as evidenced in their desire to create new university places within their communities. We might argue that these outreach programs experience some degree of success because their place realities eschew the limitations of the in–out dichotomy. In other words, outreach students, whether in the kitchen, the flat, converted cinema, or religiously aligned place, and in which notions of insider/outsider and belonging can be challenged and remade, manage to reinvent both what notions of inside and outside might come to mean in terms of HE. Redrawing and reimagining these outside/in positions, these programs have enabled the creation of what could be understood as feminist community HE in the places in-between.

Notes

1. I draw from Kent's chapter title *Making Room for Space in Physical Geography* (in Holloway et al., 2007: 109).
2. I draw on the definition offered through the European Lifelong Learning Project 2008–2010, Access and Retention: Experiences of Non-traditional Learners in HE, which suggests that nontraditional can be understood as follows (RANLHE, 2009: 3): "we mean students who are under-represented in higher education and whose participation in HE is constrained by structural factors. This would include, for example, students whose family has not been to university before, students from low-income families, students from (particular) minority ethnic groups, mature age students and students with disabilities."
3. Within Lesbian, Gay, Bisexual, Transgender (LGBT) communities, the process and being of "coming out" in order to "be in" their non-heteronormative community is a classic example of this paradox where lesbians and others come out of the metaphorical closet in order that they can come to be within their community (see Fuss, 1991).

References

Apple, M. W. (1982) *Education and Power*. London: Routledge and Kegan Paul.

——— (1996) *Cultural Politics and Education*. Buckingham: Open University Press.

Armstrong, F. (2003) *Spaced Out: Policy, Difference and the Challenge of Inclusive Education*. Dordrecht: Kluwer Academic Publishers.

——— (2010) "Disability, Education, and Space: Some Critical Reflections," in K. N. Gulson and C. Symes (eds), *Spatial Theories of Education: Policy and Geography Matters*. London: Routledge.

Barr, J. (1999) *Liberating Knowledge: Research, Feminism and Adult Education*. Leicester: NIACE.

Blunt, A. (2007) "Geography and the Humanities Tradition," in S. L. Holloway, S. P. Rice, and G. Valentine (eds), *Key Concepts in Geography*. London: Sage, pp. 73–91.

Bourdieu, P. (1991) *Language and Symbolic Power: Pierre Bourdieu*. Cambridge: Polity, Basil Blackwell.

Burke, P. J. (2002) *Accessing Education: Effectively Widening Participation*. Stoke on Trent: Trentham Books.

——— and Jackson, S. (2007) *Reconceptualising Lifelong Learning: Feminist Interventions*. London: Routledge.

Castree, N. (2003) "Place: Connections and Boundaries in an Interdependent World," in S. L. Holloway, S. P. Rice, and G. Valentine (eds), *Key Concepts in Geography*. London: Sage, pp. 165–186.

——— (2005) "Whose Geography? Education as Politics," in N. Castree, A. Rogers, and D. Sherman (eds), *Questioning Geography: Fundamental Debates*. Oxford: Blackwell, pp. 294–307.

Clarke, J., Harrison, R., Reeve, F., and Edwards, R. (2002) "Assembling Spaces: The Question of "Place" in Further Education," *Discourse: Studies in the Cultural Politics of Education*, 23 (3): 285–297.

Cousin, G. (2010) "Positioning Positionality: The Reflexive Turn," in M. Savin-Baden and C. Howell Major (eds), *New Approaches to Qualitative Research: Wisdom and Uncertainty*. London: Routledge.

Crang, M. and Thrift, N. (eds) (2003). *Thinking Space*. London: Routledge.

Cresswell, T. (2004) *Place, A Short Introduction*. Oxford: Blackwell.

Davies, B., Browne, J., Gannon, S., Honan, E., Laws, C., Mueller-Rockstroh, B., et al. (2004) "The Ambivalent Practices of Reflexivity," *Qualitative Inquiry*, 10 (3): 360–389.

Fleming, T. and Murphy (2002) *From Common to College Knowledge: Mature Student Experiences at University*. Maynooth: MACE.

Freire, P. (1979) *Pedagogy of the Oppressed*, trans. M. B. Ramos. London: Sheed and Ward.

Fuss, D. (ed.) (1991) *Inside/Out: Lesbian Theories, Gay Theories*. London: Routledge.

Greene, M. (2005) "Teaching in a Moment of Crisis: The Spaces of Imagination," *The New Educator*, 1: 77–80.

Hanson, S. (1992) Geography and Feminism: Worlds in Collision? *Annals of the Association of American Geographers*, 82 (4): 569–586.

Haraway, D. (1991) *Simians, Cyborgs and Women: The Reinvention of Nature*. New York, London: Routledge.

Harvey, D. (1993) "From Space to Place and Back Again: Reflections on the Condition of Postmodernity," in J. Bird, B. Curtis, T. Putnam, G. Robertson, and L. Tickner (eds), *Mapping the Futures: Local Cultures, Global Change*. London: Routledge.

Hesse-Biber, S. N. and Leavy, P. (eds.). (2006). *Emergent Methods in Social Research*. London: Sage.

Holloway, L. and Hubbard, P. (2001) *People and Place: The Extraordinary Geographies of Everyday Life*. Essex: Pearson Education Limited.

Holloway, S. L., Rice, S. P., and Valentine, G. (eds) (2007) *Key Concepts in Geography*. London: Sage.

Hubbard, P., Kitchin, R., Bartley, B., and Fuller, D. (2005) *Thinking Geographically: Space, Theory and Contemporary Human Geography*. London: Continuum.

Knox, P. and Pinch, S. (2006) *Urban Social Geography: An Introduction* (5th ed.). Essex: Pearson Education Limited.

Leathwood, C. and Francis, B. (eds) (2006). *Gender and Lifelong Learning: Critical Feminist Engagements*. Abington, Oxon: Routledge.

Lynch, K. (2006) *The Role of the University in Serving Public Interests: A Challenge to the Neo-Liberal Model*. Paper presented at the University and Society: From Newman to the Market.

Macdona, A. (ed.) (2001) *From Newman to New Woman: UCD Women Remember*. Dublin: New Island.

Massey, D. (1999) "Negotiating Disciplinary Boundaries," *Current Sociology*, 47 (4): 5–12.

––––– (2004) *Space, Place and Gender* (1994 First ed.). Cambridge: Polity.

––––– (2006) *For Space*. London: Sage.

––––– (2007) *World City*. Cambridge: Polity Press.

Mc Dowell, L. (ed.). (1997) *Undoing Place? A Geographical Reader*. London: Arnold.

––––– (1999) *Gender, Identity and Place: Understanding Feminist Geographies*. Cambridge: Polity Press.

McKittrick, K. and Peake, L. (2005) "What Difference Does Difference Make to Geography?" in N. Castree, A. Rogers, and D. Sherman (eds), *Questioning Geography, Fundamental Debates*. Oxford: Blackwell, pp. 39–54.

Moane, G. and Quilty, A. (2012) "Feminist Education and Feminist Community Psychology: Experiences from an Irish Context." *Journal of Community Psychology*, 40 (1): 145–158.

Pallasmaa, J. (2007) *The Eyes of the Skin: Architecture and the Senses*. Chichester: Wiley.

Pereira, M. d. M. (2012) "Uncomfortable Classrooms: Rethinking the Role of Student Discomfort in Feminist Teaching." *European Journal of Women's Studies*, 19 (1): 128–135.

Pinar, W. (2004) *What is Curriculum Theory?* Mahwah, NJ: Lawrence Erlbaum Associates.

Puwar, N. (2004) "Fish in and out of Water: A Theoretical Framework for Race and the Space of Academia," in I. Law, D. Philips, and L. Turney (eds), *Institutional Racism in Higher Education*. Stoke-on-Trent: Trentham Books.

Quilty, A. (2010) *Special Species of Space: Towards a Geography of Education* (Doctoral Thesis), National University of Ireland, Maynooth.

Quinn, J. (2003) "The Dynamics of the Protected Space: Spatial Concepts and Women Students." *British Journal of Sociology of Education*, 24 (4): 449–461.

RANLHE (2009) *European Lifelong Learning Project 2008–10, Access and Retention: Experiences of Non-traditional Learners in HE*. www.dsw.edu .pl/fileadmin/www-ranlhe/index.html

Rose, G. (1993) *Feminism and Geography: The Limits of Geographical Knowledge*. Cambridge: Polity Press.

Stake, J. E. and Hoffman, F. L. (2000) "Putting Feminist Pedagogy to the Test. The Experience of Women's Studies from Student and Teacher Perspectives." *Psychology of Women Quarterly*, 24: 30–38.

Thompson, J. B. (1991) "Introduction," in P. Bourdieu (ed.), *Language and Symbolic Power: Pierre Bourdieu*. Cambridge: Polity: Basil Blackwell.

WERRC (1999) *A Study of Feminist Education as an Empowerment Strategy for Community Based Women's Groups in Ireland*. Dublin: University College Dublin.

CHAPTER 10

"Watch Your Language": Speculative Theory and the Poetry of Rita Ann Higgins

Moynagh Sullivan

And for Christ's sake
At all times
Watch your language.
"Be Someone."

—*Rita Ann Higgins* (*Higgins,* 2005: 39)

In this chapter, I explore how looking and watching, speculation, and the specular informs question of class and gender in the poetry of the Galway poet Rita Ann Higgins. In an essay in which Ailbhe Smyth questions the validity of boundaries that empathically separate genres and "disciplines," Smyth embeds a Rita Ann Higgins poem between two dictionary definitions in order to perform a critique of the claim to objectivity of institutionally endorsed and reproduced critical and philosophical practices and to test the much-vaunted boundaries of the "disciplines." Smyth chose lines from "Oracle Readers" (Higgins, 1988: 40–43), as part of her anzalduan mediation on how feminist practices that complicate the relationship between the creative and the analytical have helped to "reveal into theory" heretofore missed, relegated, or neglected aspects of humanity and experience to change the shape and codes of knowledges. Higgins was an inspired choice, for like the work of Smyth herself, Higgins's engaging poetry not only makes those who are overlooked emphatically perceptible, but her work also directs the reader to reconsider theories of the proper place and function of poetry. Like the work of Smyth, which champions those without representation and voice, Higgins's poetry provides a testimony to and an interrogation of the intertwining of aesthetics and politics in Irish culture, and of the interlocking of culture and aesthetics in Irish politics. Although Smyth and Higgins write from different histories and spaces, each woman, according to her own gifts, addresses the complicated intersections among gender, class, sexuality, (dis)ability, and age, if not to unravel, then at least to acknowledge the trickiness of the speaking human subject in all her or his relations with a view to overturning discriminatory and unjust practices. The work of each woman, although compelled by a vision of justice and fairness, resists the lure of so-called objectivity, claims to infallible authority and its attendant moral high ground, and is humble and self-questioning, written from an acceptance of the limits of one's own understanding and coherency, of the necessary speculative character of theory, and with a compassion that extends even to those who appear to be an impediment to the achievement of the justice their work seeks.

REVELATION (OED): Select an appropriately relevant meaning. 1. Disclosure of facts made by a person; exposure of something previously disguised or concealed.

> *And we saw*
> *what we saw*
> *and we didn't see*
> *what was hidden*
> **(Rita Ann Higgins)**

What are the facts? Some call them "data," some "empirical research." Some don't call them at all. Constructing airy immaterial edifices.

THEORY (OED): Contemplation, speculation, sight. From the Greek, *Theory*, the root, spectator. (Smyth, 2005: 136)

By using the poetic to question the philosophical, Smyth thus suggests a speculative theoretical paradigm rather than a denotative one, and I draw on this emphasis on the specular/speculative to look especially at how Higgins's framing of how language is "watched" invites the reader to reflect on how questions of proper form are underpinned by intricate positioning of class and gender in discourse. As Smyth points out, the root of theory can be declined back to spectator, which in turn comes from the Greek, *thea*, a viewing and *oros*, seeing, and here I contemplate the revelatory aspects of Higgins's poetry—asking how the poetry theorizes, with a "viewing" that lets us see what is often beyond the subject of poetry (Smyth, 2005: 136). Responding to how watching language works in Higgins's poetry requires a consideration of the specific located aspects of her womanhood that Smyth outlines as fundamental to a continuing ethical feminist framework:

> Feminism has been a major transformational force in modern Ireland for the past three decades, but the changes it has generated and expedited are volatile, incomplete and unevenly beneficial. Gender transformations impact on people differently and above all unequally, and always intersect with other experiences, locations and regimes of social control, including class, ethnicity, and sexuality, age and (dis) ability, among others. To consider feminism is therefore a complex business, requiring attentive, knowing, empathetic and imaginative scrutiny of the ways in which specifically-located women can and do live their lives. (Smyth, 2007: 11)

Higgins's poetry addresses the complicated intersections to which Smyth refers. Originally from Galway city, Higgins now lives part of the year in *An Spiddeal*, on the edge of the south Connemara Gealteacht in Co. Galway. She grew up in a working-class area of Galway, married young, and famously became a writer after discovering reading during a convalescent stay in a sanatorium when recovering from Tuberculosis in her early twenties. Her work includes *Goddess on the Mervue Bus* (1986), *Witch in the Bushes* (1988), *Goddess and Witch* (1990), *Philomena's Revenge* (1992), *Higher Purchase* (1996), *Sunny Side Plucked* (1996), *An Awful Racket* (2001), *"Throw in the Vowels": New & Selected Poems* (2005), *Hurting God: Part Essay Part Rhyme* (2010), *Ireland is Changing Mother* (2011). She has also written a number of plays and screenplays. Higgins's work challenges some of the most well-established orthodoxies, not only of Irish Literature, but also of the economies of Irish Literary Tourism, with its post-Revival fetishization of the west of Ireland as a misty retreat, peopled by artists and writers in blissful quiet, a haven to which one escapes the imprecations of city and urban life, a place to get away from it all. Higgins writes about the lives of those who "cannot get away from it all," but who live in the often devastated cityscapes occluded by the city–country dialectic of Dublin and the "west." Higgins does not salve the liberal conscience of a predominantly middle-class poetry readership with characters who survive lives blighted by utilitarian and disrespectful urban and social planning with plucky humor and hope, but instead focuses on the coping mechanisms of commodity fetishization and self-medication/abuse that shore up the privileges and inequities of class-based capitalism. Higgins rejects the exhortation to "be someone" by watching her language, and initiates a shift away from the individual subject of poetry to an ethics of "some people," an indeterminate number, a community rather than a humanist individual. As such, her work repudiates the fetishization of the individual as the propelling agent of upwardly mobile culture, as exemplified in the poem, "Be Someone":

> Learn to speak properly,
> Always pronounce your ings.
> Never smoke on the street
> (Higgins, 2005: 39)

Higgins declines to "watch her language" and to "learn to speak properly" epitomizing the "impropriety" that Claire Wills's groundbreaking work elaborates.[1] In interview, Higgins recounts how writing poetry was based on an improper relationship to language from the first. When she began writing, she wrote short stories:

> The prose was going in and out of tenses—the past, the present and the future. And someone at the workshop said, "You can't do that. You have to stick to the same tenses. You can't be doing what you're doing." I thought, "God, there must be an easier way." So I started to write poems. You didn't have to worry about tenses and verbs. You could write a poem without a verb, and if you didn't know what a verb was—and I didn't—it was okay. (Wallace, 2005: B16)

Instead of trying to fit what she wanted to say to the grammatical and syntactical rules of narrative that also represent middle-class propriety, Higgins asked language to fit her world instead. Molly McAnailly Burke noted that "Rita has no intention of betraying her own background by slipping into the literary middle class, where she would surely wither and die of boredom" (McAnailly Burke, 1997: B36). Higgins is a seeming anomaly in Irish poetry—a working class poet who is "inassimilable" to a literary middle class, a woman who resists gentrification in favor of her unique poetic vernacular, with its insistence on the uncomfortable thematics of class and social inequity, its aural patternings influenced by liturgy, prayer, and idiolects of local parishes and communities of working-class Galway. The poem, "Poetry Doesn't Pay," addresses the conflict between the speaker's desire to write poetry and her need to keep a roof over her family's heads: "People keep telling me / Your poems, you know, / You've got something there, / I mean really" (Higgins, 2005: 21). Adrienne Rich notes that middle-class women exchange "self-respect for respectability" and Higgins emphatically refuses this exchange, instead highlighting the ineffectiveness of the "exchange" of her poetry, her possible permit into the middle classes. Instead of "watching" her language in order to move into the literary middle classes, she makes "some" a recurrent subject in her work in place of becoming a "some-one" herself, and in this repetition, the definitional indeterminacy of "some" becomes determinedly class specific, simultaneously panning back on how the term references anonymous and non-individuated lower socioeconomic sectors in media and popular cultural representations, and zooming in to reveal the lived pain of such occlusions. Claire Bracken writes that Higgins's "poetry has sought to aestheticise and poeticise Irish working class culture—a space left relatively unsymbolised and unexamined in the poetic sphere" (Bracken, 2007: 166). Bracken elaborates:

> Speaking from the margins, Higgins's work problematizes the universally legitimated visions of Irishness and Ireland (urban prosperity and rural idyllicism respectively), constructing another perspective—a partial vision which makes evident the perspectivism inherent in the act of looking itself. (Bracken, 2007: 166)

This "some-body" challenges traditional formalist and inherited views of poetry primarily conditioned by the lyric "I," as Higgins remains far from specifically situated in canonical terms, and her poetry sits uneasily in accounts of contemporary Irish poetry. Critics often note the importance of Higgins's work, but are shy of writing about it. Lucy Collins's 2003 essay, "Performance and Dissent: Irish Poets in the Public Sphere," is a notable exception to this, and Collins's subtle analysis explores how Higgins's poetry acts in a culture where "the critical attention to poetry still far exceeds popular readership," as a potentially disruptive interface between the performance of poetry and the enshrinement of writing (Collins, 2003: 219). Likewise, Catriona Clutterbuck's fine argument that Higgins's work stages formal interventions as part of a remapping of the borders of the physic Irish republic situates her work politically (Clutterbuck, 2000: 17–43); while Patrick Crotty's sensitive review of *An Awful Racket* notes importantly that it operates at a "tiny, crucial remove" from everyday speech (Crotty, 2001: 53). Despite this, Higgins is often positioned uncomfortably in relation to her contemporaries, and her work is often left out or nominally mentioned in descriptions of contemporary and recent Irish poetry.

It appears that one of the most troubling aspects of Higgins's poetry is not so much that it highlights class as a component of social and political life, for in this respect, her subject matter is accepted as "worthy," but that her work more disturbingly insists on class as a structuring factor of aesthetics. It was speculated that Higgins's delayed entry into the artists union *Aosdána*[2] was because "what she does isn't exactly considered poetry but 'prose with short lines'" (McAnailly Burke, 1997: B36), a put-down that demonstrates that her work can fall foul of discriminations that are fundamentally about class, but are shrouded in a language of formal art. The title of *An Awful Racket* appears to be a playful recuperation of the criticism levied at her. Will the reader/listener hear an awful racket, a harsh collection of seemingly unaestheticized political moans, or the nuanced and crafted interpellations of voices across discourses? As well as refusing to "watch" her own language in literary circles that emphasize bourgeois concerns, she also turns an eye to the reader's expectation of the poetic, specifically the "I"/eye-centered lyric, in order to throw our perspectivism on art itself into question.

In *War and Cinema: The Logistics of Perception*, Paul Virilio's landmark text on the ideology of looking, he describes the act of taking aim—an act of looking that allows us to obliterate that at the other end of our sight—as a "geometrification of looking, a way of technically aligning ocular perception along an imaginary axis that used to be known in French as the 'faith line' (*linge de foi*)." He goes on to note that "the word faith is no longer used in this context in contemporary French: the ideal line appears thoroughly objective, and the semantic loss involves a new obliviousness to the element of interpretative subjectivity that is always in play in the act of looking" (Virilio, 1989: 3). In Higgins's work, the act of looking itself becomes "playful" with deadly seriousness: the act of looking comes into focus as a destroyer of the Other, and the faith that allows the over-seeing of Others is simultaneously demolished. In "It's all Because We're Working Class" (Higgins, 2005: 34–36), one of Higgins's earliest poems, a drama unfolds in the form of a monologue that is itself a meditation on the politics of looking. The lines spoken are not "in perspective": "Fuckin' coal bag washers / And grass eaters / The whole fuckin' lot of them; / And it's all because we're working class" (Higgins, 2005: 35). But rather than pillory the long-earned chip on the shoulder of the speaker that seems at first glance to be the subject of the poem, Higgins returns the "element of interpretative subjectivity" to literary middle-class perspectives about rhyme, reason, and space. The speaker in the poem is the parent of a child, Ambrose, who has had a serious accident as a result of being prescribed "big thick spy-glasses" (Higgins, 2005: 34) when his eye patch to cure a lazy eye was prematurely removed, and the speaker laments the helplessness and powerlessness s/he feels in the face of poverty and patronizing medical authority. Through these glasses "you could see / no rhyme reason / or gable end" and these distorting spectacles were prescribed by "that coal bag washer / and grass eater / from the Shantalla clinic" (Higgins, 2005: 34). The glasses intended to bring Ambrose's "wrong" eye back to the "middle" distort the natural rhythms of his life, the reason of his rhyme, although the prescribing optometrist promises him enhanced vision:

> Burn your patch
> He said
> And be a man;
> Slip these on
> And see into
> The souls of men
> (Higgins, 2005: 34)

In the optometrist's exhortation, poetry and class are explicitly linked, as the altered perception lent by the prescribed middle glasses is supposed to allow Ambrose to see through the liberal humanist discourse of literary "soul" and shared "manity" of mankind. In this poem, where poetry and spatial reasoning are interlinked through acts of looking, the reader is send back to look, as is almost always the case in Higgins's work, at the objectivity of reading itself, as tacit faith in the universal subject of lyric poetry is disrupted. No purchase can be made along the *linge de foi*, the faith lines that run into the vanishing point of perspective, and as we swing from perspective to perception, the moral compass alters, so that the reader is prevented from finding a stable point of view from which to establish a "balanced" symmetrical and coherent "perspective," in which the Other at the end of the faith line can be obliterated in a transcendent act of in-sight. Ambrose's sight is forever damaged because the glasses that allowed him to look into the "souls of men" hampered his ability to steer his own course, detached him from his own sensory perception of his life, and he "walked into / the gable end / and his life / was in splinters / thereafter" (Higgins, 2005: 34).

Ambrose had had a "lazy eye" that was a "wrong eye" to his "right eye" and simultaneous rightness and wrongness had served him well and he knew his ground; he had eyes that were not in accord, that did not look in the same direction, yet he could see to navigate his own "pointing." However, after the corrections of perspective by another's script, his vision is "splintered" by the broken middle glasses, which are specifically related to questions of poetic framing by alliteratively bringing rhyme and reason into focus.

Higgins's feminist politics are powerfully inflected by her class consciousness, and as such the gender issues her poems highlight are often a study in intersecting formations of inequity, and she describes herself as:

> more for people than for specific gender. I'm conscious of the imbalance of power in Irish society in general. There's a lack of understanding between the bureaucrats and the ordinary person. There's an abuse of power that goes on which is very subtle. (Donovan, 1996: 16)

Power is investigated as traversing language as desire for things, recalling the concerns and title of her powerful 1996 collection *Higher Purchase*. Her work exposes the ways in which capital operates through desire to make men and women both complicit in their own abuse by each other, and through an economic structure that traps people in debilitating debts from hire purchases, often in an attempt to buy some respectability in a culture that always keeps respect beyond buying. Higgins recounts how having the time to read during her long convalescence, combined with the realities of her life as a young mother in Galway's Rahoon Flats, where she was "so tired having to carry the pram up and down the steps because there was no lift" to the fourth floor began to "create a class awareness" (Donovan, 1996: 16).[3] Thus, Higgins's "Ode to Rahoon Flats" is not a meditation on a vision of beauty, temporality, and art, but about the broken dreams laid waste by the cycle of poverty invigorated by unplanned pregnancies, drugs, and the indignities of low-income housing:

> O Rahoon, who made you
> To break the hearts
> Of young girls with
> pregnant dreams
> of an end of terrace,
> crisp white clothes
> lines and hire purchase
> personalities?

> (Higgins, 2005: 26)

Although class awareness forms a deep seam of political bedrock throughout her poetry, Higgins, as McAnailly Burke points out, resists "cheap categorising" as a "housewife-poet," or as the "voice of the working class" (McAnailly Burke, 1990: 20). However, given that her initials RAH appear imbedded in the first syllable and stressed phoneme of Rah-oon, we are given a hint that Higgins's poetry potently explores the tensions between self-growth and community responsibility, the conflict between personal dream and ethical demand, and the growing pains that accompany the act of personal, political, and relational metamorphosis. The final lines of "Ode to Rahoon Flats," visualizes the downfall of the salvational machine for modern living, when the Christological flats are undone in a "cruxificional" crumble with no promise of resurrection or renewal. The undoing of this inhospitable space is echoed in her ideas of poetic form itself. For her, poems should not be static, privatized sites of authority and meaning, but shape-changing in and of themselves, although open to reinterpretation, and specifically to intervention by others, a view demonstrated when she recounts the story of an encounter with a reader in Belfast: "Young lady," he says, "poems should not be arguable with." And I thought, "You fool: everything should be arguable with" (McAnailly Burke, 1990: 20). Understanding her poems as arguments is central to seeing how she theorizes her poetry as a set of formal interventions in discourses outside itself, and outside the self-enclosing language of poetry, to challenge hierarchical interpretive communities through exegetical privileging and generations of textual decoding that promote inclusions and exclusions.

Taxing the exclusions of the privatized poem extends to testing the enclosures of the privatized nation. *An Awful Racket* (2001) moves from Galway to a number of other sites, including Majorca and Jerusalem, and it includes "They Never Wear Coats," a poem about Newcastle, a Northern English working-class town, which shares its name with a historically working-class area in Galway city. This is one of her most powerful poems and it explores the spiritual and psychic diminishment, the emotional deadening, and the brutal sexual economies that result from poverty, addiction, and abandonment. This poem focuses on extra-national connections between the "underbellies" of the "nations"—at that which is topographically "under the belly": Carol as always has to pee, / "have ya a good look like, / I'll shove your face in it for ya?" (Higgins, 2005: 172). The promise to "shove your face in it" is made good by many of Higgins's poems, but in what is the reader's face being shoved?

Her poems shove the reader's face in the spectacle of the bodily place from which a woman pees as well as pee itself, revealing the

woman's body hidden in language and text itself, each in turn intimately politicized around the issues of woman's authority, especially
around her own body as a site of reproductive politics and of the generation of meaning. So, when Higgins does not watch her language,
but brings into view that which was "hidden," as a woman, she takes
considerable risks with her own self-authority. The "C" word remains
the most powerful curse, the most offensive word in English, linguis-
tically hidden in its euphemism, and in respectable clothing, and it
is this that Higgins repeatedly makes us "see" and "watch": "[s]ome
people know what's it's like, / to be called a cunt in front of their
children" (Higgins, 2005: 58). She exposes, "something previously
disguised or concealed."

In "Be Someone," gender, sexuality, and language are revealed as
even more emphatically intertwined when the cunt is ironically exposed
through watching watchfulness itself: "Don't be caught dead / In
them shameful tight slacks" (Higgins, 2005: 39). The shameful tight
slacks emphasize a woman's genitals, and put the curve of her vaginal
lips on show—to be "watched," and this line gestures to the relationship between outspokenness and sexuality. In this paradoxical
exhortation to "watch" the lips, we are asked to acknowledge that
watching your language does not just mean watching your tongue.
In "Anything is Better than Emptying Bins," when the poet tries to
send her poems away for publication, initiating the transition between
writing for self and claiming the right to a public platform she encounters "[m]ore lip and less tongue" (Higgins, 2005: 44), announcing
how her public voice reveals the relationship between female sexuality
and the economies of discourse in her work, from the "C wearer's"
of "People Who Wear Cardigans Are Subversive" (Higgins, 2005:
67–68) to the "bitch" "collapsin" engine of "Misogynist" (Higgins,
2005: 69). The lips reveal the "w" shape made through the "shameful
tight slacks," the watchword at the center of the body, and of a symbolic order predicated on the prohibition of female desire. The "w"
tells the disruptive desire of the woman, a shibboleth that betrays the
inside of the outsider, the desire hidden within discourse—the witch
in the bush. "Witch in the Bushes," dramatizes how fear of female
sexuality and genitalia becomes sublimated for one man into lifelong
anger fueled by an avuncular inner voice's paranoiac warning to be
vigilant: "About/the witch in the bushes," it said, "Watch her, / She
never sleeps" (Higgins, 2005: 43).

"Watching" language so that the prohibited does not erupt into
its accepted codes and practices is the activity of many institutions
and social practices, and the modification of language to exclude the

taboo is a primary indicator of social and political positions. Given that middle-class indexes of emphasized femininity valorize and reward minimized body space, sexuality, and speech in a woman, Higgins's work breaks at least two taboos by being "unfemininely" outspoken and by cursing not only publicly but in public poetry. The use of "dirty words" involves the rupture of proper language by the unseemly, and like the excrement and urine it often references, like the toilets it uses as dramatic stages, her work allows seepage of social discontent into discourses designed to keep it at bay, or hidden. Obscene language is an act of violence in speech and writing; it is an aggressive act, however affectionately the "curse" word has been declined or parsed. Increasingly, since modernists used crude or dirty language in their work, it has been acceptable as an indication of authentic vernacular and of a certain sort of working-class muscular masculinity in writing.[4] However, valorization of the plain and crude language of the working and soldiering man as an index of social truth is often made without due attention to the sexual violence implicit in such language. That is not to say that women do not use or access crude language, or even enjoy it, but rather that when the language iterated publicly is primarily from a masculine point of view, then women tend to be the objects of it, and not the shapers of it. Cursing, acceptable for men, is often read as a form of linguistic bravery and audacity, or even as politically strategic and necessary. Cursing in an Irish literary context has often been read as a postcolonial "talking back," a calibaneqsue riposte to the empire. Why does the same sexiness, bravado, or cool swagger not attach to a woman "talking back to patriarchal capitalism," an equally imperial economy? The intrusion of male sexuality into public discourse no longer disturbs social codes, but is seen as underwriting its generational logic, whereas the incursion of female sexuality and embodiment from a woman's pen undoes this logic.

Women's disingenuous management of their sexuality within the economics of capital leads to reward, and in "Be Someone," being "caught" works in two senses, for in not being caught in shameful self-revealing slacks, one can pass, can "marry up," and, like the aphorism where a man chases a woman until she catches him, the sensible woman can be "caught" for reproduction of a social order that needs the regulation and hiding of her desire: "Learn to speak properly, / always pronounce your ings," "spare the butter" (Higgins, 2005: 39). Manage your commodity, don't let yourself go (free) but make sure you get a good price: "Have nothing to do / with the Shantalla gang, / get yourself a right man / with a Humber Sceptre" (Higgins,

2005: 39). The Humber Sceptre is a niche car that denotes social status, recalling all of the imperial scepters from the rods and staffs to
Bishop's crooks to that function as a ceremonial emblem of authority
and sovereignty and that are passed on from one generation of men
to another. The addressee of this poem, being exhorted to "watch"
her body/language, is being asked to climb a social ladder that may
improve her material lot, but that structurally serves to keep patriarchal heterosexual marriage and the legitimate family firmly in place
as the site of reproduction. Sexuality in Higgins's work is most often
tied to the reproduction of social and gendered inequities. Female
desire is often specifically linked to maternity and a lifetime of unpaid
labor as in "Mamorexia" (Higgins, 2005: 123) and "Tommy's Wife"
(Higgins, 2005: 16). While the emotional richness of maternity is also
explored, the material realities of a pronatalist state that neither supports nor values actual maternal production are never far from the sur-
faces of her work, as in "Light of the Moon" (Higgins, 2005: 72–73),
which begins with playful delight in abandon and intimacy, but ends
with the labor cycles of unpaid and unvalued domestic life and childbirth, which are shown to be initiated and sustained through socially
accepted and government-supported practices of self-anesthetization
through drink:

> The glare from the moon
> Which makes you say
> In seagull Russian
> "fuse me bix foot skew
> In your stocking wheat
> Bould you kind werribly if I jay on the bat of my flack
> For the bext three-quarters of a bour
> The boon is milling me"
>
> (Higgins, 2005: 73)

Drinking alcohol is often underscored as the mechanism by which
people become inured and bound to poverty and sexual and emotional
violence. "They Never Wear Coats," illustrates young girls whose
self-worth is injured to the extent that they will not even protect themselves from the bitter Northern English winter with a coat. Their senses
are so spoilt that they do not even feel the cold; they cannot walk away
from repeated brutal and unhappy encounters with rough men:

> They know all the words of all the songs
> They sing them all day in the work place
> "I try to say goodbye and I choke

I try to walk away and I stumble."
That night they sing louder
Helped by vodka and gin.
                              (Higgins, 2005: 172–173)

The embedded lines from Macy Gray's 1999 hit song, "I Try," reveals a focus on popular song and culture in Higgins's work, shown here to have the same narcotic effect as drink (Gray, 1999). The closed poetry of its formulaic repetitions becomes the tranquilizing looping sound-track to the seeming inescapability of their lives, operating in much the same way as it does in "Work On," to prevent the critical thinking that would help them "walk away" from choking. In "Work On," the bore-dom of the factory is relieved by anticipation of the weekends' drink-ing and courting, and the soundtracks of the nightclubs are blared on the radios on the factory floor, keeping the women working there in a permanent "disco," and in a state of heightened romantic and sexual arousal, discursively centered around the ritual sucking of cigarette ends, so that they "work on" regardless of the indignities of the job that are hidden by the narrative of hope of romantic rescue by a "hero" with "acreage, physique" and a "car": "Two jived to the beat, two killed the smoke / And seven sank further into hand basins" (Higgins, 2005: 18). This poignant couplet, a vignette of a high-spirited stolen break, underscores how cruelly young women invest their hope in the romance that they are sold as a means of changing their life. Smoke is the real killer, not the girls who swat it away, and the use of "killed" in the past tense suggests the inevitable stillbirth of their dreams, where most will end in sink estates, unsalvaged by a "thousand Ranch House fantasies" over cigarettes in the factory toilet.

When desire is tied to reproduction in Higgins's poetry, it is most often linked to the reproduction of inequality and poverty and seem-ingly inescapable cycles of unmet needs. The heartbreaking poem "Mothercare" explores how desires function as capital for the child or teenage mother caught in chains of reproductive poverty. Mothercare is the well-known trademark of a chain of shops specializing in the para-phernalia of parenting, and the use of the compound brand name, rather than the phrasal "mother care" in the title, suggests that the poem's subject will be the commodification of reproduction and the reproduc-tion of commodification. The concatenation of desire and capital is explored when the emotional hunger that haunts this poem is revealed in displacement: when the terror of feeling the full force of helpless-ness is staved off by an overarching need for power, approval, and con-trol that is partially, but never completely met in the fetishization of the commodity—the status buggy, which has "underbelly things we hadn't seen" (Higgins, 2005: 117). Here, the "underbelly" revealed is not what is under or in a woman's belly, but what obscures a loving relationship to that belly and its children. The buggy is described in the coded terms of a sports car, a high-status signifier of speed, upward mobility, and totem in a culture in which social movement is improbable and in which ambitions for a life outside physical reproduction are short circuited. The poem directs us to the underclass status reinforced by such desire, a social reality that the young girls cannot see, for the underbelly delights that distract them from the revelation of their own cyclical and intergenerational relation to poverty are specifically phallic—specifically, in a lacanian sense about imagined display, pleasure, and power. The buggy visibly responds to touch:

> A little touch here
> And it collapses
> A little touch there
> And it's up like a shot
> You barely touch this—
> And you're in another street
> Another town.
>
> (Higgins, 2005: 117)

Although designed as transport for the baby, part of its powerful draw for the teenage mother is that it appears to have the power to convey her into another life, another street, another town, reaffirming what Adorno identifies as the infantilization at the heart of commodity culture, as the child–mother herself becomes the baby in the buggy highlighting her own need to be mothered and cared for.[5] Desire for this transporting buggy offers the mother the illusion of control in a life in which she has little or no control:

> A mind of its own
> A body like a rocket
> It's yours to control—
> Just like that.
>
> (Higgins, 2005: 117)

The overcompensatory veneration of the buggy/phallus is not mere social climbing, not simple vanity and self-aggrandizing, but a bid for psychic survival in the midst of her own helplessness in a culture in which single mothers are a social tabloid scourge. In this culture, Freud's formulation of femininity describes the operations whereby value is attributed to gender. He argues that a child is the means by which finally a woman "achieves" femininity, and thus, the buggy/ phallus also stands in for the child, providing the penis substitute that finally makes a woman feminine. The child–mother also makes the buggy her child, and the commodity comes to occupy the place of the baby, as it is cooed over and receives the pride, affection, and care that should be Tomma-Lee's: "the girls came over / to see the new buggy" (Higgins, 2005: 117). However, it is not the birth of a child, but of a son that finally fulfills this feminine destiny and thus, the child mother calls her daughter, "Tomma," a feminized version of the boy's name "Tommy," and to this affixes a hyphenated androgynous suffix— "Lee," which functions as a surname, or father's name where there is no father. Furthermore, Freud's essay also suggests that a woman must not only bear a male child, but she must also make her husband her child, and the buggy functions as the object that mediates the public world for her, and confers a visible status on her. In this way, the law of the father remains the means of identification for the child–mother who struggles to survive as one part of a half in a system that confers identity on her only through the mediation of the missing half—the father/husband. The over-devotion to the phallus/buggy is also a means of staving off what Luce Irigaray calls symbolic dereliction, for without identification with the phallus, she cannot feel herself exist. It mediates belonging to a symbolic system that threatens to exclude her on her own terms.[6] Here, a cycle of diverted love becomes evident, as the echoes of the child/ mother's own childhood resound in the early emotional emptiness she seeks to fill with the buggy, perpetuating a dislocation between herself and Tomma-Lee, as she touches the buggy but not her child, and mediates kinship through the commodity and not through her own kind.

It seems that the real enemy of intimacy in Higgins's work is not poverty, although the poems make clear how it generates powerlessness and fear that is detrimental to spiritual and psychic well-being; instead, the real impediment to closeness is the power of desire for the "thing." Higgins's work brings into focus the chasms between people who cannot touch as their bond is mediated through objects that serve to alienate both from the self and the other. Long before the Celtic Tiger roared its last, "Between Them" questioned the emotional soundness of a society that envisaged social renewal through material aspirations alone (2005: 83). It addressed a culture in which an abyss was placed between people by advertising, the "Berlin walls" of which are represented by the chasm between "two McInerney homes"—a reference to the most-desired object in Irish social economy in the late twentieth century and early twenty-first century, the self-owned house. This triumphalist symbol is necessarily the site of the phallic mother, the ideological habitus for the reproduction of patriarchal capital.

In "They Always Get Curried Chips," the semiotics of the kitchen extension are parsed with a strong sexual emphasis on risings and erections: "the extension means more than space / her status will rise in the estate." It "will take your eye out," so that the wrong eye can no longer guide, and instead the right eye will measure "every doodad": "they talk shape, they talk size / when it comes to it / size is everything" (Higgins, 2005: 156–157). In contrast, by refusing the investment of pleasure into estate, into size, the speaker in "The Did-You-Come-Yets of The Western World" brings a man and women into relationship in the folding of the "house" where ideologies cross. In this, the "privatised space" of the woman/house becomes open, but not "public." Higgins's work charts the edges of public and private spaces, negotiating the conflicts between a class-inflected political desire for an undoing of privatization, and a desire for safety and equal ownership of "public" spaces as a woman, in a culture in which a woman's body and sexuality are very often considered "public property." In "The Apprentices," a group of young men "perch / during factory lunchtimes / on their man-made Olympus," and from this panopticon, they pass hurtful and denigrating judgments on the women who have to pass by. The speaker asks, "who will attempt to pass / through their veil of lust unscathed / by Henry Leech-along's recital / of his nine favourite adjectives? (Higgins, 2005: 19) while the apprentices claim the street. In contrast, the women from the factory in "Work On" occupy a toilet to discuss acreage and intention. In "Space Invader," this relationship is reversed and the poet–speaker is on the street, while the man who harasses her "lived in a toilet" (Higgins, 2005: 85–86).

Higgins challenges the terms of poetic authority itself, and she recognizes that she too is the "space invader," invading the space of public poetic discourse. "Consumptive in the Library," in many ways her "manifesto poem" plots the coordinates for the materialist aesthetic that she would make her own. Whereas Seamus Heaney's "Digging" set out his poetic agenda as a journey into history, etymology, and the unconscious, collective, and individual, Higgins is diverted from this by the insistent interruptions of a consumptive homeless man:

> I started with Heaney,
> You started to cough.
> You coughed all the way to Ormsby,
> I was on the verge of Mahon.
> Daunted, I left you the Ulster Poets
> To consume or cough at.
> I moved to the medical section.
>
> (Higgins, 2005: 12)

The awful racket of an ill man without care persistently interrupts her earnest study of the poets whose writing about the Troubles formed a major part of Irish poetry at that time. In a space where silence is demanded so that people can read, Higgins listens. By following the coughing man's cues, she turns away from the notion of poetry as occurring between the pages of a book in a dedicated section of the library, and is taken on a different orphic journey by the homeless man who wears a St. Christopher's medal round his neck. The patron saint of journeyers directs her obliquely to the medical section, where the body is the object of enquiry and subject of learning, and thus she announces the body, not as a closed form, but as a political and social space as her subject: the conflicts and interlinks of desires, needs and wants of the poet and the homeless man in the public library come to stand for this interspatial aesthetic in which relationship has to be affirmed. She remains specifically situated at the interface of public and private, at text and sound, at body and utterance, and refuses an enclosed "room of her own."

Higgins's poetry exemplifies theory on the edge, writing from the threshold spaces between conflicted public and private spaces, between rasping sounds and fetishized text, negotiating the psychic, physical, and emotional needs for boundaries and safe spaces with lived knowledge of the inequities of an economic and political system derived from private enclosure. Unlike the subject of the poem "Prism," the "man / up our street" who "stuck broken glass / on top of his back wall / to keep out / those youngsters / who never stopped / teasing his / Doberman Pinscher" (Higgins, 2005: 129), Higgins's work does not function to keep anyone out, but invites them sit on the back wall with her, looking in all directions from this edge. Whereas he "watched the Castle Park sun / divide the light / and scatter it / all over his property" (Higgins, 2005: 129), a transcendent subject surveying his enclosed space, Higgins's prismatic refractions are not about illuminating meanings that are her poetic property, but about setting readers and meaning alike and unalike on edge.

NOTES

1. See Wills (1993).
2. "Aosdána pays an annual stipend to its members and the membership procedures and policies are explained by its own website thus: 'The Arts Council established Aosdána in 1981 to honour those artists whose work has made an outstanding contribution to the arts in Ireland, and to encourage and assist members in devoting their energies fully to their art. Membership of Aosdána, which is

by peer nomination and election, is limited to 250 living artists who have produced a distinguished body of work. Members must have been born in Ireland or have been resident here for five years, and must have produced a body of work that is original and creative. The current membership is 246" (http://aosdana.artscouncil.ie/).

3. Rahoon flats were tower blocks built on outskirts of Galway in 1971, as a low-cost housing project provided for people with lower incomes. They were notorious for a number of reasons, including being a dangerous place for children and a dumping ground for rubbish. They were demolished in 1998 and replaced by houses that were designed to be more family friendly and to provide more dignity and safety for those living there.

4. See Glass (2007) for a discussion of class and gender in "dirty" modernist words.

5. See O Connor (1990).

6. See Irigaray (1985).

References

Bracken, Claire (2007) "Partial Visions." *The Irish Review, Special Issue: Irish Feminisms*, 35: 165–167.

Clutterbuck, Catriona (2000) "Irish Women's Poetry and the Republic of Ireland: Formalism as Form," in Ray Ryan (ed.), *Writing in the Irish Republic: Literature, Culture, Politics 1949–1999.* Basingstoke: Macmillan, pp. 17–43.

Collins, Lucy (2003) " 'Performance and Dissent': Irish Poets in the Public Sphere," Matthew Campbell (ed.), *The Cambridge Companion to Contemporary Irish Poetry.* Cambridge: Cambridge University Press, pp. 209–228.

Crotty, Patrick (2001) "The Different Islands of Personal Verse." *The Irish Times*, June 23: 53.

Donovan, Katie (1996) "A Right Terror." *The Irish Times*, Thursday, November 7: 16.

Glass, Loren (2007) "#$%^&*!?: Modernism and Dirty Words." *Modernism/ Modernity*, 14 (2): 209–233.

Gray, Macy (1999) "I Try." EMI Publishing.

Higgins, Rita Ann (1986) *Goddess on the Mervue Bus.* Galway: Salmon Publishing.

———— (1988) *Witch in the Bushes.* Galway: Salmon Publishing.

———— (1990) *Goddess and Witch.* Galway: Salmon Publishing.

———— (1992) *Philomena's Revenge.* Galway: Salmon Publishing.

———— (1996) *Higher Purchase.* Galway: Salmon Publishing.

———— (1996) *Sunny Side Plucked: New and Selected Poems.* Glasgow: Bloodaxe Books.

———— (2001) *An Awful Racket.* Glasgow: Bloodaxe Books.

———— (2005) *Throw in the Vowels: New and Selected Poems.* Glasgow: Bloodaxe Books.

———— (2010) *Hurting God: Part Essay Part Rhyme.* Galway: Salmon Publishing.

———— (2011) *Ireland is Changing Mother.* Glasgow: Bloodaxe Books.

Irigaray, Luce (1985) *This Sex Which Is Not One.* Ithaca, NY: Cornell University Press.

McAnailly Burke, Molly (1990) "The Iron Fist." *Sunday Independent,* February 11: 20.

———— (1997) "Educating Rita." *Sunday Independent,* March 16: B36.

O Connor, Brian (1990) *The Adorno Reader.* Oxford: Blackwell.

Smyth, Ailbhe (2005) "A Reading from the Book of Beginnings." *Estudios Irlandeses: Journal of Irish Studies* (E-Journal), (1): 127–140.

———— (2007) "Momentary Views: A Personal History," Wanda Balzano and Moynagh Sullivan (eds), *The Irish Review, Special Issue: Irish Feminisms,* 35: 7–24.

Virilio, Paul (1989) *War and Cinema: The Logistics of Perception.* London: Verso.

Wallace, Arminta (2005) "Lovely Rita Metre Maid." *The Irish Times,* June 11: B16.

Wills, Clair (1993) *Improprieties: Politics and Sexuality in Northern Irish Poetry.* Oxford: Oxford University Press.

CHAPTER 11

Knowing the Landscape: Navigating the Language—Chinese Women's Experience of Arrival in Ireland

Edith Shillue

Consider a contrast of two Chinese women and their experiences of arrival in Ireland: one arrives as a professional, with significant cultural capital; another arrives as a refugee/immigrant. Each narrative yields distinct experiences of the same nation. Both stories reveal Ireland as a place wholly removed from its invented image.

It is well noted that Chinese women and men have migrated to Ireland since the 1950s, moving from Hong Kong's New Territories to Britain and then to Ireland/Northern Ireland. Early immigrants established businesses and settled largely in cities (Dublin, Belfast, and Cork). Later twentieth-century migrations were grounded in university recruitment and English-language school enrollments. By 2006, the overwhelming majority of Chinese people living on the island were those with high levels of education, working in a non-Chinese sector of the Irish labor market, and bringing a significant degree of cultural capital (O'Leary and Li, 2008: 3). However, the latest twenty-first-century migration sees an increase in people requesting humanitarian protection from Mainland China.

This chapter utilizes concepts in Michel de Certeau's essay *Spatial Stories* to challenge readers' understanding of women's movement *into* Ireland. de Certeau's focus on narrative and motion generates two definitions that help to clarify understanding of the different experiences of Chinese women in Ireland in the twentieth and twenty-first centuries. Consider the experience of women who move from "space" (China) to "place" (Ireland). As applied in this chapter, consider "space" as an arena in which familiarity and flexibility of action are defining, empowering characteristics, and "place" as an arena fixed in its categorizations, one in which one's actions are impotent without the intervention of a domestic or indigenous (read white) advocate. A scholar's experience is contrasted with the narrative elements of women who have been trafficked or smuggled into the island. The narratives or "spatial stories" contrast harshly with received ideas of nationalist cultural identity and reflect broader social problems with the historical concept of belonging in the Irish nation. Asylum-seeking and trafficked women volunteer their arrival narrative(s) in Mandarin in the safe environs of a nongovernmental organization for asylum seekers in Belfast. (All excerpts have been anonymized.)

ESTABLISHING THE BOUNDARIES: DEFINING THE CULTURE

In generating definition(s) of the Irish nation in the early twentieth century, Éamon deValera, famously referred to as Irish "maidens" at hearth side and "sturdy" children in active, stable homes.[1] Part of a broader movement defining the contours of Irish culture, de Valera's discourse consistently returned to images and institutions that centered on concepts of purity of race, religion, language, and sex. It was not uncommon for politicians or cultural activists to set out a framework to influence thinking about an independent Ireland. Set up largely as "anti-Britain," the cultural image was, nonetheless, grounded in concepts of racial purity and sectarianism. As Ireland sought to "fix" its image as a nation and "race," it delimited admission—managing exclusions according to a predefined formula. Cultural capital in Ireland of the early twentieth century was gained through ethnic and religious association, setting up a dualist framework of identification—one is either Irish, (not-British) or ethnic Irish (i.e., not Traveller and not Protestant). In implementation, Gellner's framework for nationalist movements applies: literacy and school-based ideological indoctrination reinforced concepts of the "Irish Nation." The resulting institutional and public discourse refuses admission based on highly specific categorizations of race and gender (Fanning, 2009: 13–16; Sisson, 2004: 22–24).

If, as de Certeau notes, "Every story is a travel story—a spatial practice," late twentieth-century Ireland, with its multiplicity of voices, makes for an interesting example of motion defining both "place" and "space." In de Certeau's definition, place and space are oppositional, the former inert, stabilized, and the latter fluid, dynamic, successively redefined by contexts. Space is, "in a sense actuated by the ensemble of movements deployed within it. Space occurs as the effect produced by the operations that orient it, situate it, temporalize it and make it function in a polyvalent unity of conflictual programs or contractual proximities" (de Certeau, 1984: 117). He refers to space as akin to the "word when it is spoken."

The radical shift James Joyce brought to literature in English was to make written text as fluid as spoken word, so that landscape too becomes fluid. Moving both character and reader through the streets of Dublin, Joyce's narration(s) in *Ulysses* puts readers into a position where inert "place" is transformed or redefined as "space" or "a practiced place." Stephen Daedalus, for example, moves through Dublin, thinking about the death of his mother and the city in which he lives in a multiplicity of languages—English, Latin, Greek, Italian, and Irish—and a multiplicity of historical contexts. Yet, Leopold Bloom, a European Jew, an Irish citizen, and an *Irishman* walks the same streets, and the languages and contexts are both different and deeply personal. Thus, Ireland, as place, wrestles with and suppresses its own diversity, generating a set of extremes for readers to consider—static melancholy or personal, dynamic, and fluid cityscape. "A nation," says European Leopold Bloom, "is the same people living in the same place" (Joyce, 1973: 329). Given the predominant outline of Irish "culture" generated by the nationalist movement, it is unsurprising that James Joyce wrote the novel in exile.

As a product marketed by the tourism industry, this moving and changing story is transformed into a stabilizing element. For the literary tourist, Dublin in the twentieth century is the pilgrimage *par excellence*—one in which each step (action) will be confirmed/ affirmed by a text-based sentence, which, in turn, recreates an early twentieth-century space. Step/action becomes enactment; the tourist's own step actuates building, doorstep, and pavement as a "Dublin," a "place" of June 16, 1904.

LITERARY ENVIRONS: THE SCHOLAR

In the 1980s, a migration of international students and professionals enhanced Ireland's image as an international player in what is known as the Knowledge Economy. Consider one narrative as initiated by an understanding of the English language and what James Joyce has done with it:

> She is identified as a scholar by her job, identified in Ireland as a "non-national", self-identified as a professional, an intellectual, with an expertise in the literature of James Joyce; her journey and arrival

are defined by responsibilities and opportunities. Ireland is a foreign place—not East Asia, not China, not her province, the city she lives in, nor her *laojia* (an inherited home town, an ancestral space)—in which she works or marries or acts as parent. In each of those places she is a woman first, with journeys to make inside a gender specific framework. In China, the words *Daughter, Wife, Mother, Grandmother* are primary forms of identification and enable her access to public and private space, her self-identification (intellectual and professional) has limited influence. At Dublin airport, one stamp (a visa)—a mere symbol—differentiates her from other Chinese, reversing the priority of identification—she is a *professional woman.* Initially merely a financial expense, the symbol quickly becomes her form of capital and release when she encounters government officials. She notices another woman, also from China, but wearing different clothing and carrying a different stamp, standing in a line opposite her at the airport. *She* is questioned and taken for interview.

On arrival at university in Ireland the scholar is told over and over how impressed people are by her command of English. The tone of the compliment makes her uneasy. She is patronized. This is a bitter reminder of some Englishman's comment that seeing a woman write is like seeing a dog dance—one is not concerned with the quality so much as being surprised she can do it at all. She comforts herself with Virginia Woolf: "as a woman I have no country, as a woman I want no country, as a woman my country is the whole world" (Woolf, 1992: 313).

For de Certeau, the most elementary travel story is the itinerary. It is a demarcation of space and a way of defining motion. Consider then the experience of the scholar as she examines a map delineating her new environment: She puts the university handbook down, like a tourist, and looks at the outline of the area in which she will live. She can walk easily from her dormitory room to anywhere. She uses her finger to follow along on the main street through the university and then marks the International Office with a red star and the library with a square. Lecture halls have a pink or yellow dot. She reads the names of streets, but moves through them with her senses first. Along her eye line as she walks is a church steeple; like an orchestra tuning, the noise of morning traffic rises to her ears and falls around her as she walks; her arms and legs relax more here, stiffen more there, as housing changes from family homes to hostels and dormitories. She can see the tower of the library and know there are only a few turns left, can hear the hum and creak of buses, and know the university gate is nearby. She walks knowing to keep the river to her right and remembers Joyce writing in *Ulysses*: "[Water]'s always flowing in a stream, never the same, which in the stream of life we trace. Because life is a stream" (Joyce, 1973: 153).

She was once told that when working in a foreign language in a foreign city, the "first day" or the day of "arrival" is only when words ring clear and full in your ears. When she walks the streets, she knows English is streaming all around her, but for the first month, the sound grates on her ears, like radio static, and sometimes a single recognizable word falls out, like a signal received just for a moment. "Appointment" or "meeting" sound clear, almost exactly as they did on her language study tapes. Every now and then, a man storms ahead of others, holding a phone earpiece up and making the same noise as a barking dog. A fat woman walks by and she is speaking softly, but crying. Two teenagers talk, but it is incomprehensible.

There are other sounds, as the weeks pass and she can hear more words, sputtering and flowing toward her ears. One day, as the library tower rises in the distance, she approaches the university relaxing into the warmth of a phrase overheard; a woman's voice rises up from a small garden: "Will you put the kettle on?"

Was that it? The moment everyone mentioned? Was this intimacy her arrival into the language of the landscape? Before she reaches any conclusion, she turns a corner by the park and passes a taxi stand: "Oh fuck, there's another chink now. They're everywhere." The words ring clearer than any other she's heard in Ireland and *this* is the moment of her arrival.

Escape, Hide, Escape, Hide: The Asylum Seeker

This same space—when experienced by the asylum seeker—has slammed doors and confusing languages (called "English" by all, but never sounding like English); it is a space in which a woman's perceptions and actions require fluidity, but her status is fixed at the margins.

For a Chinese woman asylum seeker, there is no central military conflict to identify as the source of her flight, and there are no refugee camps or other officials to record her journey. Frequently unmarried, she has been told to leave China with forms of coercion that start with family tension, then abandonment, both of which escalate into the economics of human trafficking. In this scenario, in China, a woman or girl cannot be identified as a wife or mother but is recognized for her capacity to work. Until the work environment is identified, she is a financial liability and a source of embarrassment.

After the work environment is found, she is an asset to be transported. Flight remains the only form of action in a situation so practically hopeless that it can only be described with the Chinese phrase "*mei banfa*"—no way, no choice. It is a verbal shrug of resignation, containing a marker (*mei*) for "never" or "none." The phrase is the cornerstone of Chinese bureaucratic culture and gender oppression. It may begin with a young girl's realization that there is no record of her birth, include a refusal to allow her access to education, and later, when she is a woman, threaten her with forced sterilization. As the itineraries and stories later reveal, the oppressive nature of relationships does not necessarily change outside China's boundaries. Working a system of agents, Chinese women simultaneously instigate migration and debt, generating narratives of moving through place after place in which a woman is indentured to an agent, and her family (if she has one) to bondage. Trucks, ships and containers, planes, cars, and multiple unknown addresses yield a limp, confusing form of "arrival" in a place that is simply "not China."

For the asylum seeker, there is no established itinerary, no mental map to reassure her of where she will land or how to navigate its landscape. Thus, rural Chinese women and girls are "taken" by snakeheads, told how and where to move by employers, and then categorized by border agencies, who have criminalized their movement entirely.[2] Unlike the scholar, the woman who has paid passage in a cargo container, or the back of a lorry, or has been secreted onto a plane as a "wife" or "daughter," can only describe her journey in terms of "following"—following an elder, following a snakehead, following an official—each successive place is a room in which she must wait until called to follow, again.

The itinerary and narrative of refugee women whose motion through borders, landscapes, and systems is governed by containment, is predicated on a concept of escape:

"They told me they could get me a good job. I have no birth certificate and cannot get education."

"I ran away when the police beat my brother to death."

"I was living on the street. He told me I would be reunited with my parents."

"My grandmother just gave me to the man. She said he would help me get a good life in the west. Sometimes I was in this city, but then I went to another city because he told me to."

"He put me in the bottom of a ship. I had to stay there for months."[3]

Understand What Is Meant by "the truth"

The discourse of the Irish and British states has already partitioned space and presupposed both knowledge and intent by women in motion across the globe. In criminal or immigration courts, the narrative of the escaping refugee is received using a discourse of containment. The requirement by border agencies for travelers to define and explain journeys calls for a "map"—a topical description of place and institutional affiliation. It is met with a toponym of experience—"the place we slept," not a house number or street name, not a city locale or border identification. "The plane we came on / the plane we moved to," not flight numbers or airport identification. "The person who brought me and gave me some papers"—nameless (but having authority).

The intimate and urgent nature of refugee travel itineraries undoes the government's presupposed narrative framework:

> "I was taken to a truck in the middle of the night. There were a lot of us gathered up."
>
> "We were in a city. Someone said it was Malaysia. I don't know where. We were in a room all day and could only go down the stairs and into the street at night."
>
> "The man told me to go into the room and wait until morning, then he put me in a car and left me at this street."
>
> "I lived in a room with six others. It was beside the restaurant and I was paid in food and accommodation and then a little bit of money."
>
> "They put me in a basement under a restaurant. When a man arrived that night he told me he had bought me. He said I belonged to him."
>
> "I sent the money back every month to the snakehead."
>
> "I didn't go out at night. It was too dark. I was afraid because the road was always so dark."

The truth value of stories, told in response to government inquiry, is found in the very inconsistencies that the state uses as evidence of dishonesty. A young girl's narrative *moves* like this:

> There were many of us gathered up and we went, I don't know where, then again to another place, I don't know where. My uncle told me to go and I followed the man he told me to. They changed the man in every new place.

Another:

> "They told me I would go here first, then there, we went to this place—[Malaysia,] then that place, [Cambodia]. I was in a truck and

the snakehead held all my papers. He told me how to do everything and took me to every place."

"The snakeheads told us we arrived, then they forced us to work in the clothing factory. Once I told them I thought my debt was paid, but they wouldn't let me go."

"They told me that I could only stay in the truck if I let them [rape] me. It happened with every new snakehead."

This, then, is the day-after-day trek of the transported woman or the trafficked girl. First: world "place"—Asia, Southeast Asia, Europe. Then, "the English speaking place"—Ireland, Dublin, Belfast, YourTown—each one having more specific, time-honored place-defining elements: North, West, and East sides of the city, The Police Station, The Post Office, Eccles Street, Cave Hill. As the journey continues, the only asset a woman has is a capacity to become *less and less* aware of specific elements in her environment. She is unable to define the countries, cities, and towns she has passed through because to identify them would be to identify those who took her.

Admission to Ireland as an asylum seeker begins with a series of questions requiring precise mapping:

"What day and time did you arrive?"
"What countries did you travel through before you arrived here?"
"Where did you claim asylum?"
"What is the reference number for your claim?"
"What is the legal basis for your application?"
"Do you know the name of the person who held your papers?"

Unlike the tableaux of bourgeois travel stories, the common element of asylum narratives is a lack of detail:

"There was a house, but I was only in one room."
"We were on a big street first, then a highway, then smaller streets again."
"I only went between the restaurant and the dormitory."
"I don't know the name of the town we were in. I cannot read and did not know the signs."

In the text of an immigration interview from 2009, one woman repeatedly answered "I don't know" to questions about itinerary, only to be told each time that if she did not tell "the truth," her application would be thrown out. Later, in a tribunal setting, she was asked to answer the question: "Do you understand what is meant by the words 'the truth'?" The fragmentary nature of a woman's traumatic experience—the bricolage—is thus found faulty or, in the language of immigration, "not credible."

Enclosed on one side by threat ("If you don't pay us back your parents will be killed") and the other side by enforcement ("You are a person subject to removal"), existence for a woman seeking asylum becomes a series of plans to move out of hiding into society, supplemented by methods for moving quickly back underground. Moving through city streets, she must be invisible but seeing. She can identify strictly defined work places (restaurants, takeaways, and homes in which she cares for children), places of assistance (charities, churches), and places of representation (solicitor firms, The Law Centre, The Irish Refugee Council). For this woman, the city streets are not embedded with the historical or literary echoes of cultural identity, but instead a rotation of threatening and nonthreatening, stable and unstable spaces, none of which has a framework to include her. Riddled as they are with "I don't know" and "I don't have," asylum narratives force listeners into a position of acceptance in spite of being unable to comprehend "the truth."

CREDIBILITY AND MEANING

When women's narratives of travel and arrival are held up next to the domestic, media, and governmental discourses on immigration, the government's use of the term "credible" is stretched well beyond its limits. In 2000, with Celtic Tiger economic development still roaring, property development growing and growing, international solidarity was jettisoned and the redefinition of support for refugee communities in Ireland came to the foreground. "Direct Provision"—a term suggesting efficiency and fairness—was put in place, signifying that nonnationals were not "in need" of welfare benefits in cash payment, but could be paid in goods and services. The resulting poverty and isolation yielded malnutrition, mental illness, and a yet-to-be-determined definition of the term "human being" as enshrined in the Irish constitution when applied to immigration law and the human rights and housing rights of asylum seekers (Breen, 2008: 634–636). The other "English speaking country," or Northern Ireland/United Kingdom, maintained its prohibition on employment for asylum seekers, enforced "no-choice" accommodation by confining people to Belfast but paid its support in cash. Trafficked women who came forward for help were given refuge but regularly told that they were "not credible."

In March 2004, The Republic of Ireland's Citizenship Referendum began a formal dismantling of Ireland's jus soli right to citizenship. The timing was predictable: An increase in immigrant family births meant an increase in "non-Irish" Irish citizens. "Baby tourism" (sic) had arrived and according to political and media discourse, there was "no diminution in the number of non-nationals arriving already heavily pregnant" (Fanning, 2009: 106). Maternity hospitals were stretched well beyond their limits and doctors were "pleading" with government officials to stem the tide of "baby tourists" (ibid.). The referendum discourse and public debate were not altered by rational evidence. Maternity service cuts from 2001 left vulnerable women in severe constraints, with refugee women suffering higher levels of post-natal malnutrition. Studies in 2003 (cited in Fanning, 2009: 107) had identified increased maternity service uptake in Dublin as the outcome of cuts in rural areas. The "non-nationals arriving already heavily pregnant" were dispersed refugees forced to use metropolitan services because they were the only ones available (Fanning, 2009: 107).

On the heels of this, the definition of being "Irish" began to unravel. In Cork, an ethnic Chinese Irish woman approached her constituency office and asked for help from her elected representative because she was being verbally abused on a daily basis. She was not Irish, people said. In the same office, a white mother of two came in looking for help because her adopted children were taunted at school. They were not Irish either. The false neutrality of the term "non-national" contained in the new government discourse left little room for doubt. Monocultural Ireland was unable to see itself in a framework of racial diversity.

Everything Changes: Everything Stays the Same

If in defining Ireland early in the twentieth century, de Valera looked inward, the century ended with a call from President Mary Robinson gently prodding Ireland to look outward: "We cannot have it both ways. We cannot want a complex present and still yearn for a simple past."[4] The Irish diaspora, she noted, was complex, "the people of Ireland" resisted any fixed or narrow definition. She said that she would "widen it still further to make it as broad and inclusive as possible." Such widening began with Robinson, and then contracted dramatically on her departure. Banks grew bigger; acceptance of human diversity grew smaller.

As banks and houses in Ireland grew bigger, the language of the tourism industry stayed fixed on a bourgeois travel narrative—staying with a simple, unimaginative notion of Ireland. Sentences by James

Joyce, in their sensual motion-filled richness remain tourism's gold, defining Ireland and Dublin for the wandering tourist. Once scorned and subject to a government ban, Joyce is now an iconic figure in both tourist literature and the academic knowledge economy of Ireland—a financial asset and a significant form of cultural capital.

Consider then the dislocating sense of movement for a tourist within a "Real Ireland" of mixed racial, linguistic, and income populations. As she makes her way to Sandycove and its Martello tower, she is less likely to hear Hiberno-English and more likely to hear Russian, Polish, or Spanish. Furthermore, she is likely to meet a Chinese woman who answers her with the rounded tones of Dublin 4. In the face of all reality, contemporary immigrant stories of arrival in Ireland are labeled "bogus" or "not credible" by government officials whose own discourse is more honestly expressed by Joyce's character Anna Livia Plurabelle in the wordplay known as *Finnegan's Wake*: "Can't hear with the waters of. The chittering waters of. Flittering bats, fieldmice bawk talk. Ho! Are you not gone ahome?" (Joyce, 1975: 215).

Notes

1. On March 17, 1943, de Valera gave a speech on RTE radio in celebration of The Gaelic League. It is commonly known as "The Ireland that We Dreamed of" and lays out an idealized vision of Ireland. Households he described as containing "the laughter of happy maidens, whose firesides would be forums for the wisdom of serene old age."

2. Under Northern Ireland/UK regulations, women asylum seekers residing in the north of Ireland are required to report to the police weekly, disallowed from leaving accomodation for more than one night (emergency accomodation) or seven nights (long-term accommodation). In the cases of pregnancy, women are allowed to suspend reporting only on request and only in advanced states of pregnancy.

3. Statements by Chinese women were collected from interviews and conversations in a refuge environment in Belfast during the years 2009–2012.

4. Address by Uachtarán na hÉireann Mary Robinson to Joint Sitting of the Houses of the Oireachtas, February 2, 1995. Available at www.oireachtas.ie

References

Breen, Claire (2008) "The Policy of Direct Provision in Ireland: A Violation of Asylum Seekers' Right to an Adequate Standard of Housing." *International Journal of Refugee Law*, 20 (4): 611–636.

de Certeau, Michel (1984) *The Practice of Everyday Life*, *trans.* S. Rendall. Berkeley, CA: University of California Press.

Fanning, Bryan (2009) *New Guests of the Irish Nation*. Dublin: Irish Academic Press.

Gellner, Ernest (1983) *Nations and Nationalism*. Oxford: Blackwell.

Joyce, James (1973) *Ulysses*. Harmondsworth: Penguin Books.

——— (1975) *Finnegans Wake*. London: Faber and Faber.

O'Leary, Richard and Li, Lan (2008) *Mainland Chinese Students and Immigrants in Ireland and Their Engagement with Christianity, Churches and Irish Society*. Dublin: Agrophon Press.

Sisson, Elaine (2004) *Pearse's Patriots: St. Enda's and the Cult of Boyhood*. Cork: Cork University Press.

Woolf, Virginia (1992) *A Room of One's Own and Three Guineas*. Oxford: Oxford University Press.

CHAPTER 12

Enjoying Substance: Psychoanalysis, Literature, and Joyce's Writing of Women

Olga Cox Cameron

Introductory Remarks

This title, perhaps rather disingenuously, compresses three quite different topics into a single space. Psychoanalysis with its perennial interest in sexuality and its not always felicitous preoccupation with literature is itself the point of linkage. It can scarcely be denied—as both theory and practice—that psychoanalysis has occupied a marginal position in Irish intellectual life since its introduction in the 1920s, and is therefore perhaps something of an intruder in a volume focused on an important figure on the literary and feminist stage over the past 40 years. In my own view, the jury is still very much out with respect to the relevance of psychoanalytic theory to literary studies. What follows therefore is by no means an apologia, but rather an experimental exploration of an exciting body of theory on the outer edges of Irish life but relevant for exactly that reason in a collection focusing on these edges. With this caveat in mind, therefore, the chapter that follows is an attempt to engage with literature from the angle of a particular psychoanalytic concept, that of the o-object or object cause of desire, introduced by the French psychoanalyst Jacques Lacan. Despite the notorious difficulty of his own written style, Lacan, via this concept, comes closer to engaging with the lure, the pleasure, the disabling "hit" of great literature than previous banalizing and reductive psychoanalytic paradigms, which have often been rightly criticized.

"Before the problem of the creative artist analysis alas must lay down its arms." So said Freud in 1928 (177), using a curiously agonistic metaphor to describe the relation between these two disciplines, and, furthermore, situating psychoanalysis in a position of regretful defeat. Why would psychoanalysis be in need of arms? In his book *Freud, Proust and Lacan: Theory as Fiction*, Malcolm Bowie, with amused irony, points out that two of Freud's preferred self-images were those of conquistador and archaeologist, invoking one of Freud's own dreams to show how frequently he privileged the first over the second (27). Many observers of the history of psychoanalysis might well detect in it a certain conquistadorial ambition, which, with dismaying frequency, has resulted in a banalizing reduction of great works of art to a small number of overused paradigms such as the Oedipus complex. Indeed, some of Freud's own writings are not completely exempt in this regard. Notwithstanding this unfortunate tendency, writers and artists in very great numbers have been generous and hospitable in their attitude to psychoanalysis, largely concurring with the views expressed by Thomas Mann on the occasion of Freud's eightieth birthday: "even should the future remould and modify one or other of his researches, never again will the questions be stilled which Sigmund Freud put to mankind; his gains for knowledge cannot be permanently denied or obscured. The conceptions he built, the words he chose for them, have already entered the living language and are taken for granted. In all spheres of humane science, in the study of literature and art, in the evolution of religion and prehistory, mythology and folklore, and pedagogics, and not least in poetry itself, his achievement has left a deep mark" (Jones, 1957: 220), sentiments echoed and amplified in W. H. Auden's later poem:

> If often he was wrong and at times absurd,
> To us he is no more a person
> Now but a whole climate of opinion
> Under whom we conduct our differing lives.
>
> (1991: 275)

These impressive and even moving tributes sidestep the question of Freud's conquistadorial defeat, focusing as they do on the contribution of psychoanalysis to human life at large rather than the specificity of how psychoanalysis can engage with literature. Disappointingly? Derrida and Lacan certainly both thought so. Freud backed off from the crucial questions—what is literature? How does writing become art?—admitting that "the nature of artistic achievement is

inaccessible to us psychoanalytically...psychoanalysis can do nothing towards elucidating the nature of the artistic gift, nor can it
explain the means by which the artist works—artistic technique"
(Jones, 1957: 444); and it is possible that this reticence has resulted
in what Derrida in "Freud and the Scene of Writing" has called the
failure of psychoanalysis to address the literary signifier. He writes:
"Despite several attempts by Freud and certain of his successors, a
psychoanalysis of literature respectful of the originality of the literary signifier has not begun and that is no doubt not an accident.
This failure takes the form of a retreat from an analysis of the literary signifier into that of the literary signified" (Derrida, 1967: 230).
This is indeed a hard-hitting observation, but in fairness, other commentators, notably Andrei Warminski, recognize that this repressive
gesture extends well beyond psychoanalysis and to a very great extent
specifies most writing about literature. Writing in *Yale French Studies*
nearly 20 years ago, Warminski accuses literary criticism of this same
tendency to retreat from the literary signifier in favor of the signified
"as though now that we know what language, text, rhetoric etc. are
we can go back to the serious business (as usual) of teaching texts
as sources and repositiories of knowledge and value—useful historical knowledge, and instructive ethical religious and aesthetic value,"
conveniently forgetting that "what happens in literature is a text, and
only a text happens" (264). In the seminar *Encore*, in which he speaks
of the signifier as enjoying substance, Lacan offers a not dissimilar
caveat to his audience in the typically mantric sentence: "the fact that
one says remains forgotten behind what is said in what is heard" (15).
The prevalence of this elision and the resistance to countermanding it
might alert us to the possibility that what is at work here is a constitutive impasse, analogous if not identical to what psychoanalysis calls
repression.

Lacan's contribution to literary studies is not easy to summarize.
Derrida has accused him of illustrative or paradigmatic readings of
literary texts, but it is fairer to suggest that he occasionally used literature to think about some of the questions that confront psychoanalysis. During the late 1950s and early 1960s, for four consecutive years,
his teaching seminar focused on a number of great literary works,
among them *Hamlet* and *Antigone*, but immediately following these,
he turned to other forms of writing, notably topology, mathematics,
and knot theory to make incursions into the fall-out of the Freudian
discovery, a fall-out that he claimed—with some justification—has
too often been tamped down into platitude. As a result of this dar-
ing project, the later seminars become progressively less readable.

In the early years, the foregrounding of language was constant but referenced to Saussurean linguistics. By the 1970s and at much the same time as this shift occurred for the literary critic Roland Barthes, Lacan had begun to signal the inadequacy of linguistics to deal with an essential aspect of language unamenable to structuralist theorization, a kind of constitutive excess that he on occasion called the remainder, associating it with jouissance, and thereafter repeatedly insisted on the distinction between language as instrumental and language as carrier of jouissance. During these years too, he had begun to elaborate what is certainly one of his most innovative concepts, that of the o-object, which has the closest possible links to an understanding of what is involved in jouissance. I do not know if Barthes attended Lacan's seminar or not, but it is striking that at the exact same moment, both men signal the inadequacy of linguistics in their respective fields, literature and psychoanalysis, specifically because of its inability to deal with jouissance and with *'signifiance'*, which Barthes defines as meaning insofar as it is produced sensually. Later writers, notably Jean Jacques Lecercle, have no hesitation in naming this outside of linguistics as the remainder, which is also one of the terms by which Lacan designated the o-object.

It is regrettably impossible to speak of Lacan's thinking throughout the 1960s and 1970s without reference to these two central, rather jargonistic terms, the o-object and jouissance, the second of which at least will be familiar to literary readers via the work of Roland Barthes. Contrary to dictionary definitions, the word jouissance does not equate to the Anglophone concept of enjoyment with its jovial, expansive, glass of wine on a summer's day kind of feel. What is in question in jouissance is a good deal less comfortable, although as Roland Barthes wrote in *Le Plaisir du Texte* what is actually needed is another word altogether, even in French, since as he says there is no word which captures both pleasure/contentment and jouissance/loss of one's bearings/fainting (*évanouissement*). To further complicate matters, these two conditions sometimes are in congruence with, sometimes in opposition to each other. As divided subjects, we oscillate between the pleasure of experiencing the consistency of the self and the pleasure of having that consistency shattered. Barthes draws a distinction in the field of literature between what he calls *textes de plaisir* and *textes de jouissance*. There is a certain type of work—often very great literature, and he includes Proust here—which is comfortable, perhaps even reassuring, inspiring a heightened sense of well-being. This type of literature he terms *textes de plaisir*, pleasure texts. Opposed to these are textes de jouissance—literature which puts us into a state of loss, discomforts us even to the extent of a certain boredom, "rocks the reader's historical, cultural and psychological foundations as well as the consistency of his tastes, values and even memories, and brings about a crisis in his relation to language" (25). Readers of *Finnegans Wake*—or for that matter some of the later Lacan—will recognize this experience. Elsewhere, Barthes describes this jouissance as opening the reader onto an immense subjective loss.

Yet, these moments are sought after, these infractions into what Beckett, writing on Proust, called "that most necessary, wholesome, and monotonous of plagiarisms, the plagiarism of oneself" (1965: 21) in order that, for a moment, "dangerous, precarious, painful myste-rious and fertile, the boredom of living is replaced by the suffering of being" (19). Writing originally in 1931, Beckett does not use the term jouissance, but anticipates much of Lacan's later thought in link-ing this experience with a dismantling of everyday identity:

> The old ego dies hard. Such as it was, a minister of dullness, it was also an agent of security. When it ceases to perform that second function, when it is opposed by a phenomenon that it cannot reduce to the condi-tion of a comfortable and familiar concept, when in a word, it betrays its trust as a screen to spare its victim the spectacle of reality, it disap-pears, and the victim, now an ex-victim, is exposed to that reality—an exposure that has its advantages and its disadvantages. (21)

Both Lacan and Beckett were readers of Bataille, Breton, and the Surrealists in general, who were in turn openly indebted to Freud; so there is as always a kind of circularity of influence here.

In his 1914 paper "On Narcissism," Freud had referred to theories on the earliest moments of subjectivity as "nebulous, scarcely imag-ined concepts" (77), and although there are numerous and deeply interesting references to this earliest pre-subjective phase of exis-tence throughout his work, notably in "Screen Memories," "A Child is being Beaten," and "Negation," these insights are scattered and somewhat episodic. In 1959, Lacan began to expand these elements of Freud's thought via a concept that he called the o-object, or object cause of desire. Over the several years of his seminar, this o-object undergoes accretions and sheddings of meaning that render compre-hensive summary impossible. In order then to avoid the pitfalls of attempted comprehensiveness, this chapter, insofar as it engages with the Lacanian concept of the o-object, will do so in the context of the central question of the literary signifier as enjoying substance (*sub-stance jouissante*).[1]

The beginning was relatively simple. When Lacan introduced the concept of the o-object, he did so via the work of Melanie Klein. In a lecture given on February 11, 1959, he speaks of Klein's emphasis on a whole series of first relationships that are established between the baby and the body of the mother (8). These relationships are theorized by Klein under the term part-objects, and by Lacan as pre-narcissistic surges that eventually become locked to elective "objects" characterized by their intermediate status. These are entities that effect both connection and rupture, belonging neither to the pre-subjective being, which is the baby, nor to the mother. As both Klein and Winnicott had already established, the breast has a privileged function in this regard, since even at a biological level, the mother needs to feed as urgently as the baby needs to be fed. For the small pre-subjective infant, the dramas of connection and rupture that ensue around these "objects" are very easily imbued with the threat of annihilation attendant upon rupture, since this small being has as yet no "I" to even begin to own or circumscribe the untrammelled surges of distress, or sometimes pleasure, attendant on these dramas. As Freud had pointed out in *Project for a Scientific Psychology*, "the very first traumas of all escape the ego entirely" (1895: 359). Parents of newborn babies, if not too harassed by newness themselves can hear when the unmitigated catastrophic earliest distress begins to modulate into something like a focused demand, when there begins to be "someone" who wants "something" rather than a kind of undifferentiated cataclysm. Indeed, it is precisely the distinction between subject and object that is lacking in this crucial pre-narcissistic existence. Lacan lists the so-called objects that most readily lend themselves to these dramas as the breast, the shit, the voice, the nothing, without indicating that this list is necessarily exhaustive, but what is actually in question is more the turbulent emotion locked to certain elective objects than the object itself. Lacan says as much in the lecture of January 9, 1963, in the Seminar on Anxiety: "to designate the little o (*sic*) by the term object is a metaphorical usage, since it is borrowed precisely from the subject-object relationship from which the term object is constituted, but this object of which we speak under the term o-object is precisely outside any possible definition of objectivity" (12). Furthermore, what is in question is not something that could be an object *of* desire, but rather that which functions as cause, as the specific tonality of *how* we desire, of what constitutes our desiringness.

At this pre-subjective stage, as Lacan says, that which will eventually appear in a transmuted form as specular image, and as ego, is there in a sense, but scattered in what he calls a disorder without image, a jumble of intensities of which there is as yet no question of having or not having, because this is not a question which presents itself at the pre-subjective level. We may say of this jumble, as Freud suggests, that in a certain sense, it has never had a real existence: "it is never remembered, it has never succeeded in becoming conscious" (1919: 180). It does not have specific properties: "(n)ot clearly sexual, not in itself sadistic, but yet the stuff from which both will later come" (182). On numerous occasions, Lacan signals the extreme difficulty of approaching this primordial moment in identification, which because it does not fall within the ambit of the vocabulary of representation, resists critical thought. Indeed, the difficulty is palpable in the various names he gives to this moment. In the Seminar on "Identification," it is a whirlwind point through which the object emerges from a beyond of the imaginary knot. Elsewhere, it is the panic point or the storm point. In the topological seminars, it is "the circle of retrogression." Other writers, notably Barthes and Kristeva, writing on the same topic, use the term "chiasmus" to designate this locus where an eventual inversion is called for within the living texture of the pre-subjective being in order to make of him or her a desiring subject.

The subsequent processes by which the small pre-subject accedes to subjectivity, theorized variously, all involve a renunciation of those earliest unowned intensities, a cutting into polymorphousness to create acceptably shaped forms of human desiringness. The contours of the specular image are profiled by means of a corresponding occultation of being, which marks the inauguration of the unconscious, and all knowledge thereafter will be conditioned by this occultation. Using a more classic psychoanalytic vocabulary, this would seem to suggest that the birth of the narcissistic ego corresponds to the coming into being of primal repression, and that thereafter, all our seeing will be marked by this constitutive blind spot. Correlative with the field of the specular as Lacan says: "there is also a whole field where we know nothing about what constitutes us as field" (Seminar on "Anxiety," 12/09/62: 5). The *Selbstbewusstein*, or conscious self, is therefore, necessarily, an indispensable illusion. Furthermore, the processes by which this conscious self emerges are never entirely successful and involve residues, remainders, hence Lacan's use of this term to designate the o-object. It is these remainders that in turn specify the most private incommunicable enjoyment of the subject, charging him or her with the hidden voltage of that which is occluded, an always unique voltage conditioning the world that the subject inhabits, along with its varying proximities and distances, its neutral zones, and its electric privacies.

In the Seminar on "Identification," 1961–1962, Lacan referred to the o-object as that which must be renounced in order that the world as world should be delivered to us (27/06/62.7). It is "*being* insofar as it is missing from the text of the world." The so-called real world that we inhabit, in particular the climate created by the ameliorative philosophies of humanism and the Enlightenment, are constructed to occlude it, to offer us accessible stabilities and happy endings in its place. Yet, repressed and invisible as it is in everyday ongoingness, "nothing has any veritable weight in the world" Lacan says, "except something which alludes to this object of which the big Other (the world as world) takes the place to give it a meaning" (Seminar on "Identification" 27/06/62: 9). However, if there is any truth in Lacan's statement, then clearly, allusions to this object which disturbs the order of things must be a pretty frequent occurrence.

The return of the repressed undoes the contours of both the self and the world as we know it. As the artist Bracha Ettinger puts it, it is as if the subject and this o-object are like the front and back of the same piece of fabric, the recto and verso of the same sheet of paper. "When the subject appears (as in everyday life) the o-object disappears, and when the o-object finds a way to penetrate to the other side … signifying meaning (symbolic and imaginary, exchangeable through discourse) disappears and goes into hiding" (2006: 41). In the Seminar on "Identification," Lacan says much the same thing when he observes that the emergence of the o-object in the phantasy is correlative to a fading or vanishing of the symbolic, of the normal supports that maintain self and world in position (9/5/62: 4)—which sounds not dissimilar to the subjective dismantling, the infraction that Barthes calls *jouissance de texte.*

Anxiety marks one of the places where this threat to ongoingness can occur, and in his 1963 Seminar on "Anxiety," Lacan opined that anxiety is perhaps the only subjective expression of the o-object. I would like to suggest, however, that in later seminars, and even the earlier one on "Identification," there is a case to be made for including the work of art, and by extension the literary signifier, as a privileged mode of access to this o-object. Indeed in his 1969 seminar "From an other to the Other," in a passing remark that he regrettably leaves undeveloped, Lacan is quite explicit when he describes the o-object as that which makes up the essential merit of what we call the work of art (12/03/69). Bracha Ettinger suggests that this is because the work of art is one of the very few places where this o-object finds a way to "appear" or at least to be perceptible, displacing the big Other and as a result causing a temporary fade out of the subject, since as Lacan put it in the seminar *RSI (Real, Symbolic, Imaginary)* : "the condition of the subject, the supposed subject, is to be only supposable, only knowing something by being himself qua subject, caused by an object which is not what he knows, what he imagines he knows, namely which is not the Other of knowing as such, but that on the contrary, this object, the small o-object removes this Other" (21/1/75). When this renounced o-object, which is the underside of the symbolic subject, does break through, it does so, Lacan says in this seminar, not as lack but as a "to be," thus recalling his earlier definition of it as "being insofar as it is essentially missing from the text of the world." The notion of the o-object breaking through not as lack but as a "to be" (what John Banville speaks of somewhere as a disturbing excess of self) links to Lacan's remark in *Encore* that to dwell on the verb to be is a highly risky enterprise (31). Are we to call this being which breaks through "I" or, as Beckett would put it, "Not I"? Both, perhaps, according to Wallace Stevens:

> I know that timid breathing. Where
> Do I begin and end? And where,
> As I strum the thing, do I pick up
> That which momentously declares
> Itself not to be I and yet
> Must be. It could be nothing else. (2006: 149)

The seminar *Encore*, in which Lacan introduces the idea of the signifier as enjoying substance, is one of a series of seminars where he is searching for a very particular writing capable of saying or at least indicating the contours of the o-object, a writing that, it seems, will have to be either mathematical or topological, devised at least in part to rip us away from the imaginary (43).[2] In *RSI* when he describes the subject as "caused by an object which can be noted only by a writing" (21/01/75: 8), he at first seems to be looking to the borromean knot[3] rather than language, since as he says, the effect of language is *pathein*, "the passion of the body." But then, and in the context rather surprisingly, he adds: "But from language there is inscribable this radical abstraction which is the object that I designate, that I write with the figure of writing o and about which nothing is thinkable except for the fact that everything that is subject is determined by it" (ibid.). In *Encore*, in the midst of a disquisition on the letter in algebra and set theory, and how this might relate to analytic discourse, Lacan suddenly urges his listeners to read Joyce in order to see how language is perfected when it knows how to play with writing (36). Furthermore, he announces, without reference to obvious echoes of Heidegger, that his stated project is to redeem the verb "to be" from its tamed auxiliary role as copula, opposing to traditional concepts of being—in other words, those supported by the philosophical tradition—the very different, and at first glance unrelated notion that we are duped by jouissance: "Behind the One of the signifier is a gap between it and something that is related to being, and behind being to *jouissance*" (6).

One could of course say that this is true of every signifier, its oneness is always permeable to jouissance, most manifestly in the joke, as Freud knew, but also in the susceptibility of even the most sedate of discourses to being fissured by impropriety. Conversing recently with other middle-aged ladies on the harmless topic of rose growing, I had the pleasure of hearing one of the said ladies describe the English rose "Lady Illingdon" as "good in a bed but much better up against the wall." As *Finnegans Wake* puts it, even syntax can become "sin talks" (269.3). And if the signifier in general can be situated at the level of enjoying substance, is there something more to be said about being and jouissance in the context of literature and the literary signifier?

The literary signifier, in the words of Maurice Blanchot, "never exists in the manner of ordinary objects or beings" (1982: 115). In Beckett's haughty phrase "it is not about something; it *is* that something," (1929: 28) an assertion both perceptible and occluded in the resonant verb that inaugurates Western literature: *Sing*. In the opening line of the *Odyssey*, it is an injunction: "Sing o Muse"; in that of the *Aeneid*, a declarative fling: "I sing of arms and the man"; in both, a gestural sleight of hand and a lure, masking the fact that it is itself that which it purports to recount, since that which is sung exists only in the singing. The American critic George Steiner speaks of the compelling needlessness of art, situating it at the exact synapse where being at its most vivid asserts itself on the knife edge of nothingness. The work of art, of poetics, carries within it "the scandal of its hazard, the perception of its ontological caprice" (2001: 29). Lacan in his later writings makes the same point via a pun on the word literature, combining as it does the words *litera*, letter, with *rature*, erasure. In grappling with these concepts in the Seminar on "Identification," he makes no claim to originality, telling his listeners that he is leading them along paths which are those of aesthetics and referring them in fact to the work of Maurice Blanchot, probably one of the greatest literary critics of our time, calling him "the poet of our literature," "*le chanteur de nos lettres.*" In one of his many essays on Mallarmé, Blanchot employs not dissimilar terms when speaking of literary language:

> If language isolates itself from man, as it isolates man from everything, if it is never the act of someone who is speaking in the presence of someone who hears him, we come to understand that to one who contemplates it in this state of solitude, it offers the spectacle of a singular and completely magical power. It is a kind of awareness without subject, that separated from being, is detachment, questioning, infinite ability to create emptiness and to place itself within loss. (1995: 42)

He goes on to point out how, "reduced to the material form of words, their sonority, their life, it gives us to believe that this reality opens up who knows what path to us into the obscure heart of things" and ends with the arrestingly lucid observation: "Perhaps that is an imposture. But perhaps that trickery is the truth of every written thing" (ibid.).

Notwithstanding his admiration for Blanchot, Lacan experimented for a number of years with the writings of topology, mathematics, and knot theory. The switch from literary to other writings is dramatic, occurring as it does in the break between Seminar 8, mostly based on Plato's *Symposium* and Claudel's tragic trilogy, *The Hostage, Stale Bread and The Humiliated Father* and Seminar 9 where the topological writing of the Moebius strip—mentioned before more or less in passing—becomes a central, even an integral, element in his theorization of subjectivity. However, in Seminars 6, 7, and 8, delivered in the late 1950s and given over to great literary texts, Lacan clearly favored tragic form as a mode of access to a jouissance that falls outside the ambit of representation. In Seminar 7, *The Ethics of Psychoanalysis*, during his lengthy discussion of Sophocles' *Antigone*, he suggests that tragedy as an art form functions in a manner analogous to that of anamorphosis in the painting and architecture of the seventeenth and eighteenth centuries. One will not find an image as such on the surface of the cylindrical *objets d'art*, which were fabricated on the principles of anamorphosis. What occurs rather is that the superimposition of fragmentary images creates a series of layered screens out of which, viewed from a given angle, a certain form that was not visible at first sight transforms itself into a readable image. It is the whirl of the cylinder or the backward glance of the departing viewer that momentarily flashes forth an image which is not represented in the actual image that is the painting itself. In a similar manner, tragedy is a form that can render perceptible a point in the coming into being of the subject on the very edges of representability. The subject at this point is unfounded, unsupported, and stripped of the trappings of quotidian identity. This is clearly visible in *Antigone*, perhaps even more so in *Oedipus Rex*, where the king, solidly established in family and kingdom at the beginning of the action, is gradually unmoored from all supports until he stands finally, stripped and solitary, in the pitiless glare of universal abhorrence. As George Lukacs put it in a celebrated article written in 1910:

> Naked souls conduct a dialogue here with naked destinies. Both have been stripped of everything that is not of their innermost essence; all the relationships of life have been suppressed so that the relationship with destiny may be created; everything atmospheric between men and objects has vanished...Tragedy...begins at the moment when enigmatic forces have distilled the essence from a man, have forced him to become essential. (1974: 155)

Tragedy offers access to one version of the subjective loss, which, Barthes suggests, specifies jouissance. Lacan in these literary years also foregrounded the work of Sade in this respect, "in the sense that it achieves an absolute of the unbearable in what can be expressed in words relative to the transgression of all human limits," and he describes the experience of reading, or probably even Sade's act of writing, as "the approach to a center of incandescence or an absolute zero that is physically unbearable" (1992: 200–201). However, these limit moments do not constitute the only access to self-shattering jouissance as of course all those who head out on a weekend night to get "smashed," to get "off their faces" know only too well. We know it too when we "crack up" with laughter. Interestingly, the only art form that stands on an equal footing with tragedy is according to the great philosopher of culture, Mikhael Bakhtin, the carnivalesque. "Tragedy and laughter equally fearlessly look being in the eye, they do not construct any illusions, they are sober and exacting" (cited in Eagleton, 2003: 185).

In the Seminar on "Identification," Lacan suggests that "there is at the heart of the o-object this central point, this whirlwind point through which the object emerges in the beyond of the imaginary knot" (23/05/62, 10–11). For those of us in love with literature, we are left with the perennial question. How does this happen? What is the constitution of the imaginary knot that permits this emergence? Dense and multi-textured as in Henry James, stripped to bareness as in Beckett, blazing from within the shards of subjective ruin as in the late mad poems of Holderlin? It would appear from the tendency to avoid this question targeted by Derrida and Warminski at the beginning of this chapter, that this emergence, this breakthrough while perceptible, even disabling for the reader, can never be entirely amenable to the appropriative gestures of commentary or criticism, although paradoxically its effects are frequently mediated precisely through these appropriative gestures of attempted mastery. In spite of this limitation, however, once the artwork is there, as Bracha Ettinger writes, "it casts some of its shadow on the cultural field, entices it, impels it to expand its frontiers and to absorb some of its traces." It even gives rise to concepts. This, however, is not necessarily a bad thing "since once you turn back to the artwork with the concepts aroused by it, it further transforms and works to seduce you from another site" (118).

And that takes us over the threshold of the final question for this chapter: How does Joyce write women?

So how *does* Joyce write women? More specifically, how does he write women in the dream that is *Finnegans Wake*? Feminist literary critics are divided in their response to this question, with some seeing it as a writing ensconced in patriarchal sexism and others—noting that in both *Ulysses* and *Finnegans Wake*, the last section is entirely given over to the word of a woman—seeing in it a writing that gestures to a beyond of the phallic economy. In the book to which Freud refers as the first dream book (1900: 98), that of Artemidorus of Daldis, a writing tablet in dreams signifies a woman since it receives the imprint of all kinds of letters. And indeed, in some ways, *Finnegans Wake*, which describes itself as a mythomatical work, does write women in all kinds of letters. I propose here to focus on the final section of *Finnegans Wake* where a letter that has periodically emerged and been submerged throughout the text reappears. This letter has apparently been written by Anna Livia herself though in some earlier versions, her sons Shem the Penman and Shaun the Post have collaborated in its composition. Its final version at the end of the book modulates into the spoken word of Anna Livia, who having been spoken of throughout the book—"o tell me all about Anna Livia I want to hear all"—now for the first time speaks herself. The lure of teleological thinking might tempt us to see in this last version something more definitive than previous versions, but the letter itself remains unambiguously ambiguous even with respect to its provenance: "Well here's lettering you erroneously" (617), thus retaining its status of error and anonymity. It is still a comedy of letters (424) or the last word in stolentelling as the *Wake* elsewhere calls it (425), which is also a writing of the sexual relation which it seems (contra Lacan) *can* be written but only so long as the woman pretends. Within a world where, as Walter Benjamin put it, "the ideas of those in power have always been the mirror thanks to which the picture of a certain order comes about" (cited in Warner, 1985: 1), what *Finnegans Wake* calls the feminine fiction stranger than the facts is largely a product of masculine fantasy. Furthermore, Joyce plays on the double meaning of letters as characters in the alphabet so that the *Wake*'s characters are also letters like HCE and ALP and the letters in turn speak a character in the sense referred to by Theodor Adorno when he wrote in 1945 that the feminine character, and the ideal of femininity on which it is modeled, are products of masculine society (1978: 95).

To some extent, both Anna Livia and Molly Bloom buy into this fiction. Anna Livia describes herself as a princeable girl (626), her identity predicated on the notion that the principal event in a woman's life is the advent of her prince, prince Charming of course. Recalling the dumb submission of an early seduction under the willing heel of her lover "I wisht I wast be that dumb tyke and he'd wish it was me yonther heel" (617), she goes on to call it "the sweetest song in the world," a sentiment endorsed by Molly Bloom's addiction to romantic intrigue and erotic reverie: "true or no it fills up your whole day and life always something to think about every moment and see it all around you like a new world" (899). It is as if in buying into this masculinist fantasy, even blindfolded—"I'll close my eyes so as not to see," says Anna—that women find their greatest happiness.

But the phallus is that which fails. Finn is sleeping under the hill of Howth. Jarl von Hoother is locked up in the castle of phallic self-sufficiency—Howth castle as it happens—"laying cold hands on himself" or "shaking warm hands with himself" in solipsistic phallic jouissance, and Earwicker, the Chapelizod publican can get it up but can't get it off, can stand but not deliver. Nonetheless, the writing is never more lyrical than when Anna Livia evokes this reluctant phallus, calling it into being as pride, turgidity, and beauty: "Rise up man of the hooths you have slept so long...And stand up tall. Straight. I want to see you looking fine for me" (619–620), amplifying this call with swashbuckling images of the romantic hero: "You make me think of a wonder Decker I once. Or some bald the saildor the man me gallant with the spangled ears. Or an earl was he at lucan" (620). These storied versions of the phallus are the very stuff of Anna Livia's desire, as the punning near homophony of yearns and yarns indicates. Yet, they are textually undercut by the recognition that this preeminence of the phallus not only engages both women and men in an impossible project, but that, in order to subsist, it requires the subordination of women. Thus, when the worship of the phallus is invoked, it is, with wonderful malice, written as "washup," suggesting that the woman who worships will also find herself doing the washup.

However, if the phallus is that which fails, how is Anna Livia to write the sexual relation on which she purports to depend? With a certain insouciance it would seem. At one point, despite having urged her husband on with masculine fantasies of rival lovers, the failed phallus has in the end to withdraw: "Withdraw your member. Closure. This chamber stands adjourned" (585)—a debacle certainly, but recounted in the carefree mocking rhythms of a nursery rhyme: "Humbo lock your kekkle up! Ambo blow your wickle out! Tuck away the table sheet! You never wet the tea!" (585). The phallus may not wet the tea but Anna Livia, it turns out, has access to other pleasures, to a languorous jouissance of her own where, as the text wonderfully remarks, "the hand of man has never set foot" (203), a world of woman's love: "How she was handsome the wild Amazia, when she would seize to my other breast" (627). It evokes a wild lesbian exultancy: "for tis they are the stormies…and the clash of our cries as we spring to be free" (ibid.), but before that the patriarchal valorization of virginity and the so-called possession of women had long dissolved and disappeared into the undulations of a whole plethora of sexual pleasurings:

> she was licked by a hound, Chirrupa-Chirruta while poing her pee pure and simple, on the spur of the hill in old Kippure, in birdsong and shearingtime, but first of all, worst of all, the wiggly livvly, she sideslipped out by a gap in the Devil's glen while Sally her nurse was sound asleep in a sloot and feefee fiefie, fell over a spillway before she found her stride and lay and wriggled in all the stagnant black pools of rainy under a fallow coo and she laughed innocefree with her limbs aloft and a whole drove of maiden hawthorns blushing and looking askance upon her. (204)

One of the most potent lures of *Finnegans Wake* is to entice its readers to pursue forms of jouissance that the text itself has already discredited. Armies of scholars document, investigate, analyze what is itself a monumental tissue of farcical investigation, analysis, documentation. Not for nothing do the letters of HCE's hundreds of names jumble into: "farCed Epistol to the Hibruws." The learned reader is lured: what is being sent up is taken up – as an object of erudite research. By the same token, it would be naive to situate how Joyce writes women

either inside or outside the phallic economy that has sustained patriarchy. As she first appears, Anna Livia is caught in the cadences of
what one might call the Ur-text of European patriarchy—the Our
Father—but right here, even within these sternly beautiful rhythms,
other pleasurings can be heard: "In the name of Annah the Allmaziful,
the Everliving, the Bringer of Plurabilities, haloed be her eve, her sing
time sung, her rill be run, unhemmed as it is even!" (104).

The appropriative and static *Kingdom* of "thy kingdom come" has
been stretched out hummingly into *sing time*, "her sing time sung,"
the mastery of an imposed will "thy will be done" ripples into a running rill—"her rill be run," and unhemmed uneven loops of plurabil-
ity foreshadow the several lures operative in her wonderful last words,
the words that "end" *Finnegans Wake*. Is it the lure of an apparent
circularity vaulting us back to the very first word of the book as is
often supposed, or can we be lured into seeing in it her signature,
as the literary critic Tony Thwaite brilliantly suggests (2001: 175),
repeated, and repeatedly incomplete: "**a** way **a** lone **a** last **a** loved
a long the ...," merging extra-textually into the signature of Joyce
himself and apparently completing itself with the final **p** coming at
the bottom of the page?

*P*aris. 1922–1939

Whichever it is, it is in the lure itself, opening up who knows what
path "into the obscure heart of things," as Blanchot put it, and as
Lacan saw, that jouissance resides.

And Blanchot, perhaps the greatest literary critic of the twentieth
century, put it best: "Perhaps that is an imposture. But perhaps that
trickery is the truth of every written thing" (1995: 42).

NOTES

1. As is evident from the current discussion, this translation does not
   capture the nuances of the French.
2. The attempts of the later Lacan to steer clear of the imaginary seem
   somewhat at variance with his earlier recognition of "the whirlwind
   point through which the object emerges in a beyond of the imaginary knot" (Seminar on Identification. 23/05/1962, pp. 10–110).
3. In his later seminars, Lacan looked to writings other than the literary to try to fly free of certain pitfalls inherent in language itself.
   The Borromean knot adapted from the medieval coat of arms of
   an Italian noble family is a linkage in which undoing any one of its
   component knots dissolves the entire thing.

REFERENCES

Adorno, Theodor (1978) *Minima Moralia: Reflections on a Damaged Life*, trans. E. F. N. Jephcott. London: Verso.

Auden, W. H. (1991) "In Memory of Sigmund Freud," in Edward Mendelson (ed.), *Collected Poems*. London: Vintage.

Barthes, Roland (1970) *Le Plaisir du Texte*. Paris: Editions du Seuil.

Beckett, Samuel (1929) "Dante…Bruno. Vico…Joyce," in *A Bash in the Tunnel*. Ed. Ryan J. London, Clifton Books 1970. Reprinted from *An Exagmination Round His Factification for Incamination of Work in Progress*. Paris: Shakespeare & Co.

——— (1965) *Proust and Three Dialogues with Georges Duthuit*. London: John Calder.

Blanchot, Maurice (1982) *The Siren's Song*. Brighton: Harvester Press.

——— (1995) *The Work of Fire*. Stanford, Meridian: Crossing Aesthetics.

Bowie, Malcolm (1987) *Freud, Proust and Lacan: Theory as Fiction*. Cambridge: University of Cambridge Press.

Derrida, Jacques (1967) *L'Écriture et la différence*. Paris: Seuil.

Eagleton, Terry (2003) *Sweet Violence, the Idea of the Tragic*. Oxford: Blackwell.

Ettinger, Bracha (2006) *The Matrixial Borderspace*. Minneapolis, MN, and London: University of Minnesota Press.

Freud, Sigmund (1895) "Early Psychoanalytical Publications," S.E.3.

——— (1900) "The Interpretation of Dreams," S.E.4.

——— (1914) "On Narcissism," S.E.14, p. 77.

——— (1919) "A Child is being Beaten," S.E.17, pp. 175–204.

——— (1928) "Dostoyevsky and Parricide," S.E.21, pp. 175–196.

——— (1953–1974) *The Standard Edition of the Complete Psychological Works*, James Strachey (ed.). London: Hogarth Press and Institute of Psychoanalysis.

Jones, Ernest (1957) *Sigmund Freud, Life and Work*. London: The Hogarth Press.

Joyce, James (1975) *Finnegans Wake*. London: Faber.

——— (1992) *Ulysses*. London: Penguin.

Lacan, Jacques. Unpublished seminars (All quotations in English unless otherwise specified are taken from typescripts of translation by Dr. Cormac Gallagher, circulated privately in St. Vincent's University Hospital, Dublin 4.)

——— (1958–1959) Le Désir et son interprétation. Le Seminaire 6.

——— (1961–1962) *L'Identification*, Le Séminaire 9.

——— (1962–1963) *L'Angoisse*, Le Séminaire 10.

——— (1968–1969) *D'un autre a l'Autre*, Le Séminaire 16.

——— (1974–1975) *R.S.I.*, Le Séminaire 22.

——— (1992) *The Ethics of Psychoanalysis*. London: Routledge.

——— (1998) *Encore*, 1972–3, trans. Bruce Fink, 1955–56. New York and London: W. W. Norton and Co.

Lukacs, George (1974) *Soul and Form*. London: Merlin Press.

Sophocles (1938) "*Antigone* and *Oedipus at Colonus*," in W. Oates and E. O'Neill (eds.), *The Complete Greek Drama*. New York: Random House.

Steiner, George (2001) *Grammars of Creation*. New Haven and London: Yale University Press.

Stevens, Wallace (2006) "The Man with the Blue Guitar," *Collected Poems*. London: Faber and Faber.

Thwaite, Antony (2001) *Joycean Temporalities*. Gainsville, FL: University of Florida Press.

Warminski, Andreij (1988) "Reading over Endless Histories: Henry James' Altar of the Dead," *Yale French Studies*, 74.

Warner, Marina (1985) *Monuments and Maidens*. London: Picador.

CHAPTER 13

Culture on the Edge: The Postfeminist Challenge

Debbie Ging

Identifying and repudiating artificially imposed boundaries—between theory and practice, feminism and gender studies, politics and culture—have always been key to Ailbhe Smyth's mission, both as an academic and as an activist. This chapter attempts to demonstrate why, at a moment that might—retrospectively—come to be described as post-feminism's heyday, Smyth's philosophical approach to gender equality is more important than ever before. Notwithstanding the phenomenal successes of the feminist movement in Ireland, the past 15 years have been witness to some disturbing developments, whereby free-market economics conspired with a broadly postfeminist culture to support a distinctly neoliberal political agenda on gender, which, beneath its liberal rhetoric, was both highly coercive and deeply regressive. Now that the "party" is over and Ireland is facing an unprecedented economic crisis, the persistence of a postfeminist "logic" built on consumerism, individualism, and genetic determinism arguably poses an even greater challenge to gender equality as the lippy catchphrases of Girl Power recede and many women find themselves hardest hit by recession, despite the ubiquity of "mancession" rhetoric. As conservative forces retrench, the ironic sexism of the noughties seems less playful, and arguments that were initially defended as tongue-in-cheek are now reemerging as more serious justifications for gender apartheid in a range of social contexts, from advertising to education.

Crucially, postfeminism is used here not to describe a chronological or epistemological period *after* feminism but rather in the sense that Yvonne Tasker and Diane Negra have described it; as a largely incohesive and untheorized, but hugely pervasive, set of cultural values around gender. As Tasker and Negra (2007) have argued, "Postfeminism broadly encompasses a set of assumptions, widely disseminated within popular media forms, having to do with the 'pastness' of feminism, whether that supposed 'pastness' is merely noted, mourned or celebrated." Unlike second-wave feminism, therefore, postfeminism cannot be understood either as a distinct mode of political activism or as a coherently developed ideology but rather as a set of discursive responses—often serving contradictory agendas—to the perceived successes and failures of feminism. For Tasker and Negra, "Postfeminism does not always offer a logically coherent account of gender and power but through structures of forceful articulation and synergistic reiteration across media forms it has emerged as a dominating discursive system." It is precisely this prioritization of the cultural and its conflation with the political that makes the contemporary genderscape so nebulous. This paradigm shift is hugely significant, not only because it represents a new set of assumptions about gender but also because it has effectively shifted the discursive arena within which these assumptions are addressed, from the realm of the political to that of the cultural.

That is not to say that culture is unimportant to gender or that culture should be apolitical. On the contrary, feminism has always been acutely aware of the significance of cultural intervention, both as a positive and negative political force. However, the Celtic Tiger years created new discursive spaces, in which ideological consensus was increasingly achieved at the level of the rhetorical, the symbolic, and the discursive. Thus, while rising costs of childcare in the noughties forced many women back into the home, postfeminism's rhetoric of free choice and revival of traditional values framed this economically motivated development as an empowered decision: it became a compliment to be called a desperate housewife, a yummy mummy or a kitchen goddess, demonstrating the power of cultural rhetoric in influencing and legitimating trends that are primarily economic or material. Similarly, reductionist labels such as lipstick lesbian, MILF ("mother I'd like to fuck"), menaissance man, metrosexual, and cougar, derived largely from television and advertising texts and their target demographics, became normalized and acceptable ways of talking about men, women, and relations between them.

These examples illustrate how certain key—and mutually compatible—developments collided and colluded in Ireland during the "boom time" to reconfigure the ways in which many people think about and "do" gender. Arguably, the most important of these are the trajectory from a feminist to a postfeminist framing of gender issues, the rise in the popularity of biodeterminist accounts of gender difference and the increasing commercialization of the media landscape. The first is crucial but its success is in large part attributable to the second and third developments, for postfeminist culture is not only deeply enmeshed within the logic of consumer capitalism but has also developed a complex, partly ironic but oftentimes sincere, relationship with the idea that gendered characteristics and behaviors are genetically ordained. In this new scheme of things, women no longer need to be liberated from the cosmetics and fashion industries because female freedom is now expressed in terms of one's ability to consume, as the l'Oréal' adverts so frequently remind us with the tagline "because you're worth it."

Perhaps, the most important defining feature of postfeminism, however, is the widespread acceptance of the notion that gender equality has been achieved, in spite of the fact that Irish women continue to be underrepresented in politics, industry, and the professions, and continue to earn less than men.[1] This optimistic rhetoric of the "level playing field" (McMahon, 1999) is a useful basis for justifying some of the more blatant inequities and contradictions of the contemporary "genderscape": with what are presumed to be the darker days of hard-line feminism now behind us, discourses of equality and empowerment facilitate a more flexible and playful discussion of gender. Thus, lap dancing is "liberating" and women retreat from public life on the basis of "empowered" choices. At the level of cultural representation, these changes have resulted in a proliferation of images of women as variously self-indulgent, narcissistic, irrational, hypersexualized, and oftentimes violent creatures who conflate pornography with freedom and consumerism with self-worth.

Finally, postfeminist culture tends to be underpinned by a postmodern aesthetics of parody, pastiche, and irony (Tasker and Negra, 2007; Whelehan, 2000), which serves as a useful escape clause (Whelehan, ibid.) against claims of sexism, elitism, or gender essentialism. It is against this particular cultural, political, and economic backdrop that the mainstreaming of a 1970s' soft-pornography aesthetic has been so successfully revived. Thus, semi-naked women drape themselves over cars at the annual Toys for Big Boys exhibition in the RDS,[2] Hunky Dorys crisp adverts purport to parody—yet simultaneously endorse—hyper-sexualized images of women, posters in third-level institutions advertising everything from table quizzes to hiking clubs feature wide-eyed, pouting females in bikinis and WKD[3] adverts trade on defiantly sexist and laddish modes of address.[4] Postfeminism gives us a fun take on the hypersexualization of women (and occasionally, though much less so, the sexualization of men), whose alleged irony resides in the claim that the stereotyping of women as coquettish minxes and obsessive shoppers and of men as domestically inept, relationship-averse larger-louts is so blatant and so passé that we can now laugh at its anachronistic nature.

The extent, however, to which these cultural texts are actually interpreted ironically remains unclear. In two substantial studies about men's media consumption and film-viewing practices (Ging, 2005, 2007b), there was very little evidence that contemporary images of male machismo and female submissiveness were understood as tongue-in-cheek references to yesterday's gender norms. On the contrary, the research showed that ironic sexism was poorly understood—at best irony was used as shorthand for "don't take things too seriously"—since the backstory of lad culture's humorously antagonistic interplay with feminism is clearly something that happened too long ago to have any real meaning for 15- to 24-year-old male audiences (Gauntlett, 2002). Moreover, the ubiquity and longevity of these images mean that they have since become part of the cultural wallpaper, with increasingly less need for recourse to the irony escape clause. This is reflected in a recent discursive shift in the tone and nature of complaints about "offensive" adverts in particular. For example, while complaints about the Hunky Dory adverts in 2011 alluded to sexism, objections to a number of recent adverts for the 48 mobile network were lodged—and upheld by the Advertising Standards Authority—on the basis that they were suggestive and offensive rather than sexist. The radio advert featured a male voiceover saying that he would "Think with my pants, heart and head. In that order. At least once, I'll spend the weekend spanking some MILF. I'll tell girls whatever lies they want to hear as long as we both get what we want." It elicited complaints that the language was "explicit, overtly sexual, offensive, damaging to young adults and encouraged promiscuity"[5] but sexism was not mentioned. The inequity underpinning the dominant male/submissive female dichotomy that pervades so much of this sexual imagery is consistently evaded in the rhetoric of liberalism, and so the debate becomes repolarized as one in which prudes are pitched against liberals, and "offensiveness" is framed as a gender-neutral concept. That there is no male equivalent of MILF is not even part of the conversation.

This de-gendering of porn makes it increasingly difficult for sex-positive feminists to argue that it is not porn or sexually graphic material per se that is a problem but rather the unequal power relations that underpin the political, visual, and libidinal economies of het-erosexual porn and its subsequent spilling over into popular culture. This goes hand-in-hand with a normalization of sex work, not in the discourse of the labor market, decriminalization, or employment rights but rather in men's magazines, in the ubiquity of lap danc-ing and pole dancing, in prostitution memoirs and in other prod-ucts that are sold for entertainment. The marketing of these products is premised upon a celebratory discourse of rights won, and evades economic and political inequities, thus making the real work that people do at the coalface of the sex industry invisible. Liberal rhetoric is also heavily invested in the notion that the sexual work women do for men, from having Brazilians to learning how to lap dance, makes them feel better and more confident about themselves, while the reasons for their feeling so bad about themselves in the first place are never addressed. According to Sara Stokes (2010), the relatively uncritical acceptance of a culture of hypersexualization in Ireland can be read as a backlash in response to the culture of fear and silence that dominated for so many decades. This pervasive fear of trans-gression, she argues, has resulted in the unquestioning acceptance of and adherence to the sexual norms, standards, and expectations set out by Raunch Culture (Levy, 2005). Stokes's (2012) doctoral research, an ethnographic study of Irish female students, shows that young Irish women's self-esteem and sense of their own sexuality has been deeply affected by the libidinal economy of pornography and that they feel pressurized to maintain their bodies and regulate their sexual performances according to the codes and conventions of porn in order to avoid being rated negatively—and in some cases, publicly humiliated—by the men with whom they have had sex.

Alongside images of hypersexism—ironic and otherwise—popular culture is also replete with exaggerated images of female power. In contemporary action films and video games, gun-toting, ass-kicking babes in hotpants engage in highly stylized acts of violence, while an antagonistic rapport of one-upmanship tends to underscore male–female relations.[6] In these genres, the use of CGI,[7] wirework stunts, animation, and timesplice/bullet-time techniques has bolstered female narrative agency in ways which, arguably, embody some of the central paradoxes of postfeminist thinking about gender: for example, that women are free to self-create, despite the fact that these characters are usually the products of male fantasy, that female empowerment is a given, or that acts of violence and sexual servility are empower-ing, even though they are, in reality, damaging to both women and men. This cultural imagery has come to equate female power almost exclusively with violence and sexual attraction and, while the entertainment industry is in the business of producing fantasies, which clearly cannot be conflated with the material realities of women's lives, there is an interesting—but arguably relational—disconnect between the two. In 1986, Molly Haskell wrote that, "The closer women come to claiming their rights and achieving independence in real life, the more loudly and stridently films tell us it's a man's world." The past 20 years, however, have witnessed something of a volte-face, whereby the kick-ass femme fatales of games and action cinema increasingly suggest female power and domination, in spite of the fact that statistics continue to indicate that for real women "having it all" means taking lower-paid, part-time work and doing the second shift with children and housework. Thus, the sexual and violent hyperbole of Girl Power, far from being removed from reality, is arguably a key symbolic part of a reality that understands female violence as both abject and sexually fascinating (Ging, 2007a).

The crucial point here is that cultural images neither reflect nor negate reality but are rather a constituent *part* of reality, intervening in the construction of meaning like any other—social, medical, political—discourse. More importantly, cultural products are not hermetically sealed within the sphere of the cultural: in an increasingly image-dominated, media-driven society, they pervade all aspects of modern life. A striking example of this is the way in which attempts are now being made to attract females into science by using precisely those gender-determinist visual strategies—pink color schemes, flowers, the chemistry of makeup—which arguably deterred them from playing with meccano and chemistry sets as children, and thus perceiving themselves as future scientists, in the first place. This irony implosion recently reached new levels in a promotional video sponsored by the European Commission to encourage girls to take a greater interest in science. Trading on highly sexualized images of female models giggling in laboratory settings and on close-ups of lipstick, nail varnish, and hair dryers,[8] and launched ahead of the Euroscience Open Forum 2012 in Dublin, the video has attracted widespread criticism from female scientists. However, the fact that the European Commission deemed this imagery to be positive and acceptable is indicative of the degree to which cultural imagery (a) becomes rapidly naturalized and (b) is mobilized far beyond the realms of entertainment. According to the European Union Commissioner for Research, Innovation and Science, Máire Geoghegan-Quinn, the campaign was designed "to overturn clichés and show women and girls, and boys too, that science is not about old men in white coats," indicating how, as ironic sexism becomes increasingly naturalized, it becomes easier for concepts of equality and power to fade from the picture.

The normalization of gender difference that underpins all of these images and discourses, from science and education to films and digital games, has undoubtedly been in large part facilitated by best-selling self-help books such as John Gray's *Men Are from Mars, Women Are from Venus*. Indeed, the explosion in sex- and gender-related self-help literature, CDs, and DVDs is both a cause and a symptom of the new essentialism. In a host of similar, best-selling publications, from Deborah Tannen's *You Just Don't Understand: Men and Women in Conversation* to Allan and Barbara Pease's *Why Men Don't Listen and Women Can't Read Maps* and *Why Men Don't Have a Clue and Women Always Need More Shoes*, the structural causes of gender inequality and the possibility of social change are ignored in favor of a more manageable, attractive, and saleable form of transformation that takes place through the individual consumption of (self-help) therapy. While most self-help therapies that address problems of gender relations give the impression of taking radical individual action to change things, they ultimately serve to preserve the status quo. Instead of tackling the root causes of inequality, they teach individuals how to gloss over and live with the symptoms. Explanations of men and women as coming from different planets are easier to digest than critiques of the unequal division of domestic labor as they do not challenge the existing economic and social structures into which people have become enmeshed (Ging, 2009). Moreover, because the incompatibilities between the sexes are presented as foreordained, the demand for dating agencies, self-help books, and sex and relationship counselling is potentially infinite. Love, sex, and procreation have become highly complex emotional danger zones, which the common human apparently cannot negotiate without the help of "expertise," bearing out John Fiske's (1990: 182) claim that, "We learn to think of our desires in terms of the commodities produced to meet them, we learn to think of our problems in terms of the commodities by which to solve them."

This shift toward essentialist thinking is increasingly evident across a range of discourses on science, therapy, and popular culture in contemporary Western society (Gill, 2003: 50–51). Terms that used to belong to the specialist lexicons of neuroscience, such as serotonin, bipolarity, and synaptic connections, have become the staple fodder of discussions about men, women, and the relationships between them on a host of Irish daytime talk shows and phone-in radio programs. According to Maija Holmer Nadesan (2002: 403):

> More recently, the public has been bombarded with a "scientific" discourse that implies a bio-genetic essentialism through its explication of phenomena such as intelligence, sexuality and aggression as neural-biological outcomes of genetic factors affected by natural selection.

Interestingly, however, in these discourses, the playful irony of post-feminism and Lad Culture disappears and is replaced by a much more sincere attempt to rationalize and justify the gender stereotypes that contemporary advertising both lampoons and simultaneously reaffirms. According to Holmer Nadesan, the discourse of "brain science" is attractive to neoliberal governments because it renders potentially threatening populations visible—and enables them to be controlled—in new ways. Thus, hyperactive children can be managed with Ritalin rather than through radical changes to diet, parenting, or state-supported services, and biochemical explanations for criminality, particularly in relation to young men, can be used to justify heightened surveillance and tougher jail sentences, while the social causes of male marginalization are ignored.

Besides fostering complex and ostensibly noninvasive forms of governmentality, "brain science" is inextricably bound up in the logic of everyday consumerism. This was well illustrated by an article written by prominent psychologist Maureen Gaffney in the *Irish Times* magazine in 2007, in which she argued that women fall in love with shoes and handbags not because they have been relentlessly objectified by Western visual culture for centuries or aggressively targeted by modern advertising since its inception but because they are "fulfilling their evolutionary destiny." According to Gaffney, women in early human societies "specialised in child rearing, nesting and foraging for food, while males hunted for meat and defended their territory. By necessity women evolved to have better peripheral vision than men, enabling them to see in a wider arc and monitor any danger approaching the nest or any subtle changes in the environment. " She went on to explain that these sensory skills make women "avid and effective foragers of luxury goods…Women lovingly fondle silk and cashmere, sniff perfume with a look of rapt attention on their faces, and talk about colours such as taupe and eau de nil."

This thinking is by no means reserved to weekend style magazines, however. Films, television, literature, toys, and children's fashion are being sold to consumers in increasingly gender-reductive ways. This is particularly evident in the growth of gender-specific cultural genres such as chick-lit, chick-flicks, and lad mags, as well as in the way television programming is becoming increasingly organized around the marketing not only of gender-specific products but also of new, gender-specific viewing contexts, such as "Girls' Nights" and "Boys' Nights." The increasing commercialization of the mediascape has therefore been a key driver in facilitating the discursive and representational repolarization of gender, since the trajectory from a public service broadcasting model to one whose core objective is to sell audiences to advertisers sets up an entirely new dynamic between the broadcast media and their audiences. As well as marginalizing demographic groups that are of little interest to advertisers, this model appeals to consumers in increasingly gender-reductive ways, since the formats supported by commercial media are highly conducive with simplified images and soundbytes. Ideas, on the other hand, which challenge commonsense assumptions, are generally not media friendly since they require complex foregrounding and contextualization (Herman and Chomsky, 1994). The proliferation of populist documentaries, vox-populi "surveys," and snippets of flawed yet highly accessible scientific "facts," which fuel the dual discourses of postfeminism and Lad Culture, mean that genetic-determinist ideas have now succeeded in assuming a central, even banal, position in Irish social discourse.

Conclusion

While the trends and developments discussed in this chapter are prevalent elsewhere in the Western world, it is arguable that Ireland embraced both the consumerism and "sexual liberation" of the boom years less critically than many other countries. The broadly celebratory acceptance of the commercialization of sex in this country has, no doubt, been intensified by a collective sense of liberation from a censorious and highly repressive brand of Catholicism. While this is to be welcomed, it is essential that one set of inequalities does not merely become supplanted by another. The increased visibility of homosexuality, the perceived freedoms of "raunch culture," and the broad acceptance of the myth that equality has been achieved have serviced a convincing rhetoric of progress and, in doing so, have ultimately served to gloss over the persistence of substantial material inequities between men and women, and between straight and LGBT people. As we have observed in recent years, both women's rights and gay rights have been mobilized on the global political stage to serve a range of agendas, from banning the burqa to military invasions, which ultimately have little or nothing to do with national sexual or gender politics. Now, more than ever before, we must be attentive to the power relations implicit in the mobilization of culture and increasingly wary of the ideological elasticity of cultural visibility and the political purposes to which it is put.

Theoretically, this must lead us back to a refusal to separate the political and the cultural, as well as to a rejection of simplistic positive/ negative analyses of cultural representation. It is important to interrogate the vague cultural use of terms such as liberation, choice, and empowerment and to map out more rigorous, systematic, and materialist analyses of power. At least three core theoretical strategies are necessary if we are to make sense of the current post-ironic genderscapes of popular culture. The first is an institutional analysis of the culture industries in question, which reveals the political economy of porn, lad's magazines, lap-dancing clubs, advertising, and the like. The second is a greater attentiveness to the mode of address that operates within cultural texts: whose point of view, whose voice, and whose pleasure is being prioritized and how are subjectivity and selfhood being constructed? Finally, more research is needed at the level of reception to understand exactly how cultural imagery and discourses are being used and understood. These approaches bring questions of power, structure, and agency back into the equation without negating the complex and heterogeneous nature of audiences and practices of consumption. They also help us to distinguish between those cultural interventions which serve to reinforce the status quo and those which work to foster gender and sexual equality. Irish women may be finally freed from Catholicism but they must now negotiate the dual forces of bio-determinism and commodification, both of which have equally high stakes in the regulation of their bodies.

NOTES

1. See Central Statistics Office (2011) *Women and Men in Ireland.* Dublin: Stationery Office. www.cso.ie/en/media/csoie/releases publications/documents/otherrelease s/2011/Women%20and%20 Men%20in%20Ireland%202011.pdf
2. Royal Dublin Society. A philanthropic Society in Dublin supported by membership subscriptions and commercial activities such as concerts and exhibitions.
3. WKD is a vodka-based alcopop marketed to a young, male demographic.

4. Text-based poster ads include captions such as "Send your girlfriend somewhere really cool. To the fridge, for a pork pie" and "Watch her face light up this Christmas. Buy her a torch."
5. See '"Spanking", "MILF," and hangover Jesus too much for the "Advertising Standards Authority" in the Journal, that is june 27, 2012. [http://www.thejournal.ie/advertisements-offensive-milf-hang over-jesus-guinness-sexual-explicit-denny-501647-Jun2012/].
6. Perhaps the most overt example is *Gender Wars*, a GT Interactive title, which imagines a future in which men and women strive to annihilate one another.
7. Computer-generated imagery.
8. See www.youtube.com/watch?v=g032MPrSjFA, accessed July 20, 2012.

References

Fiske, John (1990) *Introduction to Communication Studies.* London: Routledge.
Gaffney, Maureen (2007) "Retail Therapy." *Irish Times Magazine*, March 10.
Gauntlett, David (2002) *Media, Gender and Identity: An Introduction.* London and New York: Routledge.
Gill, Rosalind (2003) "Power and the Production of Subjects: A Genealogy of the New Man and the New Lad," in B. Benwell (ed.), *Masculinity and Men's Lifestyle Magazines.* Oxford and Malden: Blackwell, pp. 34–56.
Ging, Debbie (2005) "A 'Manual on Masculinity?': The Consumption and Use of Mediated Images of Masculinity among Teenage Boys in Ireland." *Irish Journal of Sociology*, 14 (2): 29–52.
——— (2007a) "All the Rage: Digital Games, Female Violence and the Postfeminisation of Cinema's New Action Heroine," *Film and Film Culture*, 4 (December): 51–61.
——— (2007b) "New Lads or Protest Masculinities?: Investigating Marginalised Masculinities in Contemporary Irish Film," in John Horgan, Barbara O'Connor and Helena Sheehan (eds.), *Mapping Irish Media: Critical Explorations.* Dublin: UCD Press.
——— (2009) "All-Consuming Images: New Gender Formations in Post-Celtic-Tiger Ireland," in Debbie Ging, Michael Cronin, and Peadar Kirby (eds), *Transforming Ireland: Challenges, Critiques and Resources.* Manchester: Manchester University Press.
Haskell, Molly, cited in Brunsdon, Charlotte (1986) *Films for Women.* London: BFI, 1986.
Herman, Edward S. and Chomsky, Noam (1994) *Manufacturing Consent: The Political Economy of the Mass Media.* London: Vintage.
Holmer Nadesan, Maija (2002) "Engineering the Entrepreneurial Infant: Brain Science, Infant Development Toys, and Governmentality." *Cultural Studies*, 16 (3): 401–432.

Levy, Ariel (2005) *Female Chauvinist Pigs: Women and the Rise of Raunch Culture*. New York: Free Press.

McMahon, Anthony (1999) *Taking Care of Men: Sexual Politics in the Public Mind*. Cambridge: Cambridge University Press.

Stokes, Sara (2010) "Who Regulates Sexuality in Ireland? From the Catholic Church to Popular Media: A Shift in Direction," conference paper presented at "Self, Selves and Sexualities," March 19–20, Dublin City University, Ireland.

——— (2012) *The Impact of Raunch Culture on the Development of an Autonomous Female Sexuality in Ireland*. PhD thesis, unpublished. NUI Galway.

Tasker, Yvonne and Negra, Diane (2007) "Introduction: Feminist Politics and Postfeminist Culture," in Y. Tasker and D. Negra (eds), Interrogating Postfeminism: Gender and the Politics of Popular Culture. Durham, NC: Duke University Press.

Whelehan, Imelda (2000) *Overloaded: Popular Culture and the Future of Feminism*. London: The Women's Press.

CHAPTER 14

A Cure for Melancholia? Queer Sons, Dead Mothers, and the Fantasy of Multiculturalism in McCabe's and Jordan's *Breakfast on Pluto(s)*

Anne Mulhall

The orientation of the Irish novel toward allegories of the nation has often been recognized by its critics. As Liam Harte and Michael Parker note, "many...bear the imprint of unresolved political and cultural narratives and debates" (Harte and Parker, 2000: 2). The history of the individual becomes the heavily freighted vehicle for the history of the collective, and the family drama the space in which long-standing narratives of the nation, real or imagined, are played and replayed. In particular, the obsessional recurrence of and recourse to the oedipal drama as an explanatory structure reveals the tenacity of the multiple sites of anxiety bequeathed by a fractured Irish past. For any stuttering in the oedipal structure, any critical interruption of its developmental narrative, the mother is to blame: the mother or the maternal function who will not, in one way or another, let her sons, in particular, go. The mother in Irish literature is a haunted and haunting figure, and the relationship between mother and son is likewise incapacitated by ghosts, subtended by the murderous, incestuous rhetoric of the son's blood sacrifice for Mother Ireland. Thus, the mother–son dyad becomes a kind of master trope for political violence in particular. Whether in relation to the "birth" of the nation in violence and partition or the internecine bloodshed of the Troubles, the failure to break away from the maternal imaginary becomes the explanatory cause of the recurrence of an atavistic and regressive violence that fractures the nation's imaginary wholeness.

While widely praised for its "subversion of actual and metaphorical borders" and disruptive "interrogations of established narratives of identity," Patrick McCabe firmly situates his 1998 novel *Breakfast on Pluto* within these oedipal dynamics, with the year of publication—1998—marking the novel's relation to the 1998 Good Friday Agreement, the official conclusion to the Troubles (Harte and Parker, 2000: 4). In making Pussy a transgender woman who was born biologically male, McCabe's novel implicitly critiques the position of the son in the murderous mother–son dyad, yet does so uncertainly, unable as McCabe seems to be to imagine Pussy as unequivocally a woman. Identified at the beginning and the conclusion of the novel as a man, and misnamed as a transvestite, McCabe's novel at times occludes Pussy in her transgendered specificity in the interests of her instrumental use within the allegory of the colonial and postcolonial nation. It is clear, however, that Patrick "Pussy" Braden is neither a gay man nor a transvestite, but a transgendered woman. In the novel, Pussy narrates the story of her traumatic past. Conceived, as Pussy imagines, during the rape of a young girl, Eily Bergin, by the local priest, Fr Bernard McIvor, abandoned by her parents and raised by "Hairy Ma Braden," a local "baby farmer," Pussy grows up in the border town of Tyreelin during the terrible early years of the Troubles. She escapes to London, where she works intermittently as a prostitute and gets caught up in the chaotic conflict and violence of both the paramilitaries and the British state, ending up an isolated figure in her flat in that English ghetto of the Irish emigrant working class, Kilburn High Road. Her main preoccupation in the novel is the retrieval of the lost mother. This lost mother inevitably speaks to the figurative construction of the "lost" nation, and Pussy's narrative is inextricable from the politics of colonization, partition, and the "national question."

As has been noted by several critics, Pussy's queering of the gender binary becomes the governing figure for a border-crossing sensibility in the novel that laments and critiques the politics of the border. Her nonnormative gender identity becomes a figurative vehicle for the deconstruction and critique of claims to authenticity and the fixed essentialism of political, national, and ethnic identities, foregrounding her performative disruptive potential. However, as Vivian Namaste has observed in relation to Marjorie Garber's influential study of transvestism in cultural texts, the reduction of "the tranvestite to a mere tropological figure, a textual and rhetorical device that points to the crisis of category and the category of crisis" undermines "the possibility of 'transvestite' as a viable identity in and of itself" (Namaste, 2000: 14–15). As Susan Stryker notes, the use of transgender as trope of destabilization proliferated during the "most recent '*fin-de-siecle*,'" becoming, like the figure of the cyborg, the "bellwethers (for better or worse) of an emergent 'postmodern' condition," the vehicle "through which contemporary culture imagined a future filled with new possibilities for being human, or becoming posthuman" (Stryker, 2006: 8). Namaste emphasizes the instrumental deployment of transgender within a particular "post-performative" strand of queer theory, a use that occludes the lived experience of, for example, "the precarious position of the transsexual woman who is battered and who is unable to access a women's shelter because she was not born a biological woman" (Namaste, 2000: 9–10), while Stryker comments on the difficult relationship between feminism and transgender, noting that "the fight over transgender inclusion within feminism is not significantly different, in many respects, from other fights involving working-class women, women of color, lesbian women, disabled women" (Stryker, 2006: 8).

In *Breakfast on Pluto*, and in Neil Jordan's 2005 film adaptation of McCabe's novel, Pussy as a transgendered woman is misnamed, her transgender specificity called into question by McCabe's identification of her as a transvestite and as a man at certain crucial points of the narrative. Pussy as a trans woman is reduced to a convenient trope for the fractured nation, whereby her trans specificity is occluded, most especially in Jordan's film adaptation, by making her emblematic of a utopian, postnational future. Nonetheless, Pussy herself resists such reductions in the 1998 novel in particular, refusing to relinquish her embodied difference, while keeping faith through her embodied identifications with the nation's abjected others, not least herself. In this essay, I will explore the ways in which Pussy both resists and accommodates the assimilationist force of the national allegory in both the novel and film versions of her narrative and the ways in which Jordan's film adaptation extends the director's assimilative urges through the displacement of the "old" Irish nation by the new queer multicultural national family, a displacement that is enabled by Kitten's symbolic "killing" of the mother whom Pussy, conversely, refuses to "give up" in McCabe's novel.

McCabe prefaced the first US edition of his novel with an authorial "Prelude" that directly references the novel's historical and political contexts. It was omitted from subsequent editions, indicating

McCabe's change of heart in relation to this explicit positioning of the novel within the frame of national and colonial history and the oedipal dynamics of the nation. The "Prelude" presents us with an idiosyncratic and skeleton narrative of colonial effects and the effects of partition, with the Battle of the Boyne and the Good Friday Agreement acting as historical bookends. McCabe situates Pussy, presented as a queer hero/ine for a postmodern age, as a figure of the nation and its fate:

> Distracted by the bombs and bullets, eviscerations, nightly slaughter. And ultimately deciding to devote his life to a cause and one alone. That of ending, once and for all, this ugly state of perennial limbo. To finding—finally, and for us all!—a map which might lead him to that place called home. Where all borders will ultimately vanish and perfume through Tyreelin Valley, not come sweetly drifting.
>
> However, will it all be so easy for him, this fragile, flamboyant self-styled emissary, or shall he prove nothing more than another false prophet, ending his days in a backstreet apartment, sucking his thumb and dreaming of Mama, a silly old hopeless Norman Bates of history? Or will he triumph, making it against all the odds through the gauntlet of misfits, dodgy politicians, errant priests, psychos, and sad old lovers that is his world, laying his head beneath a flower-bordered print that bears the words at last: "You're home"? (McCabe, 1999: x–xi).

Thoughts of "Mama," tied explicitly as they are by McCabe to "silly old Norman Bates," a paradigmatic figure for the murderous consequences of the failure of oedipal teleology, are far from harmless sentimentality. Rather, a refusal to let the mother go is the mark of failure, regression, and derangement: the etiology of the melancholic, and of the queer.

The refusal to let the mother go is the paradigmatic instance of what psychoanalysis describes as melancholic incorporation. Freud makes a distinction between two different responses to the loss of the object, mourning and melancholia. In mourning, the lost object is gradually decathected, let go "bit by bit," so that eventually the "work of mourning is completed [and] the ego becomes free and uninhibited again" (Freud, 1991 [1917]: 253). Melancholia, on the other hand, is pathological and interminable. In melancholia, the relation to the object is "shattered." Rather than then cathecting another object, as is the case eventually when "normal" mourning reaches its resolution, instead there is "an *identification* of the ego with the abandoned object" (258). According to Freud, "[t]he narcissistic identification with the object then becomes a substitute for the erotic cathexis" (258). In other words, the melancholic regresses to primary narcissism, rather than negotiating his or her loss and moving on. Melancholic incorporation of the lost object marks a return to the oral fixation of primary narcissism. Orality is cannibalistic, and indicates the sadistic, murderous aspect of incorporation, where the ego takes the lost object into itself "by devouring it" (258).

As Diane Fuss has noted, this regression to primary narcissism and to the cannibalistic orality of incorporation is one of the etiologies of homosexuality suggested by Freud. In his essay on Leonardo da Vinci, Freud describes the homosexual as "stuck" at this primary stage, constituted by his refusal to relinquish the primary object, the "maternal breast and all its phallic substitutes" (quoted in Fuss, 1995: 89). Refusing to "move on" to "normal" oedipal, heterosexualizing development, "the male homosexual *ingests* the (m)other, "puts himself in her place, identifies himself with her, and takes his own person as a model in whose likeness he chooses the new objects of his love" (Fuss, 1995: 89). As with melancholic incorporation, homosexual identification is represented as sadistic, murderous, devouring the object in order to take its place. Homosexuality is thus understood in this model as a pathological and murderous cross-identification with the object of the opposite sex. Freud's conflation of gender inversion and sexual object choice inscribes this as a developmental stuttering that likewise, within a Freudian logic, pathologizes what we now recognize as transgender subjectivities. By the lights of this schema, then, both homosexuality and transgender are indistinguishable from melancholia; such subjects are intrinsically, constitutionally melancholic. Fuss goes on to make a crucial point, however. Elsewhere, in *Group Psychology*, Freud describes *all* identifications as forms of cannibalistic absorption of the object into the ego: "At the base of every identification lies a murderous wish: the subject's desire to cannibalize the other who inhabits the place it longs to occupy" (Fuss, 1995: 93). In other words, all identifications are a kind of melancholic incorporation. Revising his model of the ego in *The Ego and the Id*, Freud claims that the ego is comprised of just such introjected lost objects; without such internalizations of the object, there would be no ego. However, despite this ever-expanding subjectivizing field of identification and incorporation, the taint of the pathological still "sticks," nonetheless, to those identifications classified as melancholic and perverse (Warner, 1990).

The specter of Norman Bates conjured by McCabe's short-lived "Prelude" positions Pussy as a pathological subject, murderously melancholic and perverse. The comparison with Bates suggests that her transgender embodiment is either a sign of or constitutive of this pathology, depending on whether we "read" her as an emblem of Mother Ireland or consider her in her transgender specificity. The recognition that the process of incorporation is constitutive of *all* identities begins to counter such pathologizing transphobic assimilations. In Judith Butler's influential model of gender melancholia, the incorporation of the lost object is performatively inscribed on the surface of the body, worn like a flayed skin (Butler, 1997: 132–159). This captures the ambivalence of melancholia. It proceeds on the knife-edge cleaving love and hate; preservation is a kind of annihilation; incorporation is both commemoration and murder weapon. However, Pussy's incorporation of the mother, both in her idealized and her traumatized aspects, also suggests a different, more generative perspective on melancholia than the pathologizing version that has held sway within psychoanalytic theory. Pussy's refusal to let the mother go can instead be understood as a way of keeping faith with abjected lives and histories—not least her own—that might otherwise be conveniently forgotten in the flight to chimerical postnational utopian futures and the premature resolutions they enforce.

Pussy does in fact meet that faltering end that McCabe suggests in his "Prelude," alone in her dreary Kilburn flat, the butt of the locals' phobic jibes, leafing through her collection of old magazines from the 1940s and 1950s, "*Picturegoer, Screen Parade, New Faces of the Fifties*—looking yet again for Mitzi and that old bubble cut of hers" (McCabe, 1999: 199). Gone are the glamor and flamboyance of her younger days; instead, she wears a "housecoat and head scarf," as she tells us in the opening and closing chapters that frame her main narrative, with the repetition of both details emphasizing their importance (McCabe, 1999: 1, 198). These framing chapters are situated in Pussy's present, from which position she narrates the story of her earlier life, addressed to the reader and to her absent psychiatrist Dr Terence who mysteriously abandoned his patient before her treatment was finished. Mitzi Gaynor on the one hand, and the drab housewife on the other, describe two aspects of the maternal object: the glamorous, idealized figure of Gaynor, star of the 1945 Hollywood adaptation of the Broadway musical *South Pacific*, and the traumatized, wounded maternal object that Pussy displays in her old housecoat and headscarf. Pussy creates a good maternal object from the image of Mitzi Gaynor after a local, Benny Lendrum, tells her that her mother Eily Bergin, "the most beautiful girl in the town" would "give your woman out of *South Pacific* a run for her money," inspiring Pussy's fantasy of the good, unblemished object as Mitzi, wearing a blonde bubble-cut, white capri trousers and checked yellow blouse. In one fantasized episode, Pussy imagines a young Eily in her bedroom reading the same magazines that Pussy leafs through at the beginning and end of the narrative: "*Picturegoer, Screen Parade, New Faces of the Fifties*" (McCabe, 1999: 126). The coincidence underlines that for Pussy, these magazines connect her to the good, beautiful, unviolated, but external object, the "before" of Pussy's imagining of her conception in violence.

Pussy's attachment to this idealized figure of Mitzi Gaynor stages an intersection in McCabe's novel between a series of "prehistories": that of a fantasized good maternal object mediated by the figure of Mitzy Gaynor, and, through this interconnection with Hollywood musicals of the 1940s and 1950s, the "prehistory" of post-Stonewall gay liberation and the closeted "prehistory" of the individual queer subject. In *A Place for Us*, an exploration of the significance of Broadway musicals for gay male culture and affective experience, D. A. Miller describes this psychic investment in terms of a "prehistory" that disrupts the progressive liberatory narrative of post-Stonewall queer culture as well as the adult subject for whom it has gotten better, as the 2010 Internet phenomenon of the anti-homophobic harassment viral video campaign "It Gets Better" has it.[1] "The archaeology of the post-war gay male subject regularly turns up a cache of original cast albums," Miller asserts, in a faux-scholarly footnote. He continues:

> These were used, scholars now believe, as a puberty rite that, though it was conducted by single individuals in secrecy and shame, was nonetheless so widely diffused as to remain, for several generations, as practically normative for gay men... they would sing and dance to recorded Broadway music (in one variant, merely mime singing and dancing) under the magical belief that, having lent the score the depth of their own abjection, they might then borrow all its fantastic hope that their solitary condition would end in glory and triumph. (Miller, 1998: 11)

While she is a trans rather than gay male subject, Pussy cleaves to the Broadway musical in just such a way. Even while Pussy exhibits the "signs" of a more liberated post-Stonewall queer subject at points in the novel, problematically signified by McCabe through Pussy's love of the commodity fetishism of the fashion industry—her glam rock-inspired clothing, her breathless lists of branded cosmetics—she is, ultimately, made to signify the melancholic pre-Stonewall queer subject partially through the sedimented "prehistories" to which both mother and queer daughter are consigned through the mediation of the Broadway musical and its particular queer investments. Moreover, this situating of the lost, idealized mother as the "prehistory" of the (queer) subject grounds a further analogical torsion, whereby the "lost mother" of fantasy and of individual history becomes irretrievably involved with the lost idealized maternal object of the nation itself.

Pussy is by no means unique in this novel in her search for the lost mother, or in her refusal to let her go. The novel is full of melancholic men, in particular, who cannot give up the lost mother. Pussy renames her politician lover, who is assassinated by paramilitaries, "Dummy Teat" because of his attachment to his mother, which is expressed in his sexual proclivities: " 'I came up with this idea of inserting my thumb into his mouth...' Oh Mammy! Mammy! he'd cry, sucking away on it like nobody's business!" (McCabe, 1999: 34). In the chapter, "Where the Fuck Is My Mammy?" Pussy describes the seedy late-night café where she meets another lover, Berts. In the café, "the nighttime flotsam and jetsam" of London congregate, many Irish emigrants among them. The knife edge of attachment and aggression manifests itself in the drunken hard men who sing sentimental Irish ballads—"yum yum Mama songs" (McCabe, 1999: 74)—and cry when they think of their lost mothers, their melancholia swiftly converting to violence: "I'll break this fucking place in two! I'll bury it in rubble if you say that I don't love her!" (McCabe, 1999: 75). The emigrant melancholia that suffuses the café underlines their interminable mourning for the lost maternal object, and the ambivalence of this attachment. Here, the lost maternal object figures the nation, the melancholic's grief troping the ungrieved abject residue of that nation, the melancholic phantom that haunts the nation's "good" image of itself.

While Pussy mocks the men in her characteristic camp delivery, she herself shares in their grieving for the lost mother. Just 16 at the time the priest raped her, according to Pussy's fantasized reconstruction at least, Pussy imagines what her mother was wearing at the moment of her violation: "a washed-out, pale blue housecoat with a ringpull zip, a pair of tan stockings the colour of tea kept in the cup for twenty years or thereabouts and an old hairnet"—an outfit that is "not entirely unlike my own!" Pussy tells us in a footnote (McCabe, 1999: 24). Pussy's physical appearances at the beginning and end of the novel "show" that it is the mother at the point of violation who is incorporated.[2] At the end of her story, Pussy searches in her old magazines for images of an unviolated Mitzi-Mother, but we can "see" the violated lost mother inscribed melancholically on her own body. Pussy carries within her, and wears like a badge of her abjection, the maternal phantom. The unspeakable, unknowable trauma of the lost mother is also the trauma encrypted within the daughter. Pussy's personal trauma is inextricable from the traumatic, traumatized phantoms of the nation itself.[3] The circumstances in which Pussy was conceived speak, for instance, to the child sexual abuse and the cover-up of such abuse that has been endemic on the island of Ireland, north and south, whether in the context of clerical abuse, the abuse of children in state- and church-run reformatories, Magdalen asylums, and industrial schools, and, of course, within the family itself. Eily Bergin's expulsion from family and nation and the abandonment of her child similarly speaks to the punitive treatment of unmarried mothers and their children in the Irish state and to the instrumental use of England as an amnesiac vault for those abjected by and escaping from its unlivable constraints. Pussy's emigration to England to escape the horrors of the Troubles and violence of transphobia conveys the life-threatening difficulties of growing up in 1970s' border-country. These abjected pasts and presents are condensed in Pussy's incorporation of the fantasized maternal object at the simultaneous moment of the mother's violation and Pussy's conception.

In her critical rearticulation of Freud's model of mourning and melancholia, Melanie Klein makes a distinction between "normal" mourning, where the mourner "reinstates" or introjects anew both the "good" parental objects of infancy and the person who has been lost, and "abnormal" mourning, where "'good' internal objects" were not properly introjected, so that the subject is "stuck" in the infantile depressive position, which can later manifest in manic depression and psychosis (Klein, 1998 [1940]: 369). Pussy is such a "failed" mourner, and the possibly psychotic consequences of this failure potentially undermine the "truth" of her narrative, itself peppered with the flights of fantasy that are symptomatic of psychosis. Are we to understand her fantasies as psychotic, however? Is her failure to mourn "correctly" necessarily as absolutely negative and pathological as such an interpretation would suggest? In their important essay on racial melancholia in Asian American communities, David Eng and Shinhee Han query whether intrapsychic processes alone can adequately account for melancholia in subjects and collectivities who have been abjected and excluded in the social realm. For them, melancholia for such subjects and communities has its source not in "abnormal" processes of melancholic incorporation, but in the social, legal, political, and juridical positioning of racialized, immigrant, and queer subjects. Shifting the ground of Freudian and other psycho-analytic etiologies of the melancholic subject, Eng and Han reveal the values that such melancholic positions express. Whereas the "suc-cessful" mourner will resolve his or her grief by finally letting go of the lost object, the melancholic subject refuses to let the object go. For those subjects whose melancholia arises from intersecting and transitive personal, intergenerational, and collective histories of exclusion, such a refusal to let go of the object becomes an ethical value: "the melancholic process is one way in which socially dispar-aged objects—racially and sexually deprivileged others—live on in the psychic realm" (Eng and Han, 2003: 364).

Those "deprivileged others" who are marked by gender, class, and ethnic othering may be likewise preserved and held by melancholic incorporation. Departing from Freud and from Klein, Eng and Han emphasize the intergenerational valence of racial melancholia, and its significance in the etiology of the "nation." The lost object is a phan-tom that is melancholically preserved and passed between generations, a shared encryption of trauma. Such intergenerational melancholia is the phantom that haunts the nation, the unspeakable repressed that cannot be faced up to, so that the "minority *subject* endures... as a melancholic national *object*—as a haunting specter to democratic ideals of inclusion that cannot quite 'get over' the histories of these legislated proscriptions of loss" (Eng and Han, 2003: 348). Eng and Han's rearticulation of melancholia as the refusal to give up the other, a tenacity in the name of both self and other that refuses the amnesia of proper mourning, resignifies Pussy's melancholic refusal to give up the lost mother. The incorporated lost object simultaneously signi-fies the real lost mother and those marked subjects and collectivities on whose abjection and "death" the nation depends for the mainte-nance of its own ideal image. Pussy's lived experience of exclusion and abjection is inextricable from such collective losses; it is precisely these *social* conditions that have constituted her as a melancholic sub-ject. Thus, England is not just a symbolic space in the novel, a trope within some abstract reconstituted allegory of the colonial and post-colonial nation. England is the actual space that Ireland uses to man-age the nation's unwanted, unassimilable populations.

Pussy ends her story back in Kilburn in the narrative present, leaf-ing through her old magazines looking for Mitzi, and fantasizing about her "dearest wish": to be surrounded by her family, having given birth to a *son* who turns out to be herself: "my family all around me, exhausted after my ordeal maybe, but with a bloom like roses in my cheeks, as I stroke his soft and tender head, my little baby, watching them as they beam with pride, in their eye perhaps a tear or two—who cares!—hardly able to speak as they wipe it away and say! 'He's ours" (McCabe, 1999: 199). Throughout the novel, Pussy fantasizes about becoming a biological woman so that she can bear children. She imagines what her life might be like "if I did somehow manage to get a vagina," and imagines her children rushing home to be with her on her deathbed (McCabe, 1999: 40). Relayed in Pussy's uniquely Irish-inflected camp melodrama, she remarks: "And who would ever to deny it dare? To say: 'They are not hers! For she has no vagina!' " (McCabe, 1999: 41). It is significant, however, that at the end of her narrative, Pussy imagines giving birth to herself as a *boy* rather than as a girl. In her persuasive analysis of *Breakfast on Pluto*, Stefanie Lehner draws on Moynagh Sullivan's influential critique of figures of partition and partuition in Seamus Heaney's writing. Sullivan argues that Heaney's work positions the male poet as pregnant with the "nation-to-be"; it "revives the national artist as a national symbol of peri-natal promise, his embodiment of the nascent nation a reinstatement of a mythological 'origin' that existed before the establishment of the border. As a national symbol, he *must* fail to deliver, for to deliver is to bring the border into existence" (Sullivan, 2005: 455–456). Lehner applies Sullivan's framework to Pussy's fantasies about biological womanhood and self-birthing, reading this as a figurative means of restoring the divided nation to an imaginary wholeness, a wholeness that is achieved by means of a masculine displacement and usurpation of the feminine and the maternal that preserves the male line at women's expense (Lehner, 2011: 173–175, 183).

This is, I think, an astute reading of McCabe's authorial intentions; and yet there is something in Pussy that resists such a positioning as male with the attendant patriarchal fantasy of the masculine birthing of the nation-to-be. The specificity of Pussy as a trans woman is misrecognized and occluded in McCabe's gender slippages, perpetuating the "fin-de-siecle" deployment of trans as utopian trope without recognizing the lived specificity of trans existence. This slippage risks an exclusionary essentialism whereby the trans woman cannot be countenanced as "really" a woman, but is rather seen as a man in drag. At the very least, the position of the transgender person, particularly a trans woman like Pussy who does not "pass," can hardly be described as a position of power or privilege. If anything, the non-passing trans woman occupies one of the most abject of gendered positions within our regulatory gender systems. That the novel situates Pussy as masculine at the crucial moment of its ending is, in a sense, a violation of its transgender protagonist in the service of reconfiguring the national allegory. If we are to read Pussy's fantasized rebirth otherwise, then, what is it that is being re-engendered in this melancholic ending? Her rebirthing expresses Pussy's desire for the mother to bear her anew and to erase the abjection of her existence. It is not difficult to see how this operates as an allegory of the restoration of the wholeness of the nation before the violence of separation. However, from the perspective of Eng and Han's recuperation of racial melancholia, Pussy's imagined rebirth can be read against the grain, as a melancholic refusal to give up on the lost object, gesturing toward the recuperation of those excluded others that the nation has abjected to maintain its own ideal image.

In an illuminating Lacanian reading of the novel, Peter Mahon notes that Pussy's dyadic relation with the mother resists the intervention of a paternal other, manifest most clearly in Pussy's psychiatrist Dr Terence, and that this resistance preserves the dyad intact at the end of the novel. For Mahon, this lack of "proper" oedipal resolution indicates "a working through of the relations of the mother-Ireland/ soldier-son in a way that points beyond the legal domain of the name of the father to a complex maternal site that necessarily remains outside of the phallic law" (Mahon, 2007: 466). This resistance of the dyad to paternal intervention does not survive Neil Jordan's 2005 adaptation of *Breakfast on Pluto* for the screen, however. The screenplay was cowritten by McCabe and Jordan; McCabe wrote the first and Jordan the two subsequent drafts. In several interviews, Jordan has emphasized the "unfinished" quality of McCabe's novel. Noting its "beautifully fractured" quality, Jordan nonetheless had "the feeling that he'd kind of not finished certain themes in the novel" (Felperin, 2006). Jordan thus sees the film, as "finishing the substructure to the book, which hadn't been expressed in a way...Patrick was aware of that himself...in the novel, he never meets his mother, and the priest doesn't return...it was like we were completing the novel, in a sense" (Koresky, 2005). Pussy is renamed as Kitten, a name change that indicates the neutering of Pussy, the domestication of the queer and the suppression of the novel's depictions of sex and violence. The novel's "substructure" is "finished" by reintroducing the penitent father to the story and by having Kitten, with her father's help, find and then renounce the lost mother. Paternal intervention demands that Kitten relinquish the mother, thus overcoming her stalled development and progressing her along a phallic oedipal teleology. This intervention and renunciation facilitate the creation of a new queer multicultural family, comprising Kitten, her best friend Charlie, played in the film as a young mixed-race woman by Ruth Negga, and Charlie's baby by her murdered lover Irwin. In other words, the "unfinished" substructure that Jordan senses in the novel is, in fact, Pussy's refusal of oedipal teleology and "normal" mourning. Pussy's melancholic tenacity is broken by the film's reconstitution of "normal" oedipal development, no matter how superficially "queer" the newly constituted family appears at the film's close. Jordan's adaptation thus radically alters the meaning of Pussy/Kitten's narrative.

The recuperation of the priest-father is the fulcrum on which this transformation turns. In the novel, there is no reconciliation with the father. Rather, Pussy is possessed by an overwhelming parricidal hate. During an acute dissociative episode while in custody as a suspected member of the Republican paramilitary group the IRA following a bomb explosion in a London club, Pussy hallucinates that she has traveled back to Tyreelin to banish the "stench that no-one knows is there," a stench that has persisted for generations (McCabe, 1999: 159, 154). The stench is manifest in the paramilitary killings that Pussy reconstructs, and in the person of Fr Bernard. She imagines herself kneeling in a pew in Fr Bernard's church. She leaps up, discarding her "drab overcoat" and headscarf—signifiers of the lost violated mother—to reveal the untarnished Mitzi in her yellow shirt and capri pants. She sets fire to the church and watches as the "flesh melted on an old man's bones" (McCabe, 1999: 177). The parricide is accomplished in the name of the mother and the daughter—as Pussy says, "I'm not your son, correct, my father, because what I am's your daughter" (McCabe, 1999: 177). Rather than positioning Pussy as a Mother Ireland figure, in this hallucination, she rather embodies the abjected detritus of that ideal: those young victims of the Troubles whose terrible deaths she recounts in the novel, along with the sexual and gendered others banished from the national family and embodied by Pussy's (and her mother's) phantomatic return in her hallucination to kill off Daddy Ireland.

In the 2005 film adaptation, however, the father-priest is recuperated and carefully quarantined from any complicity with the punitive exclusionary logic of the ideal nation and its actors. In a scene that references *Paris, Texas*, Fr Bernard tracks Kitten down to the sex workers' coop where she works. Speaking through a two-way mirror, Fr Bernard reveals that he and Eily had been in love—banishing the specter of rape—and gives Kitten her mother's address. Posing as a surveyer from British Telecom, Kitten calls to Eily's house, but decides not to disclose her identity. Kitten learns from a pregnant Charlie that her boyfriend Irwin has been executed by the IRA, and that Fr Bernard has taken her in. Pussy returns to Tyreelin, and moves in with Fr Bernard and Charlie. The locals, however, are scandalized by the priest's new queer family. In a scene that directly precedes an arson attack on the priest's family, four drably dressed middle-aged and elderly Tyreelin women sit in the Bishop's palace, demanding action. In the foreground, the Bishop conveys his distaste and exasperation, thus positioning these local women as the key agents of the church and state's narrowly pious moral surveillance, pressurizing the Bishop to act against his inclination. In the following scene, the locals have set fire to the church and the priest's house. In a scene that is significantly out of kilter with the aesthetic and tone of the film, Fr Bernard courageously braves death to save Charlie from the flames while Handel's "Zadok the Priest" builds to a crescendo, the slowed motion of the scene heightening the portrayal of the priest-father as salvific hero. Charlie and Kitten depart for London, driven out by the intolerance and bigotry of the local community. In the final scene, the film cuts to Charlie in labor, and then to Kitten with the baby outside a medical clinic as Charlie has her postnatal checkup. Kitten sees her half-brother Patrick, who is waiting for his (and Pussy's) pregnant mother Eily. Again, Kitten chooses not to disclose herself to her mother, and the closing shot, zooming out to a crane shot, explicitly foregrounds the two different "paths" of "development" as the new queer family of Kitten, Charlie, and Charlie's baby walk past Eily and her son Patrick and the two families go in their opposite directions.

The differences between the film and novel could hardly be more extreme. In Jordan's film, Fr Bernard becomes the savior of the excluded and the marginalized from the murderous wrath of an unforgiving community. Neeson's screen presence—particularly in the arson scene—resonates with his portrayal of Michael Collins in Jordan's film of the same name. This piece of casting suggests a connection between Fr Bernard and the popular Irish mythic figure of the heroic and betrayed Collins, positioning the noble priest against the reviled collective DeValerian monster of the undifferentiated and literally murderous community that have been explicitly associated in the previous scene with Irish *women* and *mothers*.[4] Jordan has explained this exoneration of the priest: "to complete that change of heart, he has to be rejected by the society that made him what he is…To me, that's very true of Irish life. I know everyone's always banging on about the church and whatever, but this situation was created by the culture here" (Maguire, 2006). There is no doubt of the collective complicity of the broader society with the violences against women and children in particular perpetrated by the Irish theocracy, but Jordan's film goes much further in absolving the key state and church actors of all blame. The guilt of the "civilian" collective is pointedly attributed solely to Irish *women*, rather than *male* clergy. This displacement of the nation state's guilt on to demonized Irish women reaches its logical conclusion with repudiation of the mother at the end of the film. Thus, the narrative ends with Kitten's silent renunciation of the mother in favor of the new queer multicultural family that Fr Bernard has "birthed." While Jordan has claimed that his film is " [d]efinitely about the past," the ending speaks directly to the contemporary moment in which the film was produced and screened (Maguire, 2006). This new queer multicultural family is Jordan's version of the utopian re-engendering of herself and the community of the excluded that Pussy fantasizes at the end of the novel. The national allegory is once more writ large: in order for the nation to move on and embrace the future, the old nation, Mother Ireland, must be let go of once and for all. However, the ending conflates the real mother with the mother of fantasy, Eily Bergin with Mother Ireland: to renounce one is to renounce the other, simultaneously erasing the violations that the real mother has endured in this reaching toward a utopian postnational future. National melancholia is thus supplanted by a "normal" mourning and letting go; the phallic oedipal teleology of the nation reasserts itself. Ireland's troubles, those ghosts that haunt the nation's past and present, can be put to rest now that their origin has been safely lodged to the account of the woman and the mother. However, as we saw in relation to the novel, the mother in *Breakfast on Pluto* is not so easily limned as Mother Ireland. Read in the light of Eng and Han's framework of racial melancholia, the lost mother that the melancholic subject refuses to give up on signifies the subject's refusal to banish those troublesome historical and contemporary phantoms—the human residue of the nation state, those subjects and populations exiled from full national citizenship. These troublesome melancholic phantoms are what this ending with its renunciation of the mother occlude, insisting that national melancholia has been cured: the film is "definitely about the past." But of course, the uncanny time of the phantom does not obey such phallic investments in closure.

The "good" mother, the mother that must be embraced is, in Jordan's logic, Charlie, who thereby, alongside Kitten, comes to signify a putatively queer dissolution of "old," prehistoric, atavistic attachments to Mother Ireland and her correlatives, as Charlotte McIvor has argued. In her analysis of Ruth Negga's performance as Charlie in *Breakfast on Pluto*, McIvor notes that the film does not "foreground Negga's difference, but rather sublimate[s] it in a move that recognizes the unlikelihood of an Ethiopian-Irish schoolgirl in 1970's Northern Ireland" (McIvor, 2010: 26). As McIvor observes, there is only a glancing insinuation of Charlie's racial "otherness" amidst a sea of overwhelmingly white Irishness. Charlie's (and Negga's) "exteriority" is made to figure "successful resolutions of 'difference', broadly construed," without exploring the ideological and material logic and consequences of that "differencing" in any way (McIvor, 2010: 31). McIvor notes that the film is inevitably situated both in its historical setting, the Troubles, and in its contemporary contexts, the intersecting logics of post-9/11 global politics and of Ireland in the early millennium (McIvor, 2009: 176). Charlie's racial "otherness" speaks in particular to contemporary immigration in Ireland, and specifically to the demonization of refugees and asylum seekers within government and media discourses, and Charlie's pregnancy and the birth of her child inevitably resonate with the context of the 2004 Citizenship Referendum (McIvor, 2009: 184). In the context of this reality, the presentation of Charlie as the "good" multicultural mother-subject, symbolic of a "new" Ireland that must be embraced as the "old" mother is left behind, as it were, at the crossroads, is revealed as the obfuscating and violating fiction that it really is. As McIvor rightly observes, Jordan's representation of Kitten's narrative as a kind of queer picaresque *bildungsroman*, coupled with the "sublimation" of Negga/Charlie's racial difference, serves to negate any political or ethical valence that the film might have had. She notes: "This lack of political focus allows him to foreground the redemption of the individual, rather than collective social liberation... Queerness stands as the force that can dissolve politics and allow individual liberation" (McIvor, 2009: 174).

However, as McIvor asserts, such a dissolution, rather than being liberatory, is instead complicit with the "homonationalism" and "sexual exceptionalism" that Jasbir Puar has interrogated in her work on post-9/11 reconfigurations of queerness, race, and citizenship. For Puar, as McIvor quotes, "The emergence and sanctioning of queer subjecthood is a historical shift condoned only through a parallel process of demarcation from populations targetted for segregation, disposal, or death, a reintensification of racialization through queerness" (Puar, qtd. in McIvor, 2009: 182). The logic of this—that some "good" queer subjects are granted (qualified) inclusions at the cost of the violent exclusion of "bad" racialized others—was amply demonstrated in the Irish context on the occasion of the 2005 Dublin Lesbian and Gay Film Festival, "Family Values." The then Minister for Justice Michael McDowell, who had just the year previously been largely responsible for the introduction of the 2004 Citizenship Referendum, was invited by the film festival organizers to open that year's program in an effort to encourage his support for the burgeoning movement toward Civil Partnership. As the Minister extolled the "new" Ireland for its inclusive, benevolent, multicultural inclusion of the white, middle-class, urbanite queer subjects present within a newly configured "European" Irishness, crowds of mostly Nigerian mothers and their children gathered in the Irish Film Institute foyer to protest the Minister's presence and policy.[5] The scene fully demonstrates the uses of "queer" in masking and perpetuating the global inequities and racialized asymmetrical tensions described by Puar's analysis of "homonationalism," occlusions, and mobilities that Jordan's film, as McIvor has demonstrated, fully participates in. As David Eng has put it, "queer liberalism does not resist, but abets, the forgetting of race and the denial of racial difference" (Eng, 2009: 4). Furthermore, "the emergence of queer liberalism depends upon the active management, repression, and subsuming of race" (Eng, 2009: 17).

The occlusion of Charlie's racial difference in Jordan's film and the repressions performed by the film's birthing of a new queer multicultural family speak to the contemporary biopolitics of Ireland. The borders of the nation state have been redrawn, so that the border that troubles is no longer that separating north and south, but rather that controlling the entry and conditions of domicile and everyday life of the immigrant "other," designating who can be included in and who must be expelled from the body of the postnational nation, here aligned with the biopolitical fantasy of a "post-racial" West.

The new queer postnational, postracial family with which Jordan's film "completes" the "fractured," traumatic, phantomatic narrative of McCabe's novel is an instance in representation of the biopolitical logic of multiculturalism. As Sara Ahmed further demonstrates, multiculturalism is vital to the self-image of the imaginary and juridical Nation, narcissistically reflecting back its image of itself as inclusive, progressive, and tolerant. Multiculturalism works, Ahmed observes, by creating "good" and "bad" multicultural subjects (Ahmed, 2004: 139): as such, in relation to Jordan's film, the desexualized, domesticated queer subject (Kitten) and the deracinated racialized subject (Charlie) function very well as "good" multicultural subjects within the post-9/11 context. These are "good" subjects whose deployment in Jordan's text serve to further occlude the realities of racial and (trans)gendered abjection through the solvent of an apolitical queer "liberation" divorced from the contemporary global conflicts and crises in which they are inevitably embedded. Considered within this framework, Pussy (in the novel) is a bad multicultural subject, unassimilable to the nation or its imaginary, signifying multiple personal and collective transgenerational traumas that must be repressed in the name of a delusion, while Kitten and Charlie are recuperated in the film as good multicultural subjects whose apparent inclusion within a newly constituted post-national family occludes the provisional nature of that inclusion, and masks the realities of the nation constituted through exclusion. This is the fiction that is doomed to repeat the traumatic violations of the past. As Jordan says of his film, "everybody in the movie, no matter how awful their journey or how badly they have behaved, arrives at a kind of peace. They become good…We should have called it How To Be Good" (Maguire, 2006).

NOTES

1. See "It Gets Better Project." www.itgetsbetter.org/, accessed July 11, 2012.
2. See also Jennifer M. Jeffers's discussion of this aspect of McCabe's novel in Jeffers, 2002: 162–163.
3. For a discussion of the phantom and transgenerational trauma, see Abraham (1994) and Schwab (2010).
4. Thanks to Emma Radley who pointed me toward these resonances with Jordan's *Michael Collins*.
5. For a longer discussion of this event and its implications, see Mulhall (2011).

REFERENCES

Abraham, Nicolas and Torok, Maria (1994) *The Shell and the Kernel: Renewals of Psychoanalysis*, ed., trans., and intro. Nicholas T. Rand. Chicago, IL and London: University of Chicago Press.
Ahmed, Sara (2004) *The Cultural Politics of Emotion*. Edinburgh: Edinburgh University Press.
Butler, Judith (1997) *The Psychic Life of Power: Theories in Subjection*. Stanford: Stanford University Press.
Eng, David (2009) *The Feeling of Kinship: Queer Liberalism and the Racialization of Intimacy*. Durham, NC: Duke University Press.
Eng, David and Han, Shinhee (2003) "A Dialogue on Racial Melancholia," in David L. Eng and David Kazanijian (eds), *Loss: The Politics of Mourning*. Berkeley, CA: University of California Press.
Felperin, Leslie (2006) "NFT Interviews: Neil Jordan and Cillian Murphy." *British Film Institute*. January 9, 2006. Accessed April 14, 2010. ww.bfi.org.uk/features/interviews/jordan-murphy.html

Freud, Sigmund (1991 [1917]) "Mourning and Melancholia," in Angela Richards (ed.), *On Metapsychology: The Theory of Psychoanalysis*. Penguin Freud Library vol. 11, trans. James Strachey. Harmondsworth: Penguin.

——— (1991 [1923]) "The Ego and the Id," in Angela Richards (ed.), *On Metapsychology: The Theory of Psychoanalysis*. Penguin Freud Library vol. 11, trans. James Strachey. Harmondsworth: Penguin.

Fuss, Diana (1995) *Identification Papers*. London and New York: Routledge.

Harte, Liam and Parker, Michael (eds) (2000) *Contemporary Irish Fiction: Themes, Tropes, Theories*. Basingstoke: Palgrave Macmillan.

Jeffers, Jennifer M. (2002) *The Irish Novel at the End of the Twentieth Century*. Basingstoke: Palgrave Macmillan.

Jordan, Neil, dir. (2005) *Breakfast on Pluto*. Perf. Cillian Murphy, Liam Neeson, Ruth Negga. Pathe.

Klein, Melanie (1998 [1940]) "Mourning and Its Relation to Manic-Depressive states," in Roger Money-Kyrle (gen. ed.), *Love, Guilt and Reparation and Other Works 1921–1945*. London: Vintage.

Koresky, Michael (2005) "Horns and Halos: Neil Jordan's Bedtime Stories." *Reverse Shot Online* (Autumn). Accessed April 14, 2010. www.reverse shot.com/legacy/autumn05/interviews/jordan.html

Lehner, Stefanie (2011) *Subaltern Aesthetics in Contemporary Scottish and Irish Literature: Tracing Counter-Histories*. Basingstoke: Palgrave Macmillan.

Maguire, John (2006) "Interview: Neil Jordan & Pat McCabe." *Confessions of a Film Critic*, January 9. Accessed April 14, 2010. http://maguires movies.blogspot.com/2006/01/interview-neil-jordan-pat-mccabe-rocky .html

Mahon, Peter (2007) "Lacanian 'Pussy': Towards a Psychoanalytic Reading of Patrick McCabe's *Breakfast on Pluto*." *Irish University Review*, 37 (2) (Autumn/Winter): 441–471.

McCabe, Patrick (1998) *Breakfast on Pluto*. New York: Harper Perennial.

McIvor, Charlotte (2009) " 'Crying' on 'Pluto': Queering the 'Irish Question' for Global Film Audiences," in David Cregan (ed.), *Deviant Acts: Essays on Queer Performance*. Dublin: Carysfort Press.

——— (2010) " 'I'm Black an' I'm Proud': Ruth Negga, *Breakfast on Pluto*, and Invisible Irelands." *Invisible Culture: An Electronic Journal for Visible Culture*, 13 (Spring): 22–36. Accessed April 14, 2010. www.rochester .edu/in_visible_culture/Issue_13_/index.html

Miller, D. A. (1998) *Place for Us: Essay on the Broadway Musical*. Cambridge, MA, and London: Harvard University Press.

Mulhall, Anne (2011) "Queer in Ireland: Deviant Filiations and the (Un) Holy Family," in Lisa Downing and Robert Gillett (eds), *Queer in Europe*. London: Ashgate.

Namaste, Vivian (2000) *Invisible Lives: The Erasure of Transsexual and Transgendered People*. Chicago, IL: The University of Chicago Press.

Puar, Jasbir (2007) *Terrorist Assemblages: Homonationalism in Queer Times.* Durham, NC: Duke University Press.

Schwab, Gabriele (2010) *Haunting Legacies: Violent Histories and Transgenerational Trauma.* New York: Columbia University Press.

Stryker, Susan (2006) "(De)Subjugated Knowledges: An Introduction to Transgender Studies," in Susan Stryker and Stephen Whittle (eds), *The Transgender Studies Reader.* New York: Routledge.

Sullivan, Moynagh (2005) "The Treachery of Wetness: Irish Studies, Seamus Heaney and the Politics of Parturition," *Irish Studies Review,* 13 (4): 451–468.

Warner, Michael (1990) "Homo-Narcissism; or, Heterosexuality," in Joseph A. Boone and Michael Cadden (eds), *Engendering Men: The Question of Male Feminist Criticism.* New York and London: Routledge.

CHAPTER 15

Quare Theory*

Noreen Giffney

> ...*we rarely see a glimpse of what queer theory means to those producing and employing it.*
>
> —Elia et al., 2003: 335

QUARE(LY) LACK(ING)

The lack of research into the history of Irish sexuality is puzzling, although it corresponds to a general lack of interest in sexuality in Irish academia. (Inglis, 2005: 10)

If Tom Inglis is puzzled, then so am I; what we find puzzling differs substantially however. He is puzzled by what he terms "the lack of research into the history of Irish sexuality," which for him "corresponds to a general lack of interest in sexuality in Irish academia." I, on the other hand, am puzzled by his ignorance of the reputation that The(e)ories: Critical Theory & Sexuality Studies, founded and co-organized by Michael O'Rourke and myself since 2002, has attained internationally as an academic site of excellence for the study of sexuality, Irish and otherwise.[1] Since 2007, Michael and I have also collaborated with Anne Mulhall on a series of one-, two-, and three-day intensive seminars to rigorously read and discuss an important recently-published book in the area of critical and cultural theories of gender and sexuality. Inglis' statements leave me wondering what Inglis means by the terms "sexuality" and "academics," what constitutes "an interest in sexuality" for him, or indeed what might count as "research." I am curious about his use of these words and phrases because the study of sexuality has been ongoing in Ireland for some time.

If I confine myself to the twenty-first century, I can think of a host of conferences, symposia, panel discussions, seminars, publications, and specialized courses, which deal with sexuality, predominantly from feminist and lesbian, gay, bisexual, transgender, intersex, and queer perspectives.[2] These interdisciplinary events have attracted the foremost experts in the field of sexuality to Ireland to discuss their work without "shame or embarrassment." They have also contributed toward the formation of an international community of scholars and activists who have traveled to Ireland to share their research findings on sexuality. Inglis' silence about this work raises questions relating to visibility, value, and respectability. What academic work is considered worthy enough to mention, or unimportant enough to ignore? What scholarly activities are legitimated by the academic establishment, and what research is trivialized, dismissed, or silenced? Who, more pointedly, is deemed to be respectable enough to speak on such matters and expert enough to be listened to? These questions are especially pertinent in light of the theme of this chapter: the development of queer theory in Ireland and its relationship with lesbian studies and feminism.

This chapter is a genealogical meditation on queer theory in Ireland, what I am terming "quare theory" (Giffney, 2007b).[3] I employ the term "quare" to articulate the specificities, nuances, and methodological tensions between expressions of queer theory in an Irish context and theoretical formulations of queer theory originating in Anglo-North American contexts. Employing "quare" also helps to differentiate the pursuit of queer theory as an epistemology, ontology, methodology, and pedagogy in Ireland from Irish queer studies (Valente, 1998), which is a loose umbrella term to describe scholarly efforts which concern themselves more specifically with the connections between Irish studies and queer studies or LGBT[4] studies more generally—in other words, work which has a firm commitment to or engagement with postcolonial theory and makes a concerted effort to think about questions relating to Irish national identity. While queer theory might have a tentative home in women's studies, Irish queer studies remains an amorphous shape haunting the contours of Irish studies and queer studies.[5]

I argue that quare theory happens at the points of entanglement between queer theory, feminism, and lesbian studies in Ireland. Thus, quare theory is useful as a qualifying term to describe a moment in time—a temporal anomaly—and to point to the cultural context within which this particular genealogy of queer theory has gestated. I have no investment in seeing quare theory develop as an area of study in its own right (hence, it is not quare *studies*), but instead cite the term to make visible the ways in which queer/feminist/lesbian works intersect in Ireland, and as a way to facilitate the interrogation of our collective investments in such fields of knowledge production. To suggest that there is no tension between queer theory and feminism and lesbian studies in Ireland would be inaccurate. What I am suggesting instead is a concentration on points of connection *in spite of* the methodological and ideological tensions between the three fields; an attendance to the contradictory impulses inherent in such interminglings and a commitment to recognizing that these three fields are not mutually exclusive but have shifting boundaries. In this, quare theory also happens at points of conflict and in the very sites where differences between the three fields get expressed. And so, I insist that quare theory operates as a methodology rather than as an identity category or object to be scrutinized, a culturally situated and historically contingent analytical tool for interrogating the potentialities and limits of areas of study founded on the internalization, deconstruction, or repudiation of identity categories.

I draw on collaborative queer/feminist/lesbian events I have been involved in (co-)organizing in Ireland, in an effort to show where and how quare theory comes into being. I focus specifically on the annual Lesbian Lives conference, the formation and development of the Dublin Queer Studies Group, the Certificate in Lesbian Studies and Queer Culture and the rationale for The(e)ories: Critical Theory and Sexuality Studies, all convened at University College Dublin. Originally set up as a community event in 1993, Lesbian Lives has grown in recent years into an international, interdisciplinary conference, which attracts hundreds of delegates from Ireland and around the world. The Dublin Queer Studies Group was established in 2001 to facilitate informal discussion about topics relating to queer interest. Convened fortnightly, the group used a single chapter or article, film or other cultural product to act as a springboard from which to launch thematic debates.

The Certificate in Lesbian Studies and Queer Culture was launched as an outreach certificate program in 2000, delivering modules on subjects such as history, film, psychology, politics, and literature to interested members of the LGBTQ community in Dublin and Cork. The(e)ories, which originated as a monthly, interdisciplinary, formal seminar series in 2002, also features occasional round-table discussions, symposia, and conferences under its rubric, in addition to hosting some of the world's leading thinkers in LGBTQ Studies as plenary speakers. As well as exhibiting a commitment to the formation of an interdisciplinary and multi-theoretical environment for discussions, all four events operate an inclusive, trans-academic policy, which means that they are attended by academics, activists, and non-academics. This also signifies that they often incorporate what are traditionally considered to be non-academic elements; for example, The(e)ories has featured a performance by a local drag-king troupe, the Shamcocks, in advance of a plenary lecture by Professor Judith Halberstam.

QUARE THE(E)ORIES

> A queer pedagogy must also try to break with the oedipal deadlock that creates and sustains intergenerational conflict. (Halberstam, 2005b: 69)

Genealogies of queer theory can be traced through sexology, psychoanalysis, the lesbian and gay liberation movement, the black civil rights movement, (lesbian) feminism, HIV/AIDS activism, as well as postmodernism and post-structuralism. Broadly defined, the term "queer theory" denotes a collection of methods all devoted to examining desire and its relationship to identity. Queer theorists interrogate the categorization of desiring subjects (i.e., the creation of identities based on desire), while making visible the ways in which some desires (and thus identities) are made to pass as normal, at the same time that others are rendered wrong, abnormal, sick, or evil. Queer theorists depathologize abjected desires (and thus identities), not by attacking or refuting untrue statements but by exercising a post-structuralist approach advocated by Michel Foucault to the processes through which norms are created. Queer theorists refuse to "play the game" of the dominant culture, and instead of asking what is wrong with queers, turn an interrogative gaze toward societal norms and the assumptions which underpin those norms.

Queer theorists expose norms for the constructions that they are, and show how norms define, solidify, and defend their shaky self-identities by excluding those (dissident Others) who fail or refuse to conform. Queer theorists show that norms need their abjected Others, because they would not exist if they did not have one or more Others to define (and protect) themselves against. Queer theorists also reclaim terms of insult; while brandishing them with pride and not as words of degradation, theorists (try to) relieve those same terms of their power to hurt or offend. The term "queer" itself is seen to have a performative power; a power to challenge (if not always successfully subvert) all norms relating to (desirous) identity.

While many queer theorists forward a fluid definition for the term "queer" and boast a capacious understanding of its epistemological and methodological potential, all too often the term is collapsed in its praxis into a synonym for lesbian and gay studies (Giffney, 2004). In addition, a growing body of criticism has developed around the misrepresentation or silencing of lesbian, gay, bisexual, or transgender issues and viewpoints by certain queer theorists. Many point to queer theorists' failure to deal adequately with how sexuality and gender intersect with other facets of our identities: race, ethnicity, nationality, (dis)ability, age, class, and religious affiliation. This has had the positive effect of spurring on intersectional analyses, which attempt to answer E. Patrick Johnson's call for "an epistemology of the body" (Johnson, 2001: 9). A variety of people within the university, in addition to activists and members of the LGBTQ community, have leveled charges of elitism at some queer theorists who bear the hallmarks of post-structuralism by employing jargon-laden prose in their explication of ideas. Despite the proliferation of queer theoretical work in places as diverse as Poland and India, an unvoiced assumption circulates within LGBTQ studies that queer theory is produced in North America and to a lesser extent in Britain, and then exported as a form of neo-imperialist rhetoric to other parts of the world. A "star system" continues to underpin many queer writings, with the result that certain individuals, locations, and disciplines have become conflated with producing theory while others are seen as simply applying it, colonized by its ideological effects (Giffney and O'Donnell, 2007).

Quare theory is produced relationally both in the spaces between queer theory, lesbian studies, and feminism, and at their loci of connection. Functioning as a concept like Gloria Anzaldúa's *La Mestiza*, quare theory exhibits "a tolerance for contradictions, a tolerance for ambiguity" (1991: 79). Certainly, queer theory holds within its expansive rubric the potential to embrace contradictory thoughts and positions and "combine methods that are often cast as being at odds with each other" (Halberstam, 2005a: 13). Having said that, certain works informed by queer theory follow a linear, developmental trajectory and posit themselves against heteronormative impulses on the one hand and a so-called normative feminist and/or lesbian discourse on the other. This becomes unhelpful when *all* feminist and/or lesbian scholarship is ridiculed, misrepresented, or ignored, or else employed as a catchall category for thinking that is reputedly outmoded, conservative, or essentialist. This is not to say that works sporting "lesbian" and/or "feminist" tags do not distort, resist, or discard "queer" insights. As Elizabeth Weed puts it, "To say that feminism and queer theory share commonalities and affiliations is not to say they are easy commensurable" (1997: vii). This is not to imply that either queer theory or feminism are monolithic entities; indeed, as Donald E. Hall comments, "there is no 'queer' theory in the singular, only many different voices and sometimes overlapping, sometimes divergent perspectives that can loosely be called 'queer theories'" (2003: 5).

In my queer/lesbian/feminist collaborations in Ireland, I have not experienced what appears to be a queer rite of passage if critical commentaries are to be believed: that is, queer theory's apparent ritualistic oedipal resistance to feminism and/or lesbian studies or its practitioners' metaphorical cannibalistic sacrificing of their (M)Others for not being transgressive, subversive, radical, or theoretical enough. This "collision model," as it is referred to by Laura Doan (2007), exists within a long series of unhelpful dichotomous standoffs prevalent at one time or another in queer theory, lesbian studies, and feminism over the past fifteen years: essentialism/social constructionism, academia/activism, and theory/materiality.

I sometimes find it difficult to distinguish between queer theory, lesbian studies, and feminism in Ireland for three reasons: first, my formal introduction to feminism was through the Certificate in Lesbian Studies and Queer Culture. In fact, the practice of queer theory has been facilitated, made possible even, by the earlier gains of feminism and lesbian studies. Second, I worked for a number of years in a Women's Studies department, which under Ailbhe Smyth's guidance had a firm commitment to lesbian studies—hosting an annual Lesbian Lives conference, for example, and exhibiting an active involvement in a variety of LGBTQ organizations and coalitions, such as the Irish Queer Archive, the Gay and Lesbian Equality Network, the National Lesbian and Gay Federation, and the Queer(y)ing Psychology Collective. Third, many of the events I have organized or participated in have resulted in a fusion of the three fields, in that they are generally put together by self-identified female, male, or transgender feminists with an investment in creating an inclusive environment. This means that explicitly "feminist" conferences, such as "Feminism Contesting Globalisation" (2004), have included a number of presentations on lesbian and queer issues, just as the "Queer Keywords" conference (2005) featured a panel on "Lesbo Words." Similarly, the Lesbian Lives conferences have always had queer sessions on their program, everything from panels on "Queering the (Non-) Human" (2003) to round-table discussions on topics such as "(Heterosexually) Married and Queer: An Oxymoron?" (2004).

Thus, my schooling in queer theory/lesbian studies/feminism has never been "pure" or disciplined; rather, I have always been offered a multidisciplinary conglomerate of theories and perspectives—academic and activist—for the study of sex, gender, and sexuality. This has encouraged an appreciation in me of the ways in which each of the three fields is co-implicated in and enriched by the others. It is this methodological eclecticism, this expressed refusal toward disciplinary coherence, this hybridization of feminist/lesbian/queer theory, which gives rise to quare theory. Quare is indispensable here to pinpoint this specific instance of an alignment between feminist, lesbian, and queer perspectives because not all Women's Studies departments are pro-lesbian or supportive of explicitly queer work. This also means that quare theory does not recognize queer theory, lesbian studies, and feminism as existing in a competitive or evolutionary relationship with one another. It is the emphasis on fluidity and indeterminacy—where does one discourse end and another begin?—which encapsulates the sense that quare theory constitutes a collection of moments, a rhizomatic temporal symbiosis without a center or locus of definition.

My concentration on what might appear to be the painless and seamless interconnections between queer theory, lesbian studies, and feminism should not be taken as a call for an all-encompassing eclecticism, which inhibits, according to Joan Wallach Scott, "rigorous interrogation" and results in "the coexistence of conflicting doctrines as if there were no conflict…to ignore or overlook differences, to create balance and harmony, to close down the opening to unknown futures" (2005: 116). Quare theory points to the creative energy which results from confrontational encounters between queer theory, lesbian studies, and feminism. It is through a discursive process that quare theory comes into being. This process incorporates the points of disagreement arising when ideological borders between the three fields are drawn and redrawn, when belief systems are reconsidered and new ideas are formed. Thus, quare theory describes the compromises entered into in order to facilitate such productive encounters as well as naming the encounters themselves.

The title of the annual lesbian conference at University College Dublin has been a subject of continued contention among delegates. Retaining the title "Lesbian Lives" in spite of criticism and calls for a more capacious moniker—"Queer Lives" and/or "Lesbian, Bisexual and Transgender Lives"—the organizers operate an inclusive policy when it comes to deciding who can attend and the topics that can be presented on. In this, the title "Lesbian Lives" operates as an anachronism, which is offered up yearly as something to be debated and is never clearly defined so that it is always open for resignification. This refusal to relinquish the term "lesbian" while at the same time not feeling the need to own its meaning(s) is reminiscent of Judith Halberstam's idea of queer lesbian studies: " 'Lesbian' is a term that modifies and qualifies 'queer', and 'queer' is a term capable of challenging the stability of identities subsumed by the label 'lesbian' " (1996: 259).

When choosing a name for the Dublin Queer Studies Group, Michael O'Rourke and I decided on the word "queer" for its use as an umbrella term for people as well as theories and subjects which could be discussed under that banner. While acting as facilitators of the group's discussions during 2001–2002, O'Rourke and I were privy to a number of heated debates as members argued over what "queer" might mean, who or what it included and excluded, what its practical uses and material effects were, its relationship to feminism and lesbian and gay studies, in addition to race, class, (dis)ability, age, and religion more widely. The group counted among its members academics and students from a number of academic disciplines and social backgrounds, with a range of political affiliations, as well as including activists and non-academics and people who identified as lesbian, gay, bisexual, transgender, queer, and straight. Conversations were often tense with people staking out particular positions and they often arrived frustrated that the articles were inaccessibly written. While some members were comfortable with divulging personal details, others pushed for more abstractly theoretical discussions at the same time that a section of the group insisted that everything be brought back to the material realities of queers and other disadvantaged groups. This caused a lot of consternation in the group at first as everyone endeavored to "convert" other members to one another's viewpoints. Those fiery arguments also encouraged dialogue, however, between a diverse range of people, who sometimes held fundamentally opposing opinions and forced all of us to try to find a common ground where we could tolerate if not always understand radically different viewpoints.

It was at the Dublin Queer Studies Group that the borders between particular forms of (lesbian) feminism and queer theory became visible, as discussants sometimes put forward opposing thoughts on topics such as transgender, bisexuality, heterosexuality, power, and identification. Many of those debates remained unresolved with participants reaching out across a chasm of assumptions, misunderstandings, and oppositional political persuasions. It is in this chasm, in the borderlands between identities and identifications, that quare theory sparks and takes flight. For E. Patrick Johnson, "quare studies," as he formulates it, "is 'bi'-directional: it theorizes from bottom to top and top to bottom" (2001: 19). This raises the question of the relationship between "queer" and "theory," especially as it relates to the Dublin Queer Studies Group, many of whom took issue with what they saw as the exclusionary language and elitist posturing of queer theorists. That is why I use the word "quare" in connection with "theory" because it points to the discussions we were furiously having early in the new Millennium. It is at the point of those unresolved—sometimes irreconcilable—tensions that quare theory can be identified, as well as in the perverse pleasure that we took in challenging one another's conceptions of self, desire, and identification.

THE "E" IN THE(E)ORIES

I shall speak, then, of a letter. (Derrida, 1973: 131)

The epigraph cited above is excerpted from Jacques Derrida's essay, "Differance,"[6] in which he discusses the neologism of the piece's title. "Differance," like "The(e)ories," is more properly a neographism because it is a silent interruption and one which cannot be spoken or heard, rather it can be ascertained only through writing and reading (Derrida, 1973: 132). Differance and The(e)ories happen in/between speech and writing—they are indistinguishable from the terms "difference" and "theories" when verbally expressed—thus indicating "this *sameness* which is not *identical*" (129). Differance describes that which makes meaning possible (Wolfreys, 2007: 52), and is, as Penelope Deutscher comments, an example of Derrida's engagement with the dichotomies organizing knowledge:

> Derrida finds or invents new concepts that can't be contained within overturned hierarchical oppositions. *Différance* is one of these terms. In relation to the opposition between "presence" and "absence" *différance* is neither present, nor absent. Instead, it is a kind of absence that generates the effect of presence. (2005: 29)

The(e)ories, as I will argue, operates similarly. While Derrida speaks of "a"—the letter he substitutes for the second "e" in "difference"—I will attend here to the insertion of an additional "e" in "The(e)ories." Unlike the "a" in "differance," which could be mistaken for a typographical error, the "e" in "The(e)ories" is encased within brackets to mark its appearance as a deliberate act. When we speak of differance, we gesture toward excess—that which cannot be categorized, reduced, known, or made possible—an interventionist exorbitance which manifests materially in The(e)ories. The "(e)" of which I speak is an assemblage rather than a letter, in a similar way to Derrida who chooses "assemblage" in reference to differance because for him it is "literally neither a word nor a concept" (1973: 132).

> The word "assemblage" seems more apt for suggesting that the kind of bringing-together proposed here has the structure of an interlacing, a weaving, or a web, which would allow the different threads and different lines of sense or force to separate again, as well as being ready to bind others together. (132)

Just as "[i]t is misleading to pose the question of differance in terms of what *is*" (Royle, 2003: 71), we might ask not what the "(e)" in The(e)ories *is* but what it *does*.

"What does the '(e)' in The(e)ories mean?" is however the question that has been repeatedly asked of us by correspondents since we coined the term. The first impulse then is a will to know, to stabilize meaning, to confirm with certainty, precisely the sort of ontological closure The(e)ories resists. Such a question also assumes that we have the answer, that we can provide a definitive statement to relieve the puzzlement that seems to result from encounters with this term. This of course reveals another assumption: just because the insertion is deliberate does not mean that we can provide *the* answer. Answers certainly, but *the* answer: impossible. Even if we *do* respond to queries of this sort, the answers we provide are not (indeed, *cannot* be) final,[7] for the meaning of the "(e)" in The(e)ories eludes even us, those who have put it there, and that is precisely the point. I am reminded here of what Derrida says of the "a" in differance: "it remains silent, secret, and discreet, like a tomb" (1973: 132).

And so, the "(e)" stands in here for a question mark and is designed to provoke thinking about the contexts within which questions, like "What does the '(e)' in The(e)ories mean?," arise. For the "(e)" is always a trace, which in Derrida's words, "is not a presence but is rather the simulacrum of a presence that dislocates, displaces, and refers beyond itself" (156). If The(e)ories is a question, it functions rhetorically by opening up the terms "The(e)ories" and "theories" to scrutiny, a destabilizing device that forces us through evasion to grapple with its slipperiness and our own desire for closure. It is performative in its interpellation of those who approach it to produce

theories about The(e)ories, The(e)ories about theories, and theories/
The(e)ories about the "(e)." It functions therefore in certain instances
as a relational metaphor in the bringing together of those who remain
troubled by its definitional circumventions. It acts provisionally as a
fulcrum which facilitates initial explorations of the "(e)" itself before
such discussions spiral outward toward other objects. In this, it evokes
the workings of queer theory.

Questions about the significance of the "(e)" invariably lead to
inquiries about what "The(e)ories" symbolizes; so it seems appropriate
at this point to mention that it has some relation to the term "queer."
We might say that it exhibits the multiple genealogies and theories of
queer that have led commentators such as Donald E. Hall to comment: "there is no 'queer' theory in the singular, only many different
voices and sometimes overlapping, sometimes divergent perspectives
that can loosely be called 'queer theories'" (2003: 5). That is, queer's
indefinability if it means being reduced to a sound bite. Then again,
the "(e)" may signal a queering of theory or the queerness of theory;
"a theoretical, rather than a sexual, orientation"[8]—we might even call
it a sextual orientation.

The relation between queer and theory prefigures another, that of
queer theory and critical theory more broadly. Queer theory is often
dismissed as a pseudo-theory, masquerading as that which is real,
respectable, and serious. It is of course the act of dismissal itself that
reifies such critics and promotes their theoretical proclivities to the
status of the real, the respectable, and the serious in the first place.[9]
There is a sense in which we have smuggled the "(e)" into a word,
"theories," overburdened as it is at times with expectations of gravitas,
just as we have ferreted away as renegades working on the edges of the
university in a field, "queer studies," which remains unrecognized in
Ireland and within a discourse, "queer theory," which provokes suspicion and derision in equal measure. All of this theorizing—we might
call it the(e)orizing—about the "(e)" reveals a process, a becoming
which recalls Derrida's words on differance: "What we note as *differance* will thus be the movement of play that "produces"…these
differences, these effects of differance (1973: 141).

CRITICALLY QUARE

"Queer" is such a simple, unassuming little word. Who ever could
have guessed that we would come to saddle it with so much pretentious baggage—so many grandiose theories, political agendas, philosophical projects, apocalyptic meanings? (Halperin, 2003: 339)

> If the term "queer" is to be a site of collective contestation, the point of departure for a set of historical reflections and futural imaginings, it will have to remain that which it is, in the present, never fully owned. (Butler, 1993: 228)

William Haver remarks that "it would be more useful to ask what queer research *does*, to ask what *happens* in queer research, than to ask what it *is*" (1997: 284). This is a common strategy put into practice by queer theorists who refuse to be defined or categorized as passive objects of knowledge by the dominant culture and by extension will not define what queer theory "is," by fixing its identity, but concentrate more on writing about its actions, in the process allowing it to speak on its own behalf. Quare theory doesn't exist independent of the interrelationship between queer theory, lesbian studies, and feminism, or indeed as something in its own right. This chapter is not trying to perform a conjuring act or birth a new field. To clarify: I am not suggesting that "quare theory" should be used as a so-called advanced replacement for "queer theory," in the reductive way that the latter has often been operationalized following (but against the wishes of) Teresa de Lauretis (1991) in relation to "lesbian and gay studies."

Quare *is* useful as a descriptor for a methodological apparatus in this instance because it does not harbor, like the word "queer" does, as much ideological baggage as an identity category. Certainly, quare is sometimes used in Irish contexts as a colloquial epithet for gay just as it can also be employed to point to something or someone "odd" or "strange"; however, the term does not have the same currency in Ireland as an identity marker in activist and academic circles. Quare theory signifies the self-reflexive interrogation of queer theory through a feminist and lesbian studies lens and vice versa. It is at the moment that one field interrupts another that quare becomes manifest. Quare theory enumerates the importance of each field in ensuring the continued relevance of the others and defines, through critique, compromise, and reevaluation, "the adaptability of queer studies to meet the challenges suggested by contexts that are never simply reducible to our sexual desires" (Hemmings and Grace, 1999: 394). This is in contrast to some individuals who see the words "lesbian," "queer," or at times even "feminist" as an opportunity to reduce an event and its participants to the sexual acts they think "lesbians," "queers," and/or "feminists" perform. It is a way of dismissing an event and rendering its participants silent.

Judith Butler has discussed what it might mean to "come out" as a "lesbian," professionally (in an academic sense) and otherwise.

According to Butler, it is at the moment of coming out, of rendering oneself intelligible in language, of taking on a term to identify oneself with, that a person becomes complicit with the technologies of a regulatory regime (1991: 13–14). By extension, what might it mean to "out" oneself as someone who does queer theory in the university in Ireland? The utterance, "My research interests include queer theory," is a double coming out of sorts: One is identifying oneself as an academic, a participant in the institutionalization of knowledge, while also professing one's relation to a subject which many mark out for ridicule or abjection, when not choosing to ignore it entirely. This pronouncement results in a double bind: While one is now visible in academic discourse, a subject of one's own creation, it is at this very moment that one also becomes an object and is thus subjected to the scrutiny of potentially hostile onlookers. This also has the potential effect of facilitating the (re-)institutionalization of queer(s) in an alienating academic discourse; a professional pathologizing of those who have always been subjected to pathologization in medical, legal, and religious discourses.

E. Patrick Johnson summons "quare studies as an interventional disciplinary project. Quare studies addresses the concerns and needs of gay, lesbian, bisexual, and transgendered people across issues of race, gender, class, and other subject positions" (2001: 20). For him, quare studies "is committed to theorizing everyday life" (20) and offers a critique of identity while recognizing, like Butler does, which terms like "lesbian," "gay," "bisexual," and "transgender" can function as politically efficacious phantasms (1991: 13). Johnson is especially insistent that queer theorists concentrate on the specific contexts within which sexualities are produced, discussing matters pertaining especially to race and class (2001: 13). Following on from Johnson, quare theory is especially cognizant of the pleasures and dangers involved in positioning oneself as a practitioner of queer, lesbian, or feminist work, whatever one's sexual identity might be.

The "Historicising the Lesbian" conference (2006) featured an open forum on "Bisexuality and Biphobia," which was facilitated by two queerly positioned women, one a self-identified bisexual, the other a self-identified lesbian. It was set up not to include any academic presentations and the facilitators arrived without a set agenda; rather, the purpose of the forum was to provide time and space in which to discuss any issues participants felt to be pertinent to the terms "bisexuality" and "biphobia." At the forum, attendees—particularly self-identified bisexuals—experienced a certain pleasure at being provided with a space in which to discuss these issues, particularly as "lesbian" spaces have not always been tolerant of difference when it comes to bisexuality. In addition, the discussion was attended by people with a range of identifications—bisexual, lesbian, straight, and queer—and from a variety of rural and urban locations. The forum worked so well because it incorporated unconsciously—no trigger papers were used, no advance preparation was required—the "quare" ideas of Johnson. The discussion concentrated, not on how subversive or transgressive bisexuality can be, but on the day-to-day lives of attendees, and their embodiment of or resistance to identity categories. People left invigorated by the discussion precisely because the taking on of labels to identify oneself with was respected, at the same time that there was a collective unease expressed at the way those same labels can function as exclusionary and sometimes self-alienating devices. This discussion made us starkly aware that, when we choose a label to define and make ourselves visible in the world, this often results in us becoming "owned" by that same label and its attendant meanings, so much so that our actions, beliefs, and practices can become dictated by reductive reasoning.

I would like to return to the two quotations—the first by David Halperin, the second by Judith Butler—that preface this section. While Halperin ponders how queer, "such a simple, unassuming little word," has been saddled with "so much pretentious baggage" (2003: 339), Butler insists that the term must remain forever open to reinterpretation. Certainly Halperin's point suggests that it has, in its definitional proliferations, inflated to sometimes grandiose proportions. Let me focus closer on Butler's words for a moment, in which she says that if queer is to be useful, it must "remain that which it is, in the present, never fully owned" (1993: 228). In diverging from Butler, I would make the point that it is not that queer must not be owned, so much as that it should not be allowed to own *us*—those who invest it with meaning, practice it, live it—it must not become another category for us to "come out" into, castigate ourselves with, disidentify from, or fiercely protect from encroachments by hostile forces. Queer is, of course, all of these things because it has developed simultaneously as an identity category and a methodology among having a host of other meanings. This is why the term "quare theory" has been so useful to me: I neither wish to own it nor contemplate a time when I will become owned by it. It is useful not in itself, but because it has facilitated the discursive coming into being (through this chapter and others like it) of the presence of queer theory in Ireland and the specific context within which queer theory has developed here, out of and alongside lesbian studies and feminism.

Notes

* This is a revised and extended version of Giffney (2007a). This piece also includes material I contributed to Giffney and O'Rourke (2007).

1. The(e)ories was first subtitled "Advanced Seminars for Queer Research" but Michael and I chose to change the subtitle to "Critical Theory & Sexuality Studies" as our interests grew in the fields of deconstruction and psychoanalysis respectively. The(e)ories was funded until 2006 by the Faculty of Interdisciplinary Studies and the Women's Education, Research and Resource Centre at University College Dublin. Following Ailbhe Smyth's retirement, The(e)ories has been funded by Gerardine Meaney through Irish Studies, the Graduate Research and Education Programme (GREP) and the Humanities Institute at University College Dublin. Anne Mulhall joined the organizing committee of The(e)ories in 2012.

2. For the purposes of this chapter, I will mention just a small sample of the activities I have been involved in either as an organizer or co-organizer: "Queer Studies: Where Have We Been? Where Are We Going?" (2002); "Queer Studies: Pros, Cons and "Futural Imaginings' " (2003); "Freaks of Nature? Queering the (Non-) Human" (2003); "Lesbian Lives, Studies and Activism since *The Lesbian Postmodern*" (2004); "A Public Lecture with Judith Halberstam and a Drag-King Performance by the Shamcocks" (2004); "A Public Lecture and Intensive Seminar with Judith Butler" (2004); "Reading Eve Kosofsky Sedgwick: A Retrospective" (2005); "Queer-Straight: An Oxymoron?" (2006); "Are We Post-Queer Yet?" (2005); "Gender, Sexuality and Horror Cinema" (2006); "Lesbian Studies and Medieval Studies: At the Intersections" (2006); "FUTURE*QUEER" (2006); "Reading Lee Edelman's *No Future: Queer Theory and the Death Drive*" (2007); "Reading Sara Ahmed's *Queer Phenomenology*" (2007); "Psychoanalysis, Queer Theory and Perversion" (2007); "Reading Leo Bersani: A Retrospective" (2008); "Reading Bracha L. Ettinger's *The Matrixial Borderspace*" (2008); "Commemorating Eve Kosofsky Sedgwick (1950–2009)" (2009); "Reading Lisa Baraitser's *Maternal Encounters*" (2010); "Queer Temporalities: Reading Elizabeth Freeman's *Time Binds*" (2011); "Reading Robyn Wiegman's *Object Lessons*" (2012); and "Reading Lauren Berlant's *Cruel Optimism*" (2013).

3. This is but one genealogy among many.

4. LGBTIQQA is an acronym for lesbian, gay, bisexual, transgender, intersex, queer, questioning, affiliated.

5. See, for example, the work of Anne Mulhall, Eithne Luibhéid, and Fintan Walsh in this volume.

6. The term in French is "différance." I reproduce it here as the anglicized "differance" in line with Nicholas Royle's rationale: "Derrida

stresses that (in French) the difference between 'difference' and 'differance' 'cannot be heard'…In English too, I propose that we try to pronounce and hear it as a homophone for 'difference'" (2003: 71).
7. "In the end it is a strategy without finality" (Derrida, 1973: 135).
8. Michael O'Rourke quoted in Giffney (2007b: 278).
9. A similar transaction occurs under the auspices of heteronormativity in which heterosexuality is set up as the origin and homosexuality as the imperfect copy. See Butler (1991).

References

Anzaldúa, Gloria (1991) "La Conciencia de la Mestiza: Towards a New Consciousness," in *Borderlands/La Frontera: The New Mestiza*. San Francisco: Aunt Lute Books.
Butler, Judith (1991) "Imitation and Gender Insubordination," in Diana Fuss (ed.), *Inside/Out: Lesbian Theories, Gay Theories*. New York and London: Routledge, 1991.
——— (1993) *Bodies that Matter: On the Discursive Limits of "Sex."* New York and London: Routledge.
De Lauretis, Teresa (1991), "Introduction," *Differences: A Journal of Feminist and Cultural Studies*, 3 (2): iii–xviii.
Derrida, Jacques (1973) "Differance," in *Speech and Phenomena: And Other Essays on Husserl's Theory of Signs*. Evanston, IL: Northwestern University Press.
Deutscher, Penelope (2005) *How to Read Derrida*. London: Granta Books.
Doan, Laura (2007) "Lesbian Studies after *The Lesbian Postmodern*: Toward a New Genealogy," in Noreen Giffney and Katherine O'Donnell (eds), *Twenty-First Century Lesbian Studies*. London and New York: Taylor and Francis.
Elia, John P., Karen E. Lovaas, and Gust A. Yep (2003) "Reflections on Queer Theory: Disparate Points of View." *Journal of Homosexuality*, 45 (2–4): 335–337.
Giffney, Noreen (2004) "Denormatizing Queer Theory: More than (Simply) Lesbian and Gay Studies." *Feminist Theory*, 5 (1): 73–78.
——— (2007a) "Quare Theory" in Wanda Balzano, Anne Mulhall and Moynagh Sullivan (eds.), *Irish Postmodernisms and Popular Culture* (Basingstoke: Palgrave Macmillan).
——— (2007b) "Quare Éire." *Journal of Lesbian Studies*, 11 (3–4): 291–305.
Giffney, Noreen and Michael O'Rourke (2007) "The 'E(ve)' in The(e)ories: Dreamreading Sedgwick in Retrospective Time." *Irish Feminist Review*, 3: 6–21.
Giffney, Noreen and Katherine O'Donnell (2007) "Twenty-First Century Lesbian Studies," in Noreen Giffney and Katherine O'Donnell (eds), *Twenty-First Century Lesbian Studies*. New York and London: Taylor and Francis.

Halberstam, Judith (1996) "Queering Lesbian Studies," in Bonnie Zimmerman and Toni A. H. McNaron (eds), *The New Lesbian Studies: Into the Twenty-First Century*. New York: The Feminist Press, 1996.

—— (2005a) *In a Queer Time and Place: Transgender Bodies, Subcultural Lives*. New York: New York University Press.

—— (2005b) "Queer Studies," in Philomena Essed, David Theo Goldberg, and Audrey Kobayashi (eds.), *A Companion to Gender Studies*. Oxford: Blackwell.

Hall, Donald, E. (2003) *Queer Theories*. Basingstoke: Palgrave Macmillan.

Halperin, David M. (2003) "The Normalization of Queer Theory." *Journal of Homosexuality*, 45 (2–4): 339–343.

Haver, William (1997) "Queer Research; Or, How to Practise Invention to the Brink of Intelligibility," in Sue Golding (ed.), *Eight Technologies of Otherness*. London and New York: Routledge.

Hemmings, Clare and Grace, Felicity (1999) "Stretching Queer Boundaries: An Introduction." *Sexualities*, 2 (4): 387–396.

Inglis, Tom (2005) "Origins and Legacies of Irish Prudery: Sexuality and Social Control in Modern Ireland." *Éire-Ireland*, 40 (3–4): 9–37.

Johnson, E. Patrick (2001) " 'Quare Studies', or (Almost) Everything I Know about Queer Studies I Learned from My Grandmother." *Text and Performance*, 21 (1): 1–25.

Royle, Nicholas (2003) *Jacques Derrida*. London and New York: Routledge.

Valente, Joseph (ed.) (1998) *Quare Joyce*. Ann Arbor, MI: University of Michigan Press.

Wallach Scott, Joan (2005) "Against Eclecticism." *Differences: A Journal of Feminist Cultural Studies*, 16 (3): 114–137.

Weed, Elizabeth (1997) "Introduction," in Elizabeth Weed and Naomi Schor (eds), *Feminism Meets Queer Theory*. Bloomington, IL, and Indianapolis, IN: Indiana University Press.

Wolfreys, Julian (2007) *Derrida: A Guide for the Perplexed*. London and New York: Continuum.

Ailbhe Smyth

Interview with Ailbhe Smyth

Medb Ruane

The path to Ailbhe Smyth's door leads up an Edwardian road and round a Ranelagh[1] corner to a modest red-bricked terrace near the old railway embankment. Thousands of footsteps have walked this way, bringing the friends, activists, writers, poets, dancers, singers, musicians, students that Smyth always welcomes for debate and fun. Subtle colors shade walls where prints and paintings hang—Alice Maher's witty *Rain*, a beautiful Françoise Gilot and, on the stairwell, a black-and-white photograph of Smyth's grandfather, with Éamon De Valera in the group.

Smyth's living area is a place for being and doing: things she values happen here. A fab photo of her daughter Lydia graces an uncluttered desk. Books witness her Renaissance Woman range of interests—and status as a writer, scholar, and public intellectual. She likes to cook: rock buns wait on a pretty plate, the kitchen promises good coffee.

Such a humble person does not prattle about her extensive professional achievements[2] but Smyth's record is about the pursuit of excellence and following through. Her caring, open persona makes her the kind of woman people ask for street directions, relationship advice, thesis pointers, as well as campaign strategy. Inside, there is a platinum core.

What follows comes from a conversation with Ailbhe soon after she had retired from University College Dublin (UCD) and been celebrated by peers and admirers with a reception at the Royal Irish Academy on Dublin's Dawson Street. The guests were an alphabet written from her work in academia, with communities and with writers and artists. Afterward, some of us danced to hot mambo music in a downtown bar while others argued politics and gender. These are her words.

On Reading and Writing

I have always found academic writing (my own) dissatisfying, because I can rarely if ever make it solve the problems I want it to solve, or lead me where I want to go. (Reading other people is much more likely to be rewarding). Of course, this is because of the short-circuits, fault-lines and involuntary elisions in my own ways of "thinking" in the first instance. It has also to do with the quite material boundedness of thought-products, their (rational) confinement within the parameters of linearity and logic, and how this limits our ways of knowing ourselves and the world. (Smyth, 2007)

Ailbhe Meehan was engaged by French sixteenth-century writers and essayists, especially Marie, Madame de Sevigné (1626–1696), and Michel de Montaigne (1533–1592), from her initial years at UCD.

"What drew me to that time? There wasn't much else for me. I didn't particularly like the Enlightenment. Education was hived off into different fiefdoms—political science, philosophy and so forth—and it's difficult to do all that in a transdisciplinary way. You didn't have to compartmentalise in the sixteenth and seventeeth centuries. It's all there. The only contemporary literature we were taught at UCD was Catholic, like [François] Mauriac (1885–1970). It was quickly clear to me that I was interested in ideas without wanting to be a philosopher. It wasn't what spoke to me directly. I looked for worlds with a material reality, with social formations and everyday philosophical dilemmas. That's why I read Montaigne. He's incredibly reflective but also very involved in the world, very political. He wrote clearly and understood absolutely the politics of his time. The kind of academic I became drew on the education I had but also from Montaigne. If you're stuck for something to read, read Montaigne!

Madame de Sevigné? I was always seeking out the women. She writes of the most extraordinary mother daughter relationship. And she was writing about life historically aeons away in Louis XIV's court, but entirely human, about people like me. She wrote about court life and exile but also about everyday things. It wasn't metaphorical, it was about what people said and did, how they managed babies, or problems with hairstyles, or what to say when you didn't know what to say. I wouldn't read Balzac in bed but I'd read her Letters.

I read all kinds of things and read fiction all the time. If I were on a desert island with only one book, it would be the collected poems of Emily Dickinson. You'd never get to the end of it, you'd never fully understand it, her writing frustrates your emotion because it's about what is just beyond your ken, about the formative relations in life, especially the intimate ones.

I don't see these writings and interests as being separate [academic, creative, personal discourses]. One's creative self is every bit as important, it's part of the person. I was brought up in words so I'm closer to writing but of course I love everything—reading, listening, going to exhibitions. I read a lot of poetry and it can so easily become too cerebral. I like listening to jazz and to baroque music. Dancing is wonderful! It's a great physical movement a great expression of oneself. Bach was one of the earliest recordings I listened to followed by The Beatles, The Stones. I'm listening to Chopin at the moment. Music and dance express in a way words can never really get to. Music and dance are different rhythms, they hold emotion in different ways."

On Growing Up in Ireland in the 1950s

Maybe they said it
sotto voce, Irish-style
compliments not being our forte
"What a dotey wee girl"
I was never wee
or dotey
and that's the truth
but they taught me very well how to be
a good learner
keen to please to prove to improve
ready to be primed, primped, preened
by all their principles
they did it for love
I did it for love
for they loved me, yes, and I loved them
which just goes to show how love
can lead us all astray

(Smyth, 1997)

"Are you a bossy girl?" I was asked on radio. "Of course!" I replied. My mother was horrified when I said I come from a long line of bossy women. My grandmother had 11 children. I am the eldest of a family of six. I was caught between the contradictions of training girls to be leaders and training them to be leaders of families. "Ailbhe will you...Ailbhe would you?" I'd be asked. "Of course," I would say.

I was educated by outsiders, by a congregation of English nuns who were brought to Ireland by John Charles McQuaid.[3] It was a different experience from most girls of my generation. McQuaid was concerned with the rate at which the middle classes were sending their daughters off to England to be educated so he brought English nuns here. However, Catholics in Britain were automatically oppositional no matter how conservative they were, because they were not part of the established church. So there was a dimension of outsiderness built into their intellectual and social apparatus. The nuns did not know that Ireland was so different from Britain. They were listening to Radio 3, not Radio Éireann. They had the outsiders' perception; they brought a very different approach.

The school was Our Lady's Templeogue, with early nineteenth-century architecture and beautifully polished floors. It was very new and there were very few other girls. The nuns did not put a foot outside the walls. We were encouraged to read books and ask questions. They actually talked to you as a human being. When you asked a question, they saw it as a sign of intelligence and encouraged you to think it was better to go out and find an answer for yourself. I really loved school.

I tended to be naughty because I had to be good at home. I used to do my hair in funny ways, odd top notches and that kind of thing. There was something very tolerant about the nuns. One day the Reverend Mother looked at my funny hair and said: "Oh Ailbhe, a palm tree on a lonely island! How nice!"

I loved the ballroom dancing we did in school. You were taught to dance because you would be going to your Debs. Games were the only thing I hated. We played lacrosse—I can still hear the games mistress shouting "Up, up, up!" I could cradle a lacrosse stick in my sleep. McQuaid was very pleased until he realized that lacrosse was a Protestant sport. I eventually shot an own goal deliberately so I would not have to play. I loathed games. I thought them really stupid, a waste of time, energy, and brainpower.

I came from a very sporty athletic family. My brother was two years younger and I learned to bowl so he could practice his batting. It was a very privileged, protected upbringing. My father inherited land on Palmerston Road when I was seven so we moved there from Terenure. He was in retail business. He was a butcher in Rathmines. We were well off in comparison with other people but we did not go on family holidays, people did not then.

Even middle-class Dublin was a tough, harsh place. They were very, very bad times. What it must have been like for working-class and rural people. I would never wish to go back there, with that repressive Church and those dark, dull politicians. Never again.

I wanted to burst out and do something different. To have fun! There was not much outlet for brainy girls; I was lucky the school encouraged me. I had lots of school friends although I also got bullied because I was plump. My mother tried to sort it out. We were all nice, middle-class girls but in my class there were a couple of very clever girls who were incredibly good to me. I learned languages from the age of eight years. Eileen O'Sullivan, my teacher, encouraged me as did Fidelma O'Sullivan, another nun. A Benedictine Hostel for boys was down the road and a Brother there spoke French to me. I quickly excelled at it. I must have known at some level it would bring me out of where I was. French was ultimately an escape route from 1950s' Ireland.

On Being a (Smart Young Older) Woman

"That girl shows what she eats"
He aimed his blow with vicious accuracy
it came so fast I never knew what hit me sliming me with
    self- disease
I couldn't eat for years
no one told him off
the premises
and out of my mother's house
where I never quite grew up
or into the woman I would become
I was twelve and tender still
open as a book or a breeze
"Hail Mary, full of grace,
Tuesday's child is fair of face
Her sense of self thou shalt not erase"
but they did
indeed, and in word
then I saw myself as I was seen
through him and them and never me
seen and framed

(Smyth, 1997)

People say now there was not so much emphasis on the body then. Women's bodies were not put up on billboards [in the 1950s and 1960s] but you had to conform to a certain silhouette. I was five foot eight inches and ten stone. I was seen by boys and girls as too fat. And I did not like being tall. I had finished school very early at 16 years and I could not go to university straight away because I was too young. I thought I was a bit dim. I didn't feel particularly clever.

My first year at UCD[4] was a terrible awakening. There were 6,000 students [her school had been small]. I did four subjects in my first year—French, English, Latin, and German. I was hauled in to lecture at 21 years.

A teacher invited me to a Sunday morning meeting where there were guitars and rock buns. Later, I was told that it was an Opus Dei place. They put their fingers on people who were going to be influential teachers.

I remember going to The Singing Kettle for coffee with my friend Nessa in the first year. There was a group of boys at a table. "You come and join us," they told Nessa, "but don't bring your big, fat friend." They were crude. I remember thinking that I may be fat but I am not stupid.

I walk now, I do my exercises. Stockard Channing [actor, 1944–] says she does various bits and bobs for health reasons. I thought, yeah, right.

It is actually still very difficult for a woman to be highly engaged and articulate. It is incredibly difficult for young women now. Gender is seen as one category among others, not as a politics. So the message is "Don't politicise our culture." Young women have to behave in certain ways but also deal with the fear that they will be seen as less feminine and therefore less sexually attractive if they demur. It is about power relations and people being fobbed off with simple notions of equality and gender.

Raunch culture was another example. It is another kind of incarnation of patriarchal heteromasculinity, favoring semi-naked young women. The power spaces and relations have not changed. It is like the way young men behaved when I was young.

I am interested in feminist politics that are transformative, not merely about tweaking or equalizing unequal relations of power. This is absolutely not the moment to be fobbed off by "equality" and "gender." Women bear the brunt of the cuts in the recent Budgets and will keep on having to manage what is often unmanageable as long as feminist politics is kept out of economics.

Why could anyone say feminism is not necessary when we see strong, feisty women still being pushed out? As soon as we shift the power relations, they are shifted right back again. Look at the British election [May 2010]. The extreme invisibility of women was very visible. Theresa May [politician, 1956–] spoke on BBC Radio 4 about being appointed home secretary. She said she was proud to be a woman and to be given such an important role. Then she was given the women's portfolio—she was double-gendered.

We are accused of our gender. We are expected to explain our-selves. And if we engage actively, a point comes where we are not welcome. In this country, women are dispirited at times. It is very difficult for a woman to be a public intellectual. There is a spectrum of presence. As soon as we advance toward the center, we are pushed toward the margins, toward the edge.

Culture has been technologized by the Internet, Youtube, and so on. Pornographic imagery is much more widely available and con-sumed. What the reality says is that a man is (a) actively exercising more power politically and economically and (b) is entitled to con-sume women. Women are consumer durables, or unendurables who are always there to be consumed. There is not a "yes" or "no" answer to why women take up the place of being the consumed. There is an attempt to actually look at ways in which we are positioned, at how we comply with our own subordination. This is not about blame. You can never really say "I am absolutely autonomous and never compli-ant." For example, I can be compliant by not speaking up, perhaps, by not being more politically explicit. We are most aware of a highly sexualized way of being compliant. But compliance is difficult to move away from—it can catch so many unawares.

Women are not essentially more ethical than men. Many around the world are in positions of extreme vulnerability. Vulnerability comes from feeling there is nothing you can do in your life. What you have to do is supply what is immediately available. That vulnerability comes out of poverty. Looking at the socio-sexual discourse where women put themselves up for sale, there is an economic transaction where the buyer apparently has so much power. Usually, men have the money. If I am at the bottom in the World Poverty Stakes [United Nations measurement], of course I am going to say "that's my choice, I'm not a victim." But it is something I do not have much of an option about. There is a high end where women can make a lot of money. But who would not be won over if there is nothing else for them where they are? How is she to exist, especially given a notion of life looking at much more privileged women? The feminist question is this: We can see why women are in this situation. What is it about our sense of sex that means men are allowed without impunity, except in Sweden?

Even in buying child sex, men are not stopped. Right along the line globally, men retain power over women and children. We need a whole systemic analysis. Of course, there are exceptions. Some women have much privilege and power. But they do not prove the rule for the rest. There are women of six feet, five inches in height, but there are very few.

On Teaching

A transformed world will never grow on trees. (Smith, unpublished-a)

UCD was an incredibly conservative place. I was there for nearly 40 years. It opened up for a while, then it regressed. It would have hooked me in if I had played the game. I would have been weighed down, burdened by the expectation that brings with it. The moment comes when you say "this matters." You bring the politics of the exterior and that is a huge challenge for an academic institution that sees itself as nonpolitical.

How do you survive and flourish in an institution that really does not want to recognize women as scholars of excellence? The resistance to promoting women is still huge. There was a brief respite when Mary Robinson was President (1990–1997), then the daggers came out.[5]

Ten to fifteen years later, the overall percentage of women professors in Ireland is only 12 percent. In UCD, it is 14 percent. If you want to kick down this old boys' system, I promise you, within five years you will be muzzled. I have seen this happen to other women in the system. They have been parked. Nothing will be said. It is a bit like turning the Titanic or the Queen Mary. It happens by degrees. By the time you realize you are headed for Argentina, not the States, the course is set and it is too late.

You get banished, like in Louis XIV's court. It is very powerful. The UCD regime was closely aligned to neoliberal policies and the emphasis was on pushing UCD higher up the list of the 100 top universities. They wanted to rationalize the university and effectively put departments under central control. Then they would reduce or stop funding to departments seen as outside the parameters. This was rather than extending the knowledge base throughout society. It will be crucial over the next decade in terms of equality and justice.

Elite systems are killing us in banking, in the university sector, everywhere. Nobody is crying wolf—and the wolf is still there.

I did not tolerate it. There are moments of transition and some people seem to summarize the pressure points of that transition. I was left wing without being aligned with any specific camp. I was nonaligned in fact. I think at some level, I may have been seen as a class traitor—and as a woman. I survived with a certain degree of resilience because I had very good support from colleagues and friends. I knew in my bones that I was, ironically, in a very good position. The public profile of women's studies was so high that UCD could not be seen to demolish it. The question for me really was how can I reposition and relocate a feminist politics of knowledge within the academy. Although we were dealing with students effectively "outlawed" by the academy…often working-class women, often older, from "outlying" communities untouched by third-level education. Openings are narrow for people marked by permutations or combinations of gender, class, age, and ethnicity. It can be lethal. So knock the doors down!

Love underlines everything you do as an educator, in a way. It is very difficult to be an educator without some sense of affect. I don't think you can go on without a sense of passion for what you do and the people you teach. Educating is about practice, methodology, concepts, technique but there must be a strong sense of human connection. We decline to think about that at our peril.

On Being an Activist

You think I exaggerate for rhetorical effect? Just the other day, I heard someone say: "We on the Left don't use the word 'opposition' any more: we prefer 'alternative' ". *Left-wing lite.* No, I don't prefer "alternative". Oppositional politics—feminist, anti-racist, lesbian, gay, queer, anti-corporatist—are not pick-and-mix, customized, consumerist options, co-existing harmoniously in the mainstream. I *oppose* (that is I confront, contest, resist, seek to change) specific socio-economic, political and cultural systems based on arbitrary hierarchical divisions which intersect with one another in remarkably consistent and persistent ways to produce and maintain unequal relations of power, with acute and deleterious material consequences for people in their everyday lives and life possibilities.

(Smyth, unpublished-b)

I have something almost visceral about injustice. It is a kind of anti-authoritarian stance that has stood me in good stead. I always want to know from what place a person derives his or her authority. By what right or privilege does anyone tell someone else what to do or try to control them? "What's this about? " I want to know. I am interested in breaking down barriers. I am not sure if I ever identified the causes in advance. Issues *du jour*, really. I did not say at the age of 38 years "This is my agenda." I belong to a generation that was defining agendas and excluding other agendas. We were dealing with urgent life issues—economic stability, the right to work, to control your fertility and your reproductive health. If you did not, you were faced by a group of people telling you what to do!

A political life does not only mean the barricades. It is something about your sense of the human condition, about something more whole. *Caritas* is a good word. It has at its core a desire for the other but not to possess them. Altruism? It receives a very bad press because we are so deeply engrained with the notion of people as fundamental egotists who operate out of self-interest. It is a very limited view of human relations because we often do things that are not in our self-interest. Altruism is complex, it is not absolutely cut off from egotism. Its motives are more fluid and more mixed. You feel very challenged and satisfied and therefore you keep on doing it. You're also motivated by something that's not just for you but for others too.

There's an ethical spectrum. Sometimes for you to stand by and do absolutely nothing would be hugely irresponsible. It is when you think some action or behaviour is absolutely unacceptable and inhuman but you're not prepared to stand by and accept it. I am a good, middle-class girl, relatively speaking, from a privileged environment who accessed education. I have no sense of a birthright except justice for everyone.

I am not being coy but really I am not so interested in power. I was not a conference junkie—there is no point in going to conferences if you do not have something to say or learn. I have attended many across the world, in Europe, the United States, India, Australia, New Zealand, though not as much in Africa. Over the years, I have been fortunate to link into global networks and I would like to do more in the future. I am involved as an activist with organizations such as Feminist Open Forum, the National Lesbian and Gay Federation, Marriage Equality, and the People Before Profit Alliance, as well as with GAZE, the LGBT film festival, and the Dublin Writers Festival. I have been working as a consultant and educator since I left UCD, mainly with community groups and organizations.

I worked with a Tanzanian women's group for a month when I turned 60. It was a one-hour walk to and from the camp every day. Now that's what teaching is about. You set up a relationship with people. At the same time, I had a huge question about going over as a white woman.

I have never had a plan and I don't have an agenda. The agenda is in the politics I pursue. I have strategies. I do not like injustice nor inequality. Usually, when others call you "radical," they want to be rude. I define myself as a radical!

Every society needs to say there are outer limits. The problem is Ireland is a small country—if you play too much ball with the mainstream, you lose the edge. A society losing its edginess will go into decline because it cannot move. Me, I am more comfortable on the edge. I have been there a long time so it is familiar.

On Sex

I can be, and sometimes am, ignored, marginalised or discriminated against because I am lesbian. Yet my lesbian sexuality is an important part of my identity and the Irish woman I am, and I want that to be acknowledged and valued in the same way as all the other connected parts of me.

(Smyth, unpublished)

I often feel because of my sexuality I have lived several lives. Love is complicated. I was a straight woman until my late thirties, now I call myself lesbian. I am actually sequentially bisexual. There is definitely a core but subtle shift to same-sex relationships. That is significant not because it is about sex and social identity but because it involves personal and familial relations, particularly for women of my generation.

There never was a moment when I sat down and thought to myself, now I am going to choose to become a lesbian. Frankly, the late 1980s were so repressive you would have to be quiet about it. The big issues now are the right to marry, and discrimination against lesbian and gays in the workplace. And I am not saying they are easier for men. They are not. Let me say I do not regret any of it. I would not have lived my life as a problematic in terms of my sexuality.

On Beauty

A man remembers Ailbhe looking dazzling in blue while balancing gracefully on a truck parading through O'Connell Street. I wonder about *New York Times* columnist Maureen Dowd's words that you couldn't be gorgeous and feminist in her youth. Smyth is both.

You ask about the parade where I was wearing a jump suit? Actually, it was a black wet suit with a red stripe. It was Pride Week and it was cold!

Ugly feminists? There is no uniform of ugliness. The culture sees what it wants to see. The visual is very important to me—where I live, the environment I am in—I have a strong aesthetic sense. Where is the contradiction in dressing smartly and wearing makeup? Visual sartorial pleasures are very satisfying. I do have a keen sense of performance, which does not mean I see my life as performance. When Lydia (her daughter) was a small girl, she asked "Mum, why do you have that funny voice on?" I don't have a sense of being diminished by style or of having to prove myself. There is a sense of liberation when you hit your fifties. I thought, I might as well enjoy myself because I cannot do everything.

NOTES

1. Suburb of Dublin, Ireland.
2. Books: 1 as sole author; 3 as editor. Articles: 37 (27 in international refereed journals). Special issue editor of 7 refereed academic journals. Book chapters: 24. Encyclopaedias: 2 as section editor, 2 as contributor. Conference proceedings (papers): 17. Research reports + non-academic Articles: 20+. Research projects: 24. Invited keynote and guest lectures (mainly international): 100+. Journal coeditor: 2. Journal advisory board member: 9. Television, film, visual arts: director GAZE LGBT Film Festival, curator OUTART, contributions to numerous television/film documentaries, regular broadcaster, writing anthologized in *Field Day Anthology of Irish Writing*, Gill and Macmillan and others. Appointments include Higher Education Authority (two 5-year periods), National Library (trustee for five years) and others.
3. Catholic Archbishop of Dublin, 1940–1972 (1895–1973).
4. University College Dublin in Earlsfort Terrace.
5. Smyth began the Women's Education, Research and Resource Centre at University College Dublin in 1990.

REFERENCES

Smyth, Ailbhe (1997) "Girl Beaming in a White Dress," in Liz Murphy (ed.), *Wee Girls*. Melbourne: Spinifex Press.

———— (2007) "Momentary Views," *The Irish Review*, 35 (Cork: Cork University Press).

———— (unpublished-a) "Layers and Loose Ends" (2010), unpublished.

———— (unpublished-b) "Resist, Fall, Fail, Resist: Diary of a Feminist Academic," unpublished.

———— (unpublished-c) "Momentary Views," unpublished.

Contributors

Senator Ivana Bacik LLB, LLM (Lond), BL, FTCD, is Reid Professor of Criminal Law, Criminology and Penology at Trinity College Dublin, and a practicing barrister. She is a Labour Party Senator for Dublin University since 2007 and became deputy leader of Seanad Eireann in May 2011. Ivana has written and published extensively on criminal law, criminology, human rights, constitutional law, and related matters, and has a long track record of campaigning on civil liberties, penal reform, and feminist issues. She is a coauthor of *Abortion and the Law* (1997) and a coeditor of *Crime and Poverty in Ireland* (1998). She coordinated an European Union–funded study on rape law in different European jurisdictions, *The Legal Process and Victims of Rape* (1998), was editor of the *Irish Criminal Law Journal* from 1997 to 2003 and coauthored a major report on gender discrimination in the legal professions in Ireland (*Gender Injustice*, 2003). Other publications include *Kicking and Screaming: Dragging Ireland into the Twenty-First Century* (O'Brien Press, 2004).

Paula Burns is a civil servant and graduate of Queen's University Belfast in Combined Humanities and Social Science with an MA in Gender and Society.

Olga Cox Cameron is a psychoanalyst in private practice who teaches psychoanalytic theory and psychoanalysis and literature in St Vincent's University Hospital and Trinity College Dublin. She has published numerous articles in national and international psychoanalytic journals.

Lisa Fingleton is an award-winning artist and filmmaker living in North Kerry. Lisa is fascinated by the diversity of human and nonhuman experience. She loves to observe and transform the mundane. Much of her current work involves working with local women's and community groups through the medium of art and film. She is the recipient of numerous awards including Bursary and Travel Awards from the Arts Council of Ireland.

Noreen Giffney works as a psychoanalytic psychotherapist in private practice in Dublin. She also coordinates postgraduate and postdoctoral researcher training in the Humanities Institute at University College Dublin. Her research focuses on critical and cultural theories of gender and sexuality, Kleinian psychoanalysis, and film studies. She is the coeditor of *Twenty-First Century Lesbian Studies* (Taylor and Francis, 2007); *Queering the Non/Human* (Ashgate, 2008); *The Ashgate Research Companion to Queer Theory* (Ashgate, 2009); *The Lesbian Premodern* (Palgrave Macmillan, 2011); and *Clinical Encounters: Psychoanalytic Practice and Queer Theory* (under review). She is currently researching the discourses of desire in the work of the psychoanalyst Wilfred Bion.

Debbie Ging is a lecturer in the School of Communications at Dublin City University. Her research focuses on gender and sexuality in the media. She is the author of *Men and Masculinities in Irish Cinema* (Palgrave 2012) and a coeditor, with Michael Cronin and Peadar Kirby, of *Transforming Ireland: Challenges, Critiques, Resources* (Manchester University Press, 2009).

Breda Gray is a senior lecturer in the Department of Sociology and Director of programmes in Gender, Culture & Society at the University of Limerick, Ireland. She is also a co-convenor (with Niamh Reilly) of the University of Limerick-National University of Ireland Galway research consortium Gender ARC (www.genderarc.org/). She is the principal investigator on the IRC research project "The Irish Catholic Church and the Politics of Migration" (www.ul.ie/icctmp) and co-principal investigator (with Luigina Ciolfi) on the Government of Ireland, Irish Social Science Platform research project "Nomadic Work/Life and the Knowledge Economy" (http://nwl.ul.ie/). Her publications address questions of gender, migration, and public religion; gender and work in the knowledge economy; and feminism and the politics of memory and emotion. She is author of *Women and the Irish Diaspora* (Routledge, 2004); coeditor with Anthony D'Andrea and Luigina Ciolfi of special issue of *Mobilities* 6(2), 2011, on methodological innovations in mobilities research; and editor of *Irish Journal of Sociology* 19(2), 2011, on transnationalism.

Eithne Luibhéid is an associate professor of Gender and Women's Studies at the University of Arizona. She is the author of *Entry Denied: Controlling Sexuality at the Border* (University of Minnesota Press, 2002); coeditor with Ronit Lentin of a special issue of *Women's Studies International Forum* on "Representing Migrant Women in Ireland

and the EU" (2004); coeditor with Lionel Cantú of *Queer Migration: Sexuality, U.S. Citizenship, and Border Crossings* (University of Minnesota Press, 2005); editor of a special issue of *GLQ: A Journal of Lesbian and Gay Studies* on "Queer/Migration" (2008); and the author of various articles and book chapters on migration and sexualities. Her forthcoming book, *Pregnant on Arrival: Making the Illegal Immigrant* (University of Minnesota Press), analyses how pregnant migrants became discursively constructed as paradigmatic figures of "illegal" immigration, thereby illuminating how nationalist sexual norms shape state designations of migrants' legal statuses.

Sandra McAvoy is a historian who teaches on and coordinates the MA in Women's Studies at University College Cork, as well as teaching adult education women's studies outreach courses. Her current research interests include the history of sexuality, with a focus on the experiences of women in Ireland in the twentieth century; the history and politics of reproductive rights issues; and women and politics.

Gerardine Meaney is a professor of Cultural Theory and Director of the Humanities Institute at University College Dublin. She is the author of *Gender, Ireland and Cultural Change* (Routledge, 2010); *Nora* (Cork University Press and the Film Institute of Ireland, 2004); *(Un)like Subjects: Women, Theory, Fiction* (Routledge, 1993); a coeditor of the *Field Day Anthology of Irish Writing: Women's Writing and Traditions*, volumes 4 and 5 (Cork University Press, 2002), and the author of numerous articles on gender and Irish culture, with particular emphasis on film, literature, and drama. She is general editor of the Liverpool University Press series of new critical editions of Irish women's writing.

Anne Mulhall is a College Lecturer in the School of English, Drama and Film Studies at University College Dublin, Ireland, where she teaches and researches in critical theory, gender and sexuality studies, and Irish literary and cultural studies. She has published extensively on queer theory, psychoanalytic theory, contemporary Irish writing, Irish periodical culture, migration and multiculturalism, and Irish popular culture. She has coedited *Irish Postmodernisms and Popular Culture* (Palgrave Macmillan, 2007); *Women in Irish Culture and Society* (Irish Academic Press, 2012), a collection of essays coedited with Gerardine Meaney and Maria Luddy; a special feature on the work of Bracha L. Ettinger for *Studies in the Maternal*; and a special feature on the work of Lisa Baraitser in *Studies in Gender and Sexuality*. She is coediting "Queer Studies and Ireland," a special issue of the *Irish*

University Review (2013), and working on two monographs, *Anne Enright: Excavating the Present* and *Intimate States: The Biopolitics of Ireland 1970–2012.*

Aideen Quilty is the director of the Women's Studies Outreach Programme at the School of Social Justice, University College Dublin. Her research is focused on developing geographies of space and place within higher education. Her most recent work seeks to combine feminist and spatial theories and practices with the aim of articulating place pedagogies for community-based higher education. She locates her undergraduate and postgraduate teaching as a form of critical civic practice and is committed to promoting educational access and participation for traditionally under-represented groups.

Medb Ruane is a writer and psychoanalytic practitioner, based in Dublin, with research interests in psychoanalysis, gender, literary, and visual cultures. She received a GREP/IRCHSS (Graduate Research and Education Program/Irish Research Council for the Humanities and Social Sciences) scholarship for her doctoral studies in University College Dublin looking at literary and visual culture in *The Táin* (Dublin: Dolmen, 1969) via contemporary psychoanalysis. She has written as a columnist with *The Sunday Times, The Irish Times, The Irish Independent,*and in many journals and museum catalogs. She has lectured at postgraduate level in Dublin Business School and Independent Colleges, Dublin. She works with individuals and as a supervisor, along with editing APPI's (the Association of Psychoanalysis and Psychotherapy in Ireland) magazine and other publications. She serves on the Mental Health Tribunals and on a range of cultural and professional bodies.

Margrit Shildrick is a professor of Gender and Knowledge Production at Linköping University, Sweden. Her research interests lie in postmodern feminist and cultural theory, bioethics, critical disability studies, and body theory. She is the author of *Dangerous Discourses of Disability, Subjectivity and Sexuality* (Palgrave Macmillan, 2009); *Embodying the Monster* (Sage, 2002); *Leaky Bodies and Boundaries* (Routledge, 1997); and many other books and articles.

Edith Shillue is an independent scholar living in Belfast, Ireland, currently working with asylum seekers and refugees in advocacy and rights work. She is a contributing researcher for the Greater Middle East Project at the University of Massachusetts/Boston and the author of two travel memoirs.

Ailbhe Smyth has been active in feminist, lesbian and gay, and radical politics since the late 1970s. Co-convenor of Feminist Open Forum, she is also Chair of the National Lesbian and Gay Federation, national convenor of the People Before Profit Alliance and a board member of various feminist, LGBT, and equality organizations. A senior academic at University College Dublin, Ireland, for many years, she cofounded the Women's Education, Research and Resource Centre (WERRC) in 1990, and was the Centre's director until 2006. She has published widely in Ireland and internationally on feminist theory and politics, on LGBT issues, and in the field of culture and the arts. She has served on several state boards, including the Higher Education Authority and the National Library. She now works as an educator and consultant with community organizations and nongovernmental organizations.

Moynagh Sullivan is a lecturer in English Literature at the National University of Ireland, Maynooth, with research interests in psychoanalysis, gender, modernism and postmodernism, and popular culture and women's writing. She was the Fulbright Scholar in Irish Literary and Cultural Studies at UC Berkeley, CA (2009), and a recipient of an IRCHSS Post-Doctoral Fellowship (2002–2004). She is currently working on a monograph on Psychoanalysis, Gender, and Irish Poetry and Culture and she has published extensively in Irish and Gender Studies. She has coedited *Facing the Other: Interdisciplinary Essays in Race, Gender and Social Justice in Ireland* (with Borbala Farago) (Cambridge Scholar's Press, 2008); *Irish Postmodernisms and Popular Culture* (with Wanda Balzano and Anne Mulhall) (Basingstoke: Palgrave Macmillan, 2007); and "Irish Feminisms," Special Issue, *Irish Review* (with Wanda Balzano), 2007.

Fintan Walsh is a lecturer in Theatre and Performance Studies at Birkbeck, University of London, where he teaches on the BA Theatre and Drama degree and the MA Text and Performance (with RADA). He is author of *Theatre and Therapy* (Palgrave Macmillan, 2013) and *Male Trouble: Masculinity and the Performance of Crisis* (Palgrave Macmillan, 2010). He is editor of *Queer Notions: New Plays and Performances from Ireland* (Cork University Press, 2010), coeditor of *Performance, Identity and the Neo-Political Subject* (Routledge, 2013), and *Crossroads: Performance Studies and Irish Culture* (Palgrave Macmillan, 2009). In 2012, he edited a special issue of the journal *Performing Ethos* on the subject of "Queer Publics" (2.2). Fintan has published in numerous journals and anthologies and is a regular contributor to *Irish Theatre Magazine*. He is a founding member and co-convenor of the International Federation for Theatre Research's Queer Futures working group.

Margaret Ward is the director of the Women's Resource and Development Agency, a regional organization located in Belfast. She was a member of the N. I. Women's Coalition. She is an active member of the women's voluntary sector and is an executive member of the Northern Ireland Council for Voluntary Action, the Northern Ireland Women's European Platform, and the Northern Ireland Rural Women's Network, and has lectured extensively on issues related to women in Northern Ireland. She is also the author/editor of several books including *Irish Women and the Vote: Becoming Citizens*, edited with Louise Ryan (Irish Academic Press, 2007).

Index

Bolded page entries denote chapters by contributors, and photographs.

Printed and bound by CPI Group (UK) Ltd, Croydon, CR0 4YY